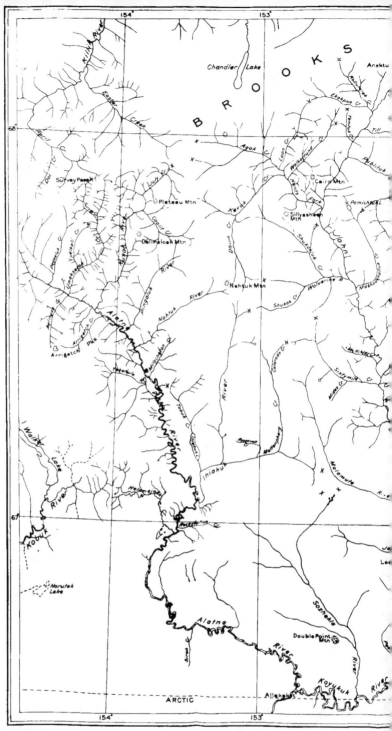

SKETCH MAP OF DRAINAG

Compiled principally from
U.S. Geological Survey maps
and traverses and records
of Robert Marshall, 1932.

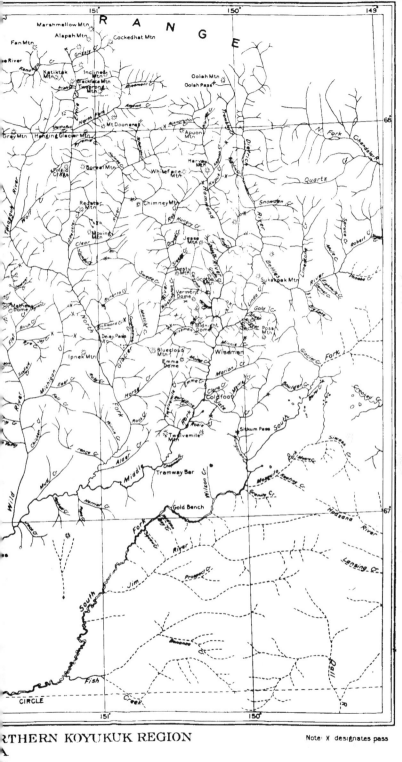

NORTHERN KOYUKUK REGION

Note: X designates pass

20   25 Miles

ARCTIC VILLAGE

WISEMAN IN THE WILDERNESS: The houses across the frozen river seem almost lost in the vast, snow buried expanse of the surrounding country.

ARCTIC
VILLAGE

ROBERT MARSHALL

UNIVERSITY OF ALASKA PRESS

Library of Congress Cataloging-in-Publication Data

Marshall, Robert, 1901-1939.
    Arctic Village / Robert Marshall.
        p. cm.
    Reprint. Originally published: New York: H. Smith and Haas.
  c1933.
      ISBN 0-912006-47-1
      1. Alaska--Description and travel--1896-1959. 2. Koyukuk River
(Alaska) 3. Eskimos--Alaska. 4. Frontier and pioneer life--Alaska.
I. Title.
F909.M372   1991   90-27265
979.8'7--dc20   CIP

Printed in the United States by Thomson-Shore, Inc.
      on Springforge, recycled and acid-free.

This publication was printed on acid-free paper which meets the
minimum requirements of American National Standard for
Information Sciences—Permanence of Paper for Printed Library
Materials, ANSI Z39.48-1984.

Cover design: Dixon Jones, IMPACT Graphics, UAF Rasmuson Library.
Cover illustration based on the original 1933 Literary Guild edition cover
by Arthur Hawkins, Jr.

To the people of the Koyukuk who
have made for themselves the happiest civilization of which I have
knowledge.

CONTENTS

ILLUSTRATIONS

PREFACE TO THE 1991 EDITION

WHEN artist Rockwell Kent first read Robert Marshall's *Arctic Village* in 1933, he thought it was "one of the great books that had come out of America," a classic work of our national literature. "I am not a reviewer of books," Kent wrote, "nor do I spend myself in generous praise of many things. I am writing about this book because it has moved me more than any book that I have read in years."[1]

Bob Marshall's intimate portrait of the community of Wiseman, Alaska, in the early 1930s is one of the most revealing and inspiring books ever written about the American frontier. Like Henry David Thoreau's *Walden*, Marshall's *Arctic Village* is one man's account of the beauty and richness of life in the wilderness, the story of his search for happiness.

Modern environmentalists know Robert Marshall to have been a pioneering wilderness advocate—the Bob Marshall Wilderness Area, of nearly one million acres in Montana, is named for him—but relatively few know of his first and most important book.[2] *Arctic Village* has been out of print for fifty years, yet it is still a favorite among old-time Alaskans, and over the years the book has prompted numerous readers to pack up and move north. No book more eloquently and accurately explains why many people choose to live in Alaska. Marshall's long-neglected classic is an original work of literature by one of America's foremost conservationists.

A professional forester, Marshall became the driving force behind the organization in 1935 of The Wilderness Society, which has been rightfully called Bob Marshall's lengthened shadow. "If any organization has been overwhelmingly indebted to a single individual," environmentalist Harvey Broome wrote in 1940, "The Wilderness Society has been, and remains so, to Robert Marshall."[3]

Marshall urged those who cherished the "freedom of the wilderness" to unite in order to resist "the tyrannical ambition of civilization to conquer every niche on the whole earth." Marshall believed the happiness and survival of the human race depended in part on the preservation of wilderness, which nourished the roots of freedom, democracy, and the American character. How could the nation of Jefferson and Lincoln exist without undeveloped land? "As long as we prize individuality and competence," Marshall wrote in 1930, "it is imperative to provide the opportunity for complete self-sufficiency. This is inconceivable under the effete superstructure of urbanity; it demands the harsh environment of untrammeled expanses."[4]

Marshall believed wilderness was not an abstract concept; it was life itself. "For me," he said, "and for thousands with similar inclinations, the most important passion of life is the overpowering desire to escape periodically from the strangling clutch of a mechanistic civilization. To us the enjoyment of solitude, complete independence, and the beauty of undefiled panoramas is absolutely essential to happiness."[5]

Marshall's quest for happiness led him in 1929 to Wiseman, an isolated mining camp in the mountains of northern Alaska "200 miles beyond the edge of the Twentieth Century." In a world tormented by the Great Depression and the rise of Fascism, many sensitive souls yearned for a better way of life. Marshall believed that on the Middle Fork of the Koyukuk River in the heart of the central Brooks Range—90 miles from the nearest church, 150 miles from the nearest doctor, and 200 airline miles to the nearest railroad, automobile, or electric light in Fairbanks—he had found the happiest civilization on earth.[6] *Arctic Village* is the story of that distant civilization. Published in 1933, the same year as James Hilton's famous novel *Lost Horizon*, Marshall's *Arctic Village* depicts the charm of a true life Shangri-La in the Alaska wilderness. From the first day he set foot in Wiseman, Marshall, like the travelers in Hilton's novel, believed he had landed in paradise.

Bob Marshall first learned to love wilderness in the Adirondack Mountains of New York State from his father, Louis Marshall, a prominent New York City constitutional lawyer.[7] Born on January 2, 1901, Bob was the third of four children. At his family's summer home in the Adirondacks, he roamed a patch of woods in which he could imagine he was following the footsteps of his boyhood heroes—Meriwether Lewis and William Clark. His favorite book as a child, *Pioneer Boys of the Great Northwest*, which he read at least once a year (or more) until age twenty-one, told of two brave young boys and their fathers who walked across the continent with Lewis and Clark. Bob's only regret was that he had been born too late to be a "pioneer boy" himself. Nevertheless, he said the woods near the house were "a real wilderness to me, as exciting in a different way as the unexplored continent which I had missed by my tardy birth."[8]

While still a teenager Marshall began his serious exploration of the Adirondacks, climbing his first mountain peak at age 15. By that time he had decided to become a forester, a career which he thought would enable him to enjoy, protect, and study nature. Forestry seemed to be the ideal profession. "I love the woods and I love solitude," he wrote while a junior in high school. "I like the various forms of scientific work a forester must do. I should hate to spend the greater part of my lifetime in a stuffy office or in a crowded city. If I can combine my greatest pleasure with a useful work, then I shall have a great advantage over most business and professional men."[9]

True to his childhood ambition, Marshall earned a B.S. in forestry at Syracuse University in 1924, a Master of Forestry at Harvard in 1925, and a Ph.D. at Johns Hopkins Laboratory of Plant Physiology in 1930. His doctoral dissertation was entitled "An Experimental Study of the Water Relations of Seedling Conifers with Special Reference to Wilting."

Marshall knew he needed to be in the woods, because climbing and hiking were a lifelong obsession. By 1925 Bob and his younger brother George had climbed all of the 46 peaks in the Adirondacks of 4,000 feet and higher.[10] Marshall became a legendary hiker; few people in America could keep up with him on a wilderness trail. With long, easy strides he covered ground with incredible speed; often he actually ran downhill. For him hikes of 20-30 miles in one day were casual walks, and on occasion he rambled as far as 60-70 miles in a single day. He always felt driven to stand on the "highest peak of the highest mountain in the country he was visiting."[11] One of his lifetime ambitions was to take at least one 30-mile day hike in every state in the Union. Rhode Island was his 35th state in 1936. Typically he was happiest when he traveled light, wearing sneakers or work shoes and blue jeans. One hiking companion remembered him carrying only a "small bag of raisins and a hunk of cheese."[12]

Hiking brought him happiness, and so did his other great passion in life: statistics. At a young age Marshall developed an insatiable thirst for precision, a love for compiling statistics that would serve him well as a scientist and an observer of human nature. As a man who would spend much of his professional life counting tree rings, statistics were both his vocation and his avocation. Never satisfied with unsubstantiated generalizations or vague theories, Marshall was constantly measuring, listing and compiling, and dreaming up imaginative ways to correlate the data he had discovered. He found the mental diversion of counting to be endlessly rewarding. "Indeed," Marshall's biographer says, "his lifelong penchant for compiling statistics was so strong as to seem compulsive."[13]

He was a baseball fan and loved to read box scores. Drawn to the study of history, he acquired an encyclopedic knowledge of dates and anniversaries; if anyone was likely to remember the birthday of General Grant, it was Bob Marshall.

Marshall devised a "composite view rating" to evaluate the scenery on his mountain hikes; he tabulated the best days, months and years of his life; he listed the best books he had read; he ranked his best friends and his top ten girl friends; he rated his friendship with the 76 whites who lived in the Koyukuk; he ranked the top 36 foresters in the United States; he counted the number of pancakes his companions ate for breakfast and how fast they ate them. He added up the number of swear words lumberjacks uttered at mealtime.[14]

One of the most unusual correlations he discovered was the relationship between precipitation and presidential elections: he claimed that his tree ring data from the 19th century proved that poor rainfall invariably caused incumbents to lose. While he claimed that rainfall was not an " infallible key to our political history," he thought "historians have so emphasized the petty actions of puny politicians that it seems worth while stressing one fact which even the largest campaign fund cannot alter."[15]

After reading "35 or 40" books on the Civil War, Marshall compiled a list ranking the top 200 military leaders of the War Between the States. A taste of his method is evident in a letter he sent in May 1922 to General Samuel S. Sumner, the son of Civil War General Edwin V. Sumner.

"While a great deal has been written on the Civil War...," Marshall wrote the retired general, "it is very hard to get any idea of the relative merits of the commanders. Writers seem to hate to be precise..." Marshall asked Sumner if he would mind evaluating his list of the top 12 Civil War commanders, which he ranked in the following order: Thomas; Sedgwick; Grant; Sumner; Sherman; Meade; Sheridan; McPherson; Hancock; Slocum; Warren; and Logan.

"Whom do you regard as the greatest among the younger generals of the war, say those who were under 30 at the end, as MacKenzie, Miles, Custer, Upton, Brooke, Wilson, Merritt, Webbe, Ames, and Harber?" He asked the general which battle was his hardest fight, and whom he would rank as the greatest Indian fighter. "If not too personal a question," he added, "which decade of your long and active career was most enjoyable?"[16] Though the general may not have had the strength to answer such a barrage of questions, the letter is charged with the same energy Marshall devoted to his exploration of wilderness.

Marshall came to the Alaska wilderness for the first time in 1929, drawn to the Brooks Range by the large blank space on the map at the headwaters of the Koyukuk River. "At that time I had the notion that exploration should have a social justification," Marshall wrote. "So I pretended to myself that the real reason for this expedition was to add to the scientific knowledge of tree growth at northern timber line."[17] He enjoyed his months in the Brooks Range immensely, saying the best part was the freshness of the country, "the feeling that at last one was getting away from the contamination of other human beings."[18]

Marshall found the 127 people living in the 15,000 square miles of the upper Koyukuk drainage to be happy and content. "I cannot say that I learned very much either about tree growth or timberline," he said. "But I did come away with a vivid impression that the few white and Eskimo people who were scattered throughout this remote region were on the whole the happiest folk I had ever encountered."[19] He thought the secret of their happiness was that they lived in harmony with nature, in what Marshall labeled a "pre-industrial civilization." Marshall believed that the lifestyle preserved in the isolation of the Koyukuk was "closely analogous" to the 18th century American frontier.[20]

After finishing his Ph.D. dissertation, Marshall returned to Alaska in September 1930 to test his theory about the happiness of pre-industrial America. With advice from anthropologist Margaret Mead, he undertook a year-long economic and sociological study of civilization on the Koyukuk. Marshall spent the next 13 months recording a wealth of intimate information in his notes about the lives of the people in Wiseman, including their gossip, finances, sex lives, political philosophies, religious beliefs, conversations, quarrels, feuds, and much more.[21] He filled *Arctic Village* with so many revealing personal anecdotes about residents of Wiseman that Marshall said his attorney claimed "he expects to spend the better part of the next two years defending me in libel suits when my friends in the Koyukuk get hold of *Arctic Village*."[22]

And, in fact, when *Arctic Village* was published in early 1933, it did come as a shock to the Koyukuk. Everyone thought he had been studying the trees around Wiseman, not its people. No one in the Koyukuk knew that Marshall planned to write a book about the community until shortly before copies of it arrived in the mail in the spring of 1933. At that time Marshall wrote a letter to Jesse Allen, one of his closest friends in Wiseman, explaining what he had done.

"I know, of course, that some of you will not agree with everything which I said and that others of you may think I did a pretty lousy job, but I really did try to paint the most truthful picture which I possibly could.... I really do feel that the civilization in the Koyukuk was the finest which I have ever seen. It was for this reason that I chiefly wanted to write this book because I felt that the outside world might profit a little bit from seeing how much better the people in the Koyukuk knew how to conduct their affairs than do the people in the world at large."[23]

Marshall said that whenever he "had to make unpleasant comments about people I always changed their names."[24] Of course Wiseman was so small that these changes did not offer much anonymity, as everyone in Wiseman knew exactly who said what about whom. But to be honest and avoid the "vague generalities" that he disliked about typical academic studies, Marshall felt he had to include many intimate details about their personal lives. Those in Wiseman who liked the book best were those who did not gossip about their neighbors. Most of the residents liked the book, but one woman claimed all the books should be tossed in a pile and burned. Another said "the only thing good about the book was the pictures."[25]

Jesse Allen reported that the book spawned numerous arguments and accusations. People in Wiseman carrying copies of the book were shouting and pointing their fingers at one another, but nevertheless, Allen said, "It's the most truthful book I ever read, a wonderful description of our life and habits written in good plain everyday language that any body (can) understand. I admire the frank way in describing sex and sex relations.... Sometimes I think that all of us up here were misfits which caused us to come here and stay after every one else had left, trying to get away from ourselves. But I think a good majority have found themselves instead."

Another admirer, Ken Harvey, echoed Allen's praise. "We all got our books and most of us liked them fine. I sure got a great kick out of mine.... The first time I went to town after they came I heard a lot about it, but the best part was they couldn't junk any one else, they were all stewed in the same pot. All they could do was stand and yell to themselves."[26]

George Eaton's only comment after seeing the detailed story of his love life repeated in *Arctic Village* (see pages 250-256 of this book) was, "Of course, Bob, when I was saying how I'd slept with more women than any man in Alaska, I didn't expect you to put it in a book, but I'm a-telling you, it's true." Some who were offended by *Arctic Village* maintained for years that Marshall got the story all wrong. When Marshall returned for his first visit back to the Koyukuk in 1938, five years after the book's publication, reporters in Fairbanks had asked if he was afraid of being lynched when he landed in Wiseman.[27]

But those who took offense had softened their criticism when Marshall gave half of the $3,609 he earned in royalties to the residents of the Koyukuk, sending every adult in the Wiseman area a check for $18 in 1934, a sum probably equal at that time to several weeks' pay. *Arctic Village* was a selection of The Literary Guild, and sold very well for a book published during the Great Depression. Marshall had promised himself that if he made any money from the book, he would split it with the people of the Koyukuk. As the author explained in a letter to a Koyukuk friend, "surely the people about whom a book is written deserve as much out of it as the man who writes it, and that was especially true in this case...(T)he main reason why the book had a pretty big sale was the fact that the Koyukuk people were such unusually splendid human beings." After getting his check one man wrote Marshall, " I was surprised to get the check and to tell you the truth it is me who should give you a check for $18 for the great pleasure the reading of *Arctic Village* gave me."[28]

Critics outside Alaska, including Rockwell Kent in the *New York Herald Tribune*, H.L. Mencken in *The American Mercury* and Ruth Benedict in *The Nation*, gave a chorus of praise for *Arctic Village*. Several called it an "Arctic Middletown," after the famed 1929 sociological study of Muncie, Indiana, by Robert and Helen Lynd. Reviewers were enchanted with Marshall's "personal biography of a wilderness settlement," and his portrayal of the freedom and happiness he found in Wiseman. As Mencken noted, with no newspapers, no politicians, and barely any police, the people of the Koyukuk seemed to live in an ideal world. "Above all," Mencken said, "they are not cursed with theologians. Thus they are free to be intelligent, and what is more, to be decent."[29]

For modern readers, the strengths of Arctic Village are its honesty, openness, and intimate detail. For instance, the chapter on "Quarrels and Unpopularity" begins with the following sentence: "The question was whether Bertha Badeau (a pseudonym) really did say: 'I hope the son-of-a-bitch dies.'" (p. 222)

The richness of statistical detail in *Arctic Village*, and Marshall's careful descriptions of the characters he met, provide readers with a window on the world of 1930, and a nearly complete record of the Koyukuk civilization as Marshall found it. We learn what the people of Wiseman thought about sex, religion, and politics. (According to Marshall, the whites included 37 capitalists, 31 socialists, and 9 "malcontents.") We know how much money they earned, what foods they ate, the books and magazines they read, and what they did for entertainment. We even know what they talked about. In the course of his 13 months in Wiseman, Marshall recorded the subject matter of 5,016 minutes of conversation (totalling more than 83 hours of talk). The most common topic was gossip (495 minutes). Other subjects included joshing (231 minutes), economics and government (197 minutes), sex from a personal standpoint (152 minutes), sex from a factual standpoint (121 minutes), foreign affairs (34 minutes), civil liberties (26 minutes), sporting events (4 minutes), etc. (pp. 285-290).

Despite all the statistical categories he could conjure up, ultimately Marshall admitted it was probably impossible to give a precise measure of happiness or freedom, just as perhaps it was impossible to give a ranking on the importance of wilderness. What he found most inspiring about life in the Koyukuk was its freedom, the freedom of the frontier. In the outside world men often felt doomed to be corporate wage slaves, but not in the wilds of Alaska. As a committed socialist himself, Marshall believed that the subsistence economy of the Koyukuk, where "each person receives directly the profits which accrue from his labor," was far more just and honorable than the cruel capitalism of the outside world with its soup kitchens and bread lines (p. 103). Though he admitted that residents of the Koyukuk suffered "greater physical hardships than they ever would in industrial civilization," and lacked "conveniences which even the most poverty stricken New York family would have," they were still far happier than the average Americans who received their "few thrills vicariously through movies, never conscious that there is a joy in just being alive...."[30]

Those who chose to stay in the Koyukuk, Marshall said, "would rather eat beans with liberty, burn candles with independence, and mush dogs with adventure than to have the luxury and restrictions of the outside world. A person misses many things by living in the isolation of the Koyukuk, but he gains a life filled with an amount of freedom, tolerance, beauty, and contentment such as few human beings are ever fortunate enough to achieve." (p. 379)

Marshall believed that the incessant march of industrialization threatened the freedom of the Koyukuk. When he returned to Alaska in 1938, his first visit in seven years, he sadly noted many changes. Nearly half of the oldtimers had moved or died, and six radios, one automobile, and two or three airplanes a week disturbed the peace of the village. Ironically Marshall himself had brought about one of the greatest changes. With the publication of his book, tourists began to fly in regularly from Fairbanks each summer to see the famed town profiled in *Arctic Village*. Roadhouse proprietor Martin Slisco printed stationery that advertised his establishment as "The Roadhouse of 'Arctic Village.'" With the new wave of tourists, Marshall noted, "Wiseman was no longer beyond the end of the world."[31]

To preserve the freedom of the Koyukuk, Marshall had proposed in a 1937 government report on Alaska's recreational potential that "all of Alaska north of the Yukon River," except for a small area near Nome, should be designated as wilderness. Marshall claimed that the "highest value" of Alaska to the United States "lies in the pioneer conditions yet prevailing throughout most of the territory. These pioneer values have been largely destroyed in the continental United States. In Alaska alone can the emotional values of the frontier be preserved."[32]

Alaska has changed in many ways since Robert Marshall died at age 38—apparently of heart failure—in November 1939, shortly after his fourth and final visit to the Upper Koyukuk.[33] Almost nothing is left of the Koyukuk civilization he once knew, except for the portrait that Marshall created in *Arctic Village*. Wiseman, the town that time forgot, "200 miles beyond the edge of the 20th century," sits nearly astride both the Dalton Highway to Fairbanks and the 800-mile-long Trans-Alaska oil pipeline from Prudhoe Bay to Valdez. The handful of current Wiseman residents enjoy most of the fruits of modern America, including satellite TV and telephone service.[34]

Yet Bob Marshall's legacy continues. Despite the construction of the pipeline and the haul road in the 1970s, the wilderness of the Brooks Range survives. The 8-million-acre Gates of the Arctic National Park and Preserve established by Congress in 1980 is almost four times the size of Yellowstone, and was inspired by the writings of Bob Marshall. The Gates of the Arctic park protects much of the wild Koyukuk country that he knew and loved.[35] What also survives is the spirit of freedom and independence that Alaskans still cherish most about life in the 49th state, a spirit that Bob Marshall captured so well in the pages of *Arctic Village*.

—*Terrence Cole*

NOTES

1. Rockwell Kent to Robert Marshall, 20 May 1933, Box 7, File 6, Robert Marshall Collection, Bancroft Library (hereafter RMC); *New York Herald Tribune Books*, 14 May 1933, p. 3.

The Robert Marshall Collection at the Bancroft Library in Berkeley, California, has been used with the kind cooperation of Bob's younger brother (and hiking companion) George Marshall, without whom this reprint would not have been possible. George Marshall has written extensively about his brother's life. See his bibliography "Robert Marshall as a Writer," *The Living Wilderness*, Autumn 1951, pp.14-23, and "Bibliography of

Robert Marshall: A Supplement," *The Living Wilderness*, Summer 1954, pp.31-35; also see his introduction to the collection of Bob's Alaskan exploration narratives which George collected and edited, entitled (in the second edition) *Alaska Wilderness* (Berkeley: University of California Press, 1970), pp. xxiii-xxxiv.The only full length biography of Marshall yet published is James M. Glover's *A Wilderness Original: The Life of Bob Marshall* (Seattle: The Mountaineers, 1986).

2. Meyer H. Wolff, "The Bob Marshall Wilderness Area," *The Living Wilderness*, July 1941, p. 5.

3. Harvey Broome, "Origins of The Wilderness Society," *The Living Wilderness*, July 1940, p. 15; *The Living Wilderness*, Autumn 1951, p. i.

4. Robert Marshall, "The Problem of the Wilderness," *Scientific Monthly*, February 1930, p. 143, 148.

5. Robert Marshall, "Impressions from the Wilderness," *The Living Wilderness*, Autumn 1951, p. 10.

6. See page 18.

7. Charles Reznikoff, ed., *Louis Marshall: Champion of Liberty* (Philadelphia: Jewish Publication Society of America, 1957); Cyrus Adler, *Louis Marshall: A biographical Sketch* (New York: The American Jewish Committee, 1931).

8. Robert Marshall, *Alaska Wilderness*, pp. 1-2.

9. George Marshall, "Robert Marshall as a Writer," p. 19.

10. Glover, *A Wilderness Original*, p. 66; "Robert Marshall's Autobiographical Outline," n.d. Box 1, File 14, RMC.

11. Chester J. Olsen, "Glimpses of Bob Marshall Afield," *The Living Wilderness*, July 1941, p. 11.

12. Glover, *A Wilderness Original*, p. 79. 206.

13. *Ibid.*, p.22.

14. *Ibid.*, p.21, 57, 78, 92; George Marshall, "Robert Marshall as a Writer," p. 19.

15. Glover, *A Wilderness Original*, p. 66.

16. RM to General Sumner, 5 May 1922, Box 1, File 1, RMC.

17. Robert Marshall, *Alaska Wilderness*, p. 3.

18. RM to "Lincoln," 3 April 1930, Box 1, File 3, RMC.

19. See page 3.

20. RM to Al Cline, 15 July 1930, Box 1, File 4, RMC.

21. RM to Margaret Mead, 28 January 1933, Box 1, File 11, RMC.

22. RM to Harrison Smith, 3 May 1933, Box 1, File 14, RMC.

23. RM to Jesse Allen, 12 April 1933, Box 1, File 13, RMC.

24. *Ibid*.

25. RM to Kenneth Hausker, 7 January 1935, Box 1, File 19, RMC; Joe Ulen to RM, 24 February 1934, Box 11, File 11, RMC.

26. Jesse Allen to RM, 8 May 1933, Box 3, File 9, RMC; Ken Harvey to RM, 2 June 1933, Box 6, File 10, RMC.

27. Robert Marshall, *Alaska Wilderness*, p. 115 (quote), 112.

28. RM to Jesse Allen, 4 April 1934, Box 1, File 17, RMC; Joe Ulen to RM, 4 May 1934, Box 11, File 11, RMC.

29. H.L. Mencken, "Utopia in Little," *The American Mercury*, May 1933, p. 126; Ruth Benedict, "The Happiest People," *The Nation*, 7 June 1933, p. 647; Rockwell Kent, "How People Live in the Arctic Wilderness," *New York Herald Tribune Books*, 14 May 1933, p. 3; Daines Barrington, "An Arctic Middletown," *The Saturday Review of Literature*, 13 May 1933, p. 589; "Books in Brief," *Forum*, June 1933, p. vi.

30. RM to Family, 26 October 1930, Box 1, File 6, RMC.

31. Robert Marshall, *Alaska Wilderness*, pp. 113-114; Martin Slisco to RM, 19 May 1938, Box 10, File 17, RMC; *Alaska Miner* (Fairbanks), 11 July 1939, p. 12.

32. Robert Marshall, "Comments on the Report on Alaska's Recreational Resources and Facilities," Appendix B, p. 213, in U.S. National Resources Committee, *Regional Planning: Alaska—Its Resources and Development* (Washington: Government Printing Office, 1938); see also, Robert Marshall, "Should We Settle Alaska," *The New Republic*, 8 January 1940, pp. 49-50.

33. *New York Times*, 12 November 1939, p. 39.

34. *Fairbanks Daily News-Miner*, "Wiseman Leaving the

Past Behind," 8 July 1990, p. C-1.

35. George Marshall, "Bob Marshall and the Alaska Arctic Wilderness," *The Living Wilderness*, Autumn 1970, pp. 29-32; Bill Brown, "Gaunt Beauty...Tenuous Life: Historic Resource Study for Gate of the Arctic National Park and Preserve," (Anchorage: National Park Service, 1988).

FOREWORD

WHEN *Arctic Village* was published in 1933, I wrote my first
fan letter. The Koyukuk country was part of the caribou country—where Olaus was carrying on his studies and where we had
travelled on our honeymoon.

In a very short time I received a beautiful hand-written letter
from Bob Marshall, in which he said: "When I left the Koyukuk
the people there said 'if you meet the Muries somewhere, give
them our best regards.'

"I figured that out of the millions of Americans, I was not
likely to find any Muries. So—next time you are in Washington
get in touch with me, please."

The following winter we were in Washington, where Olaus
was reporting on his studies for the U.S. Biological Survey (now
the U.S. Fish and Wildlife Service), and we were the house
guests of Dr. and Mrs. Robert Griggs. Robert Griggs had been
the leader of a National Geographic Society expedition to the
Mt. Katmai area—Valley of Ten Thousand Smokes, and he
knew Bob Marshall. Bob was invited to their home for dinner.
I recall so vividly coming into the Griggs' living room that
evening. There, in front of the fireplace, stood Robert Griggs,
and Olaus, and Bob Marshall. I stepped over to shake hands with
Bob; he and Olaus and I looked at one another, and I am sure that
we all knew immediately that this was the beginning of a very
special friendship.

The following summer Bob visited us in Jackson Hole, Wyoming, where Olaus was studying the elk herd. And again in 1939—only weeks before his death. In the meantime The Wilderness Society had been established and Olaus was a member of the first council.

One of my most precious memories—which I often recall—is how delighted our three children were with Bob's visits. He always had some wild and humorous and outlandish stories to tell them; his visits were never long enough.

But the memories are still fresh.

—Margaret E. Murie

ACKNOWLEDGMENT

THE first acknowledgment for assistance in the preparation of Arctic Village must go to all the people of the Koyukuk for their delightful frankness, their good nature about explaining and demonstrating the features of their life, and their unfailing cordiality which made the fifteen months spent in the region constantly profitable and delightful. There was not a single one of the 127 citizens of the Upper Koyukuk who failed to treat me kindly, and with many of the Koyukukers there has been a mutual friendship such as I have seldom experienced.

Specifically I want to thank Verne Watts, Jesse Allen, Ike Spinks, and Harry Foley for the outstanding assistance which they rendered. To Ernie Johnson, with whom I spent some seventy-six days on the trail, I owe an especial debt for his patient demonstration of the art of Arctic travel, winter and summer, and his great store of Arctic knowledge. I am also indebted to Martin Slisco, my kindly landlord, who helped me with so many services that I can not even begin to enumerate them and who was better than a newspaper in disbursing the latest local gossip. From Clara Carpenter, the schoolteacher of Wiseman, I received heartiest coöperation in the giving of intelligence tests to the children.

Among the Eskimos I am especially obligated to Ekok, Big Jim, and Big Charlie Suckik for their eager and thoughtful instruction in the language, beliefs, customs, and activities of their race. Bessie Suckik performed the same sort of service for me with the Indians. To Ekok and Kaaruk goes the credit for the English translation of Eskimo legends and love songs. I want to thank Jennie Suckik for permission to use her drawings which are reproduced in this book.

In the writing of the book I received very valuable assistance from a number of sources. By far the most valuable was that furnished by Lenore Marshall, who read the entire first draught, offering several excellent major criticisms, and instructed me in many of the details of getting a book published. Elise Untermyer also read the book in manuscript form and made a great many desirable suggestions. George Marshall reviewed critically the entire economic part of the book. Eleanor Nelson was kind enough to perform the tedious drudgery of reading proof. Dorothy Coggeshall, from a combination of my abominable voice and outrageous notes, succeeded in transcribing the Eskimo music in what very closely approximates the actual tunes. Magda Skalet gave me much helpful advice and training, before I left for the Arctic, on the use of intelligence tests. Elna Anderson, Carol Bedell, Huntington Cairns, Broadus Mitchell, and Helen Smith offered very valuable suggestions concerning individual chapters. It must of course be stressed that none of the faults of Arctic Village may be blamed on these people, but many of its virtues may be directly attributed to them.

The photographs in this volume were all taken by the author except for the one of General Allen which was supplied by his widow.

ROBERT MARSHALL

January 7, 1933

INTRODUCTION

INTRODUCTION

BLANK spaces on maps had always fascinated me. So when I found in the spring of 1929 that I had a summer ahead in which to do whatever I desired, I took the atlas from my shelf and turned to the map of Alaska. Carefully examining it, I observed that only two really large sections were left uncharted, the one on the South Fork of the Kuskokwim River, southwest of Mount McKinley, the other at the headwaters of the Koyukuk River, north of the Arctic Circle. Mount McKinley was a great temptation, but on the whole the notion of a summer in the Arctic was even more alluring. I decided that there ought, however, to be some purpose back of this spree, so I rationalized a scientific investigation as a reason for my expedition. As a forester and plant physiologist, it seemed eminently appropriate that I should make a study of tree growth at northern timberline.

I cannot say that I learned very much either about tree growth or timberline. But I did come away with a vivid impression that the few white and Eskimo people who were scattered through this remote region were on the whole the happiest folk I had ever encountered. It is so easy, however, to found an erroneous impression on the superficial contacts of a couple of months that I decided to return for at least a year in order to make a detailed study of this civilization of the North.

Consequently, in August, 1930, I set out for a second so-journ in Arctic Alaska. It took me about two weeks' travel by train, boat, and train again, to get from New York to Fairbanks, which, with its 2,000 people, is the metropolis of interior Alaska. At Fairbanks railroads and highways cease, so after a week of waiting for good weather in this city, I took the 200-mile airplane flight into Wiseman, the major settlement in the Koyukuk.

The welcome awaiting me when we landed would seem preposterous to any one with the conventional notions about the stolid frontiersman. Suddenly I realized to what good friends I was returning in Wiseman. The instant I stepped out of the plane, Martin Slisco, jovial roadhouse proprietor, ran up and threw both arms around my neck. Little Willie English, seven-year-old Eskimo boy, with whom I had hop-ping races the previous summer, was next, and he jumped all over me. Pete Dow, cynical old sourdough of thirty-two Arctic winters, nearly pumped my hand off, and his face was cracked with smiles. And following them came all the others, for every one in town, Eskimo and white, was out at the field.

The next two days were spent in Wiseman, conversing happily with friends whom I had known for a few weeks the year before, but who acted as if we were lifelong acquaintances. They were so eager to pour out the events of the past year to some one to whom they were not stale stories long ago. So I heard over and over, from a dozen different persons, each giving a slightly different version, the chief landmarks in the life of the community.

These two days were also spent preparing for a trip which Al Retzlaf, my previous year's partner, and I were taking to the sources of the North Fork River. Al was interested in gold prospecting and I in tree growth, but in spite of these mixed purposes, our partnership worked splendidly. We

THE AUTHOR'S CABIN—INSIDE.

THE AUTHOR AND ERNIE JOHNSON.

panned for gold and measured trees separately, but gloried together in nearly a month of travel up unvisited valleys, in scaling the summits of unknown mountains, in camping more than 100 miles from the closest neighbors, in discovering scenes of natural beauty fully as splendid as the world-famous Yosemite or Glacier Park.

When we got back from this trip at the end of September, Al returned to Fairbanks and I started to prepare a home for the ensuing year. I had rented from Martin Slisco a log cabin next door to the roadhouse. It was sixteen by eighteen feet, eight feet high, and had a board floor, canvas lined walls and ceiling, and a roof of split logs covered over with dirt and sods. On the south side, where it would admit the maximum sunlight, was one large window, five and one-half feet long and two feet high. Through it I could look out across the still unfrozen Koyukuk River to a range of steep, rugged mountains, all covered with snow.

The furnishings of my room included a spring bed, a double-decker wooden bunk, three chairs, a bureau with two deep shelves instead of drawers, a large, flat table for writing, located directly under the window, a cupboard for my kitchen utensils, a table for my wash basin and toilet articles, and a high, home-made cabinet for storing my medical, scientific, and photographic equipment. An iron heater in the middle of the room served the triple purpose of cooking, keeping the cabin warm, and drying damp clothing.

On top of the bureau was an analytical balance, my phonograph, and thirty precious records which I had shipped all the way from Baltimore. Near the window I had a crude bookcase made of old egg crates which contained some sixty-six volumes which I had brought with me, including works as varied as *The Magic Mountain, Mrs. Dalloway, Anna Karenina, Plays of Euripides, Erewhon, The Life of Sir William*

Osler, The Decline of the West, Ordeal of Civilization, Middletown, The Sexual Life of Savages, The Dance of Life, The Quest for Certainty, Social Psychology, Physics of the Air, The Universe Around Us, Minor Surgery, Medical Biometry and Statistics, and Thermodynamics. It was a splendid collection for a year of isolation, but the isolation proved so extremely social that I did not have time to read a quarter of the books.

This sociability commenced the first day I moved into my house, while I was still unpacking my belongings. Three veteran white inhabitants of the Koyukuk and one Eskimo dropped into my cabin, ostensibly to listen to my new records, but actually, I am sure, because they were afraid I might be a little homesick. Thereafter, there was scant opportunity for homesickness. Scarcely a day went by that at least five or six different people did not visit me. During the course of my year in the Koyukuk, every person around Wiseman except one three-months-old baby, and one Eskimo woman who could not speak English, spent at least several hours alone with me in my cabin.

Intimacy with these friendly people was also enhanced by many visits to their own homes. In addition to constant association with those who lived right in Wiseman, I paid about a dozen visits to each of the two nearby gold mining centers on Nolan Creek and Hammond River. Here the miners would invariably welcome me with glowing hospitality, banter with me in unfailing good humor, provide a comfortable bed for as many nights as they could induce me to stop with them, cook delicious meals for me, allow me to work with them in their mines, lend their magazines to me, and borrow my books in return.

Sometimes I took longer trips. Toward the end of October I indulged in my first dog mushing on a four-day journey with Bobbie Jones, when the sky was sparklingly clear and the snow freshly white. The Stanich brothers and Tom Kovich, with whom we stopped along the way, were brimming with eager cordiality. A few weeks later Jesse Allen, Kenneth Harvey, and I went out on a ten-day expedition to haul sheep meat from the head of the Middle Fork. Later we were joined by Albert Ness, and the four of us spent vigorous days in the unique fellowship which comes from enduring mutual hardships, and snug nights in snow surrounded camps where we conversed on the widest variety of subjects. Then in March Ernie Johnson and I occupied a month in exploring the course of an unknown river, and returning to Wiseman by way of the most remote mining camps in the region, where we were welcomed as if we were long-lost friends. Finally, for fifty days during July and August Ernie and I were mapping the source streams of the Alatna and John River drainages, and meeting now and then, scores of miles from the closest human being, some solitary prospector.

But it is not the purpose of this introduction to go into the details of these different expeditions which I made by mushing, boating, and back packing. It is enough to state that a third of my 452 days in the Koyukuk were spent on such journeys. Sometimes they would lead me to isolated cabins, miles from the closest neighbors, where under the stimulation of unanticipated companionship, lonely men would speak to me of yearnings and strivings, of secret satisfactions, of long-buried tragedies, of splendid ideals, and of constant gropings through many years of contemplation for the meaning and significance of life.

However, the major share of my fifteen months in the Koyukuk was passed in the town of Wiseman. My typical day started around seven, when I arose, during much of the time before daylight, started my fire, crawled back into bed while the cabin warmed, and then breakfasted with Martin Slisco. After breakfast, while we waited for the dawn, he would regale me with the latest details of his contemporary love affair, or we would play the phonograph to drive away the last vestiges of drowsiness. I would spend most of the mornings in my cabin, reading, writing, fixing up my notes, and talking with visitors. After cooking my lunch I might spend the afternoon visiting around town, working at home, or going for a walk. I recall a number of evenings when I walked out along the trail, while the far below freezing weather made my nose tingle. The southern sky would be brilliant with sunset colors, the snow all around would change from a strange purple to a dark gray, and diminutive Wiseman when I returned would be twinkling with lights. Then I would repair to the roadhouse, which was at the same time a shelter from the trail and a social center for the community. Supper would always be a loquacious meal, with those who were eating there, and those who merely came to chat, talking back and forth without intermission. After supper I would sometimes remain at the roadhouse until bedtime, either listening to the conversation or dancing, sometimes receive visitors and play the phonograph in my own home, but most often drop around from one cabin or igloo to the other, talking with different friends until far into the night. Then I would walk home through the freezing air, while the northern lights rolled brightly across the heavens, and feel that life could not possibly be more splendid. While I was undressing I might play the *Hungarian Rhapsody*, the *Gymnopedie*, or perhaps Schubert's *Unfinished Symphony*. The last record for the evening I always put on just before turning out the gasoline lantern, and then I listened to it comfortably from bed. When the final note was over and the automatic stop had clicked, it generally took me about thirty seconds to fall asleep.

In the long days of spring and early summer, when there was no darkness at all, we often chatted or danced until two or three in the morning without noticing the time. I remember one night when Kaaruk and Oscar and I set out at midnight to tramp the hills for seven hours, picking cranberries, shooting ducks, stopping now and then to catch grayling at some deep hole in the river, watching the sun rise at one in the morning, and joking and laughing continually. I recall another night when Jennie Suckik and I climbed to see the midnight sun from Smith Creek Dome, and I shall probably never forget the strange light which saturated the vast expanse of wilderness. About this time Jesse Allen, Kenneth Harvey, and I set out on another trip, traveling by the cool daylight of night, and sleeping without blankets in the warmth of mid-day, and feeling that the whole world was a trifle upside down.

Those were days which made life seem a constant romance and adventure. To-day, when I am back in the more prosaic cities of the Atlantic seaboard, it sometimes seems difficult to realize that such events were ever real. But almost every month I receive letters from my Arctic friends, some from the Eskimo girls running to thirty pages, so I have sound evidence that my fifteen months in the Koyukuk was more than a glorious dream.

However, it is not my desire to write about my own adventures, but rather to describe in an objective manner the unusual civilization in which these adventures were set. For I think it would interest many readers to learn something about the independent, exciting, and friendly life of the Arctic frontier. Consequently, I am writing this book with the purpose of painting a complete picture of the civilization of whites and Eskimos which flourishes in the upper reaches of the Koyukuk, 200 miles beyond the edge of the Twentieth Century.

PART I

THE BACKGROUND

I

GEOGRAPHY

IN THE vast domain beyond the Yukon is a distinctive civilization which spreads across the entire drainage of the Koyukuk River lying north of the Arctic Circle, an area embracing approximately 15,000 square miles. While this territory seems rather small when blocked out on the map of Alaska, in comparison with more familiar places it takes on a greater significance. Belgium contains in all less than 12,000 square miles. New Jersey has but 7,500 and Massachusetts barely 8,000 square miles. It would take Massachusetts and New Jersey combined to equal the area of the upper Koyukuk.

But there is this striking difference between the places mentioned and the Arctic Koyukuk. Belgium has a population of 8,060,189 people. New Jersey has some 4,041,334 citizens. Massachusetts shelters 4,249,614 people, while the two states together have a population of 8,290,948. The upper Koyukuk has a total population of 127.

Stated in terms of density of population, it is interesting to compare this region with more familiar places:

Region	Population per Square Mile
Upper Koyukuk	0.0085
Alaska	0.101
Nevada (least densely populated state)	0.8

Region	Population per Square Mile
United States	41.3
New York	264.2
Rhode Island (most densely popu- lated state)	644.3
Belgium	686.0
England	734.2
Manhattan Island	84,113.2

In other words, Alaska as a whole is some twelve times as densely populated as its remote segment, the upper Koyukuk. The least densely populated state in the Union has about one hundred times as many people to the square mile. The United States as a whole has five thousand times, England has nearly 100 thousand times, and Manhattan Island has ten million times as concentrated a population as the civilization of the Arctic Koyukuk.

The 127 people who make up this Arctic civilization include seventy-seven whites, forty-four Eskimos, and six Indians. The following table analyzes this distribution in a little greater detail:

Race	Men	Women	Children	Total
White	70	7	0	77
Eskimo	9	11	24	44
Indian	1	4	1	6
Total	80	22	25	127

It may seem that in taking an arbitrary fraction of the drainage basin of a single river as a unit of civilization, an artificial and illogical boundary has been set. Actually, however, the Arctic drainage of the Koyukuk represents a remarkably unified culture, and the break with an entirely different culture occurs just about at the Arctic Circle. North of the Circle is a civilization composed of a mixture of white men and Eskimos with their central occupation gold mining and their major language English. South of the Circle is a civilization composed almost entirely of Indians who have felt very little the influence of white culture, where the central occupations are still hunting, trapping, and fishing, and the major language is still Indian.

Practically on the Arctic Circle is the Episcopal Mission of St. John in the Wilderness. Around this focus on the north side of the Koyukuk is the Eskimo village of Alatna, and on the south side of the river the Indian village of Allakaket. Both villages show markedly the influence of the white man, much more so than do the Indians lower down the river, but they still remain closer to the down river than the up river culture.

The main Koyukuk River and the lower reaches of its five chief tributaries (the Alatna, South Fork, John, North Fork, and Middle Fork Rivers) flow through a flat, swampy country with no conspicuous relief. But in their upper reaches these streams cut through one of the most rugged terrains imaginable, with precipices rising sheer for hundreds and even thousands of feet, with deep, glacial canyons as sensational as Yosemite, and with great rock mountains jutting almost straight up from the valleys. This back country is virtually unknown even to the inhabitants of the Koyukuk. A few have been into it on hunting or prospecting expeditions, but there are still many areas which have never been visited by man.

The entire population of the Arctic Koyukuk focuses around two towns. Before going further it is necessary to explain that the word town as used in this region has a very different connotation than in the outside world. One can liken this difference to the diversity between the new and the old conception of the atom. The old conception was simply of one solid, substantial mass. But the new conception pictures the atom as consisting of a nucleus and everything in space which it affects. Similarly, the ordinary town consists of a solid, consecutive mass of houses occupying a limited position on the map. But the Koyukuk town consists of the nucleus of the store and everything in space which it affects; in other words, everybody throughout the entire region who comes regularly to the store to trade.

Actually only sixteen of the seventy-seven white people of the upper Koyukuk live permanently around the centers of trade. The majority, some forty-six people in all, live in mining communities of from two to eighteen people at Nolan Creek, Hammond River, Jim Pup, Emma Creek, the Porcupine, and Wild Lake. There are eight people who live close to some community (that is, from one to ten miles away), where they can easily get into contact with human beings, but where they are too remote for neighbors to hear their shouts or observe that no smoke rises from their chimneys in case of some disaster. One of these people, taken violently sick last summer, lay for three days alone in his cabin, too feeble to travel the necessary mile for help. But there are seven men who live in far more genuine isolation than this man. Their homes are from twenty to sixty miles from the closest humankind. The Eskimos almost always live in groups, residing around the towns chiefly in the winter and camping among the caribou hills or along the rivers in summer. It is only their hunters who live in isolation for periods of a few days or at most a few weeks.

Both of the upper Koyukuk towns are located on the main artery of the region, the Koyukuk River. Bettles is the first one reached on ascending this stream. It is thirty-eight miles by trail and ninety miles by the sweeping bends of the river

BETTLES

WISEMAN: The large building in the foreground is the roadhouse,
and the second cabin beyond is the author's home.

UPSTREAM FROM WISEMAN.

DOWNSTREAM FROM WISEMAN: The town is at the left margin of the photograph and the airplane field in the center.

from Alatna at the Arctic Circle. It is located at the confluence of the John River and the main Koyukuk, and merely consists of a dozen occupied houses on a willow flat about eight feet above the river. Some twenty-four of the Koyukuk inhabitants do their trading at the Bettles store and make its roadhouse the social center of their lives.

The term roadhouse too has a different connotation in Alaska than in the outside world. It is not primarily a place for wild parties and intoxication, though these are surely not barred, but is chiefly a haven of shelter along the dogteam road. Every old sourdough [1] in Alaska has recollections of plowing with his dogs through some blizzard, half frozen, half exhausted, wondering whether he would ever reach the end of his dark trail, when into the night would suddenly shine the cheering lights of habitation. He would drive his weary team up to a large log cabin, overjoyed in the assurance at last of a night of warmth and safety. Later, with his dogs tied up, he would sit by the glowing heater, removing his damp moccasins, rubbing his hands together, thawing out his whole chilled body, while the ever ready proprietor would be busy in his kitchen, no matter what the hour, preparing a sumptuous supper. Then while eating he would listen to the gossip of the country, give in exchange the news of the people from whom he had just departed, and feel the glow of friendship so distinctive of the northern hospitality.

Eighty-five miles up the Koyukuk from Bettles, upon a low flat where Wiseman Creek flows into the Middle Fork from the west, is the metropolis of Wiseman. Here some 103 people come to do their trading, of whom as many as eighty-one actually were in town at one time during the

[1] A sourdough is a veteran of the North country. The term is sometimes used to include any one who has witnessed the Yukon and its tributaries freeze up in the autumn and break up in the spring.

Christmas festivities. Wiseman boasts forty-eight occupied houses, located chiefly along three streets which run parallel to the river and two more avenues which extend back from the Middle Fork. However, when I speak of avenues please do not imagine paved boulevards. In summertime a Wiseman street is represented by a brown streak through the surrounding weeds and willows. In winter it is marked by a hard groove made by the passing sleds and walkers in the soft snow. In spring it is merely a part of town even a little muddier than the rest. At most places it is bounded by fences and cabins, except for the outside of the front street which is the bank of the river. This riverside road is the longest street in town, being about half a mile between its two extreme cabins.

It is not, however, the minor dimensions of town which are most impressive in Wiseman. It is instead the huge expanse which separates this lonely settlement from the outposts of Twentieth Century civilization. It is 200 miles airline to the closest pavement, the closest auto, the closest railroad, or the closest electric light at Fairbanks. The nearest hospital or doctor is 150 miles to the southwest at Tanana. Even steamboat navigation ends eighty-five miles down the river at Bettles, while the closest church is ninety miles further still at Alla-kaket. For many things which a person desires he must send 3,500 miles to Seattle. Such great distances give the Koyukuk an inaccessibility reminiscent of the Nineteenth Century frontier of the West, and an isolation which lies beyond the conception of most people in the closely populated regions of Twentieth Century mechanization.

II

CLIMATE

THERE are few civilizations set in such a varied yearly climatic cycle as is the Koyukuk. The difference between the short, sunless, snow-filled days of December, and the verdant, twenty-four-hour days of June and July, is almost the difference between two worlds. All the economic activities of the people, all the social habits, even the psychological reactions are revolutionized by the passage of the seasons.

Viewed from a scientific standpoint, the basic force behind all these differences is the fact that the earth's axis is tilted at an angle of 23° 27′ away from a perpendicular to its orbit. This tilt, as we all learned in fourth grade geography, means that in summer the northern regions of the earth are pointed toward the sun, while in winter they are faced so much away that even at mid-day the sun in many places cannot clear the horizon. The Arctic Circle is an imaginary line the same number of degrees from the North Pole as the earth's axis is tilted. As one travels north from the Circle there is a constant increase in the number of sunless days of winter as well as the days of midnight sun in summer, unless local topography happens to alter theoretical conditions.

Of course, in any mountainous country local topography does. Thus at Wiseman, which is only one degree north of the Circle, there are thirty-one consecutive days, from December 7 through January 6, when the sun can never be seen. This is because the 3,000 foot mountains which wall in the valley of the Koyukuk hide the sun even when it rises several degrees above the horizon. At the other extreme, although in theory one should be able to see the midnight sun for a couple of weeks in summer, the high mountains block it out entirely from Wiseman, and one must climb several hundred feet up some surrounding hillside before it becomes directly visible. But right in town one can always see some color in at least the northern sky for four and one-half consecutive months, from April 15 through August 28.

The amount of light in Wiseman on clear days at different periods of the year may best be indicated by the following chart:

Condition of Light	Dec. 21	Feb. 21	Apr. 21	June 21
First color in sky	8.00 A.M.	5.50 A.M.	. . . .	. . . .
First daylight	9.10 A.M.	6.40 A.M.	2.20 A.M.	. . . .
Sunrise	. . . .	10.40 A.M.	4.50 A.M.	1.25 A.M.
Sunset	. . . .	3.15 P.M.	7.35 P.M.	9.30 P.M.
Last daylight	2.40 P.M.	5.20 P.M.	9.40 P.M.	. . . .
Last color in sky	3.50 P.M.	6.10 P.M.	. . . .	. . . .

I have defined daylight as that amount of light necessary for trees to appear three dimensional and colored, in contrast to darkness when they are merely flat, black objects. In the shortest days of winter I could only read comfortably, without artificial light, for an hour and a half at midday, even when seated next to my south-facing window. On cloudy days at this time I had to burn my light all day long. At the schoolhouse the gasoline lantern is continually lighted during December and January. At the other end of the year it is unnecessary to use artificial light even at midnight from May 1 to about August 10.

THE CANYON OF THE KOYUKUK: Between Bettles and Wiseman.

THE RIVER CROSSING AT WISEMAN—WINTER.

THE RIVER CROSSING AT WISEMAN—SUMMER.

Of course the winter is featured by cold as well as darkness. The coldest thoroughly authentic temperature was one of — 70° F. recorded at the Weather Bureau Station at Allakaket, just at the south edge of the region. In December, 1901, a standard Green thermometer, hung outside the old roadhouse at the mouth of Minnie Creek, registered — 72° F. There have been scores of days when the thermometer passed 60° below. In the winter of 1929-1930 this happened every day for two consecutive weeks. On the other hand, there have been relatively mild winters. One of these, according to all accounts, was the one which I spent in the Koyukuk, when the coldest temperature was merely minus fifty.

In summer the weather becomes as warm as in many mountainous parts of the United States. On July 29, 1923, the temperature in the shade rose as high as 90° F. at the Weather Bureau Station at Allakaket. It had been —69° F. on January 26 of the same year, making a six month span of 159 degrees Fahrenheit. In general any temperature over 70° F. is considered very hot weather.

The seasons in the Koyukuk are of considerably different definition and extension than those of the temperate zones. Winter, the dominant season, I would define as that time of the year when the ground is continuously covered with snow and when a person in traveling must be constantly prepared for below zero weather. Summer is the time when the rivers are open for navigation, the ground is free from snow except on the higher mountains, the leaves are out on the hardwood trees, and the mosquitos, and later the gnats, make life thoroughly miserable for any one not prepared to cope with them. Spring is a brief transition period between the two, when the snow is melting, the rivers breaking up, the ground exceptionally muddy, and travel an extremely difficult matter. Autumn is another brief transition period when the rivers are freezing and the ground is alternately bare and covered with snow. It would not be possible to set hard and fast limits to these seasons, but in a general way they have the following approximate duration at Wiseman:

Winter	October 10 to May 10	7 months
Spring	May 10 to June 10	1 month
Summer	June 10 to September 10	3 months
Autumn	September 10 to October 10	1 month

If you come to Wiseman for the first time during the summer months there is little to suggest the Arctic. You see green hills rising all around you to end in rocky summits three thousand feet above the valley, yet not a trace of snow on any of them. There is dark green timber in all of the valleys and well up on the south-facing mountain slopes. The muddy flats are covered with clumps of sedges, and many delicate flowers are in bloom from the valley floor to the highest summit. The turbulent Koyukuk boils along, now tumbling over shallow riffles, now racing squarely into cut banks, now flowing in orderly procession for a brief distance down some spruce-girded lane. The bright gravel bars which fill its valley are cut into innumerable abandoned channels where it has flowed along in former years, and where it may start to flow again at any moment. Almost everything at this season could find its counterpart in any wild temperate region. It is only when one walks about in the full daylight of midnight that there is a sense of the exotic, and the weird feeling of mystery that one anticipates at the ends of the earth.

There will come a night, sometime about the middle of August, when the thermometer will drop well below freezing, and in the morning when you rise to look outside your cabin you will notice the whole valley tinged with yellow.

From then on summer will keep building toward autumn. First the birches, then the cottonwoods, then the willows become bright golden. The hillside herbs turn red and purple and yellow. The muddy flats are frozen every morning, and every evening the winds down valley from the unexplored north bring promise, though summer has not yet departed, that winter is almost at hand. By the end of August there is a brief period each night when darkness settles down, and on clear nights one sees the first mild flashing of the aurora.

Early in September the birch leaves come down in great numbers, and soon after the cottonwood commences to lose its foliage. The rivers grow very shallow, and one knows that their source streams in the high Arctic Divide have frozen. On cold mornings the river is filled with slush ice which may keep flowing for several hours after the sun strikes the surface of the water. The ground becomes frozen even in midday, making walking delightfully easy after all the mud of summer. Some cloudy day the falling rain will commence to turn to snow, and in a few hours everything will be white. But it is still only autumn, and the sun is sufficiently high that a few hours of shining will melt all the snow in the valley. However, on the mountaintops the bare ground will not show up again for nine or ten months. Some time early in October there will be a little heavier snowstorm than before, and then one morning you will wake up to find that the ground is buried to remain so, and that winter is really at hand.

Shortly after the snow has come to stay the main river freezes solidly. The days grow rapidly shorter, so that where there were ten hours of sunlight at the autumnal equinox in September, two months later only an hour and a half is left. On the sixth of December half of the sun skids along the horizon for ten minutes, and then disappears, not to return until the seventh of January. During the sunless days, if it is clear weather, there is a continuous sunset effect in the sky to the south from the first break of dawn to the last twilight. I remember vividly, one clear, cold Sunday afternoon, walking back toward Wiseman from Hammond River. About three o'clock, just at dusk, I came to a place where the trail swung out on a high point overlooking the Middle Fork, and there below me was a barren plain of snow stretching half a mile through the twilight to the cold, black forest. Beyond that was the most gorgeous sunset you can imagine, a whole sky warm and glowing, and everything so quiet and beautiful that I wondered what commensurate value the outside world could possibly provide.

There are many crystal clear nights, when the whole sky is covered with surging waves of the aurora, bands of green and blue and purple and white which go shooting and rolling and twisting across the heavens in a display of brightness which is never the same for two consecutive seconds, which sometimes almost fades into oblivion, at others bursts in full vividness over the entire expanse of the sky, and even seems to dip down below the mountaintops and race along the surface of the earth. The full moon at this time of year is so bright that you can read fairly fine print by its light, and each star is a clear, sharp, twinkling beacon, almost a solid, substantial mass in its certain outlines. And as a frame for everything, above and below, are the cold, moonlit mountains rising whitely against the sky.

Early in January there is great excitement. The sun has returned again. The first time it shines in town old and young alike are exuberant. I walk down the street and an old sourdough, cutting wood in front of his cabin, shouts and points to the sun. At another cabin a man who has spent thirty-four

winters in the North is all beaming. He laughs and quotes
these lines from "Paradise Lost":

> *"Oh thou that, with surpassing glory crowned,*
> *Look'st from thy sole dominion like the god*
> *Of this new World—at whose sight all the stars*
> *Hide their diminished heads—to thee I call."*

I drop in at an Eskimo cabin where three old women are
seated on the floor sewing moose hide and gossiping. They
point excitedly to the wall where the sunlight is shining, and
one of them chants an Eskimo nonsense rhyme about the sun.
Another says in broken English: "Me feel pretty young to-
day. Old fellow come back again." Then they all laugh. I go
out and pass by an igloo. A five-year-old Eskimo girl who
can hardly speak English runs up to me.

"See that down there?" she says, pointing to sun, and then
she jumps up and down in excitement.

At first the increase in sunlight is slow. It is almost two
weeks before the sun shows up for even an hour. But around
the beginning of February the days do noticeably lengthen,
and by March they stretch so rapidly that one can readily
observe that each day is longer than the one before. On the
first of April there are six more hours of sunlight in town
than on the first of March.

During these months of increasing daylight Wiseman
shows its most typical appearance. The roofs of the houses,
the fences, and the summer gardens which they surround are
buried under a deep layer of powdery snow. Only the streets
and the entries to the cabins are well packed down by the constant passage of sleds and walkers. By day a blue smoke rises
from each occupied cabin, at night the light gleams out from
the yellow windows in cheery warmth.

Viewed on clear days, the setting of Wiseman is inspiring

until one becomes so accustomed to it as to forget the fact that men grow up and die without ever beholding even a small fraction of the beauty which constantly surrounds this village. As far as one can see, up and down the Koyukuk, the flat valley floor is flanked by pure white mountainsides, jutting into rocky pinnacles which catch the sunlight hours before the lowlands are out of shadow. Behind the town a series of terraces ascend to the base of sparkling summits which rise in opposition to the deep blue sky. Across the Koyukuk is a cut bank, projecting about fifty feet upwards. It is pleasant to climb to its top late in the afternoon and watch the evening and night come down on the valley. At first, backed by the bright, setting sun, Wiseman is an imposing-looking village, with its well-spaced group of houses arranged in orderly rows, up and down the river. But as the sun dips behind the mountains, and the chill evening winds arise, the town seems to shrivel and the all-abounding wilderness grows larger and more impressive. Dusk keeps on deepening, a single light shines from a cabin window, and before long all of Wiseman is aglow. Its brightness, however, seems very trivial in the infinite extension of the uninhabited mountains. As darkness descends, the wilderness keeps on expanding, until when night has fallen the sparkle of town seems only the tiniest oasis of warmth and comfort, almost lost in the all-pervading desolation and freezing and mystery of the Arctic.

But even an Arctic winter has an end. By the middle of April there is no more total darkness. The snow commences to melt on the roofs under the influence of the high sun. By the end of the month, here and there in the town, out on the river bar, along the lower south-facing hillsides, bare spots of ground appear. Early in May the niggerheads are already in blossom, though most of the ground is still buried under snow.

Before the middle of May there is so little snow left in the flats that sledding becomes impossible. Then some day, without any warning, you perceive that the ice is gone from the river and the water is running free. Day by day the snow continues to disappear until the flats are all bare, and the mountainsides show a spectacular speckling of white and green. Only the north slopes still remain a pure white. But not for long. Under the constant vigor of the sunlight, which is already shining more directly than it ever does in temperate zones, the snow is taken away so rapidly that you can almost see it disappearing, hour by hour. The side streams now are brim full of water, and little trickles which you can cross in summer without wetting the soles of your shoes are absolutely unfordable. A week or two after the streams around Wiseman are at the full, the ones up valley reach their peak. Then the flood comes down the river, covering gravel bars and little islands and everything from rim to rim of the valley floor, a wild, surging, absolutely uncontrollable torrent, sweeping along willows and large logs and even entire, uprooted trees, which go bobbing up and down as they ride the crest of the inundation.

Meanwhile the flowering plants are at the height of their glory. The delicate white blossoms of the Arctic anemone are sprayed along the warmer banks as early as the middle of May. They are shortly followed by the golden dandelions and buttercups, the purple violets, the goldthread, and the angowuk. Early in June the spruce forests are carpeted with the large, white blossoms of the Dryas, most widely distributed of all the Arctic plants. Throughout the month this eight-petaled flower makes the woods glorious. It's place of prominence is followed by the golden California poppy and the Arctic sage and later still by a myriad of blue forget-me-nots.

But long before the forget-me-nots are in bloom the insects come out so fiercely that most men must wear a head net and gloves constantly when they are working, to protect themselves from the mosquitoes. These are taken philosophically and jocularly. "Only about two more months of them," says Wes Ethrington, the day after they appeared, "and then a month of gnats, and then the snow again."

Sometime around the middle of June the first hot spell sets in. The temperature rises above 70° and feels more like 95° with the direct solar radiation. Then at last your mind, which has not quite been able to keep up with the rapid changes, drops the last thought of winter, and suddenly you realize that summer has come again.

III

HISTORY

FOR AT least a hundred years before the advent of the
white race the Arctic Koyukuk was largely a no-man's land.
The settlements of the Indians extended only up the main
river for a short distance above the mouth of the South Fork.
The Eskimos did not live in the region at all, but came across
from the Kobuk and Noatak Rivers and over the low passes
from the Arctic, to hunt and fish in the watersheds of the
Alatna and John Rivers. But, in spite of these minor inva-
sions, the greater portion of this 15,000-square-mile territory
was as untraveled as it had been when it was buried under the
last ice sheet.

The first white men to enter the Arctic Koyukuk were
Lieutenant Henry T. Allen and Private Fred Fickett of the
U. S. Army. Allen, later nationally famous as the commander
of the Ninetieth Division of the United States Army in the
World War, and internationally admired for his humane and
tactful administration of the duties of commander of the
American Army of Occupation in Germany after the War,
had been commissioned to make an exploration of the almost
unknown interior of Alaska. During the course of a 2,200
mile wilderness journey he reached in August 1885 a place
about five miles above the mouth of the John River. Upon
his return to the United States he made a remarkably accurate

map of the Koyukuk River which the best previous sketches had made to head about 400 miles off course. This initial exploration of Allen's was augmented the following March by a journey of Lieutenant Stoney of the Navy across the drainage of the Alatna River. As a result of these two expeditions the outside world received its first knowledge of the upper Koyukuk.

During the subsequent years a few adventuresome prospectors commenced to search for gold in the remote sources of this river. John Bremner and Peter Johnson were the first to brave its isolation, coming there in 1887 and several years following. The dangers were genuine, but the isolation not quite sufficient, for Bremner encountered some Indians on the Hog River who murdered him in 1891. In that same year Johnnie Folger made his first journey to the Koyukuk, and for four years with a series of different partners he mined the placers on the South Fork, Chapman Creek, and Tramway Bar. The first gold in paying quantities was discovered at the latter place in 1893. In all there were probably eighteen or twenty different prospectors who visited the upper Koyukuk between 1887 and 1897.

Then came 1898.

From all over the world 80,000 people went stampeding to the North country, certain of a fortune in exchange for a few weeks, a few months, or a few years of adventure, depending on the degree of their optimism. Many of them knew nothing about the outdoors, most of them knew nothing about gold mining, and all of them knew nothing about the requirements for existence in the North. Possessing various degrees of stamina and adaptability to totally new conditions, some died, most gave up, a fraction remained and founded the present civilization of Alaska.

The great focus for the stampede of '98 was Dawson and

the Klondike. However, the good claims had already been staked in 1897. All one could do was to buy one of these for a huge sum of money, work for wages, prospect on worthless creeks, or move to some other part. A great many chose the latter course. About 1,000 people from this Dawson over-flow boated to the Koyukuk in the late summer of 1898. Some 200 of these found their way north of the Arctic Circle, and staked out a great swath of country on the South Fork, Middle Fork, and Alatna drainages. Caught short by the early freezeup, they had to spend the winter on these bleak and frigid rivers, a pathetic band, isolated, incompetent, hor-ribly homesick for the outside world from intercourse with which they were entirely severed. One can still see the crum-bling remains of the cabins they built for themselves in clus-ters which they optimistically christened Arctic City, Beaver, Rapid City, Union City, Peavey, Seaforth, Soo City, Jimtown. One can still imagine the smoke rising from the chimneys of these long-forgotten settlements, while lonely men clustered around stoves, wondering if winter would ever end, wonder-ing if they could outlast scurvy or starvation, wondering al-most if there really were other people anywhere in the world. By a miracle only two out of the two hundred men marooned in the Arctic were frozen to death, one drowned, and one died of a fatty heart. The others, as soon as the river had broken in the spring, pulled stakes and dropped down to the Yukon, leaving as their only permanent record the names of their wives and sweethearts on most of the creeks flowing into the Koyukuk for a hundred miles north of the Arctic Circle.

Following their departure a hardier and more permanent group of miners entered the country. Four of them are still resident there to-day. The first real money was struck by Knute Ellingson on Myrtle Creek that summer. The first store was opened at the mouth of John River that autumn by

Gordon Bettles, after whom the settlement which grew up around it was named. The prospectors were still, however, leading a nomadic life, and they were still very much cut off from the normal comforts of even frontier existence. Probably the best picture of those nomadic days can be given by quoting the reminiscences of an old German named Carl Frank who still resides in the Koyukuk.

In those days we didn't have no time for prospecting anywhere. We was just running around wild, stampeding. It was in February, I remember, I was living just as comfortable as can be in a little cabin in Bettles, big stove, big woodpile, plenty of blankets, what more could I want? Only I was a little low in grub. Then some fool—we had awful liars in those days—we have them now—he whisper about something up North Fork, so we all wanted to get a claim of course there too. I got tangled up with Argo Bill as a partner. I had a hell of a time with him. He was a tough fellow. He always want to shoot the gun. He growl: "You do what I say or I blow out your brains." I don't understand much English in them days, but I understand that. Plummer, he come along with us. I didn't bother about getting snowshoes, I think I can just walk along the trail, it will be good and hard. So we set out along the trail, pulling and pushing on our sled. There wasn't hardly any dogs in the country in them days, and it cost you nearly a whole winter's outfit to buy one.

We met John Tobin, oh, what a liar he was. He whisper, something awfully rich on Alder Creek. There is no trail to Alder Creek broken out, just the deep snow. Plummer has snowshoes, Argo Bill has snowshoes. I want to get in on the rich creek, so I make snowshoe out of a young spruce tree and some board. I have to practice first. Of course you can slip along, slip along, but the thing gets so awfully sidling, and it's very slow. Bill and Plummer start out first, and so soon as I am ready I start along, tracking after them. I walk and I walk, but I can't see anything of them. I came to a creek and I see where they blaze for me to write my name on, to stake out my own claim. But it get darker and darker and I still don't see anything of them. They climb right up over a mountain and I have awfully hard time with my boards. Pretty soon I come to a place where I can't see their trail no more, and then I really am lost. The snow gets hard and I take off my boards and walk on the snow. Then pretty soon it gets soft again and I have left my boards behind. I slip down under the trees and all over, and the snow gets down my neck and the snow gets up my sleeves and the snow gets inside my pants. Then I come to a creek and pretty soon I see a trail. Oh, my God, I feel good. I saw this must be Alder Creek. I don't know which way to follow trail, but I think maybe I go downstream. In a little while I see light through the trees, and then I see a fire, and pretty soon I find Plummer and Argo all set up comfortable there in the snow for the night. We all talk, but the worst was I couldn't make myself understood what I had done, I speak such awful English, and they just laugh at me. I say: "If I could only explain myself," and then they laugh some more.

After we get finished up with the Alder Creek business I go down to the mouth of the North Fork to rest up. I had hardly any food left, and I sit alone in my tent wondering what I should do. All at once I hear some one walking very quick up to the tent. I go outside and there is Tom Dowd. He looks as if he is pretty nearly crazy. He says: "Oh, an awful thing has happened. Andy Seaman shot himself." Andy was his partner, a nice young chap, about 27 years old, only he was so awful religious.

I say: "Where is he and how did it happen?"

Tom says: "He's on the North Fork, near Florence Creek. He was pulling his sleigh in front, and he had his shotgun lying on it all cocked, and the trigger must have caught on some willow, and now he's dying."

We went right out to Florence Creek, and find the poor

fellow. He was suffering terribly. He was wounded all through the bowels, and the pain and the worry drive him crazy. His mind was in a terrible way. He kept shouting: "God forgive me, God forgive me, oh, my God, my God, forgive me, forgive me, oh, forgive me," all day long. What he wanted Him to forgive I don't know, but it made me feel bad. I think it was awful. If religion is any good for any one it should be to ease your dying moments. But his religion put him through the worst agony I ever saw a man go through.

"My God," I thought, "if religion is only that the last hour of the poor religious man is made so miserable, my God, I say, the hell with religion."

After three terrible days like this he died. We hauled him on a sled to Pope Creek, just across the Koyukuk from the mouth of the North Fork. There was a cabin there, and we put his body inside. Then we start to dig a hole, but the ground is so hard and frozen it take us two days just to dig a place big enough for his body. We finished it the evening of the second day, but we didn't bury him that night. We cooked our beans over a fire in the snow. The bacon was rotten. After a while I go in the cabin to get something. There was no window in it, no light at all. I open the door and all at once there was a rumpus there, a r-r-r-r. "I'm not afraid," I think, but I am though. You know how a man feels, you have a dead man there. I don't believe in a ghost but I think a little there was a ghost anyway. I stand perfectly still for a few seconds, and then all at once something rush by my leg, and out into the snow, and I nearly fall over. But it was no ghost, only a marten that had gotten inside some way.

The next day there was the funeral. We hauled him out of the cabin—it was 60° below zero that morning and the sun was blood red. Dowd was an Irishman, born in America, a nice, fine, slow spoken gentleman.

"Carl," he said, "I'm not a good talker, but I'll pray the Lord's prayer anyway."

Then we let him down. I was not religious, I never was,

but it comes so funny to a man when you remember back how we put the fellow down, there was no one around, only us two ragged stiffs kneeling there at the grave, and the sun so big, and the air so cold.

Then, when we had that fellow buried, that Tom Dowd, he want to go prospecting then. He say: "What we do now, Carl?" I say: "We go to Florence Creek, that is Get-Rich-Creek, but—" I say: "I have no grub." Dowd say: "That's all right, I have no grub either, we get some from Jack Hood."

We go down to Bettles and talk to Hood, and he agree to grubstake us. But he was awful much in love with the natives down in Bettles in those days. He is too busy to haul grub for us, but we haul a little grub ourselves to Florence Creek, just enough to last a couple of weeks, till Hood gets up with the team. But Hood does not come. My partner goes out to get ptarmigan and he fall and sprain his ankle. I have a partner down at Bettles, and a partner in the hospital, and the grub thirty miles away. It was an awful time. Every day I go out to get ptarmigan, but I do not know how to do it very well, and we get pretty empty. A whole week more pass. Still Hood did not arrive. I don't know what we will do. I don't think people ever starve to death any more, but still I think, how can you live without any food? Finally Hood came just before the snow melt.

Then we start to prospect like the deuce. But we don't find any gold. We prospect four weeks, but still we don't find anything. Finally we think it's no use prospecting this way any more. So we come back to river to go up to Twelve-mile Creek. But meantime the river had broken up, and there was so much water everywhere we had to wait in the Canyon five or six days for the water to go down. We decide to cache our stuff here while we go up the river so we won't have so much junk to haul. I had a good feather bed and my pillows I brought from 'Frisco and lots of good clothes. Tom had his lots of clothes too. We made a big cache in a swampy place, and left everything there.

Then we set out for Twelvemile. Tom set out by river, but I said, no I will walk across country, it will be shorter and easier. They all draw us maps and tell us just where it is, back of big mountain range. But something go wrong. There was a mountain range all right, but it was the wrong mountains. I got lost for three days. It was the worst thing I ever had happen to me. I wander and wander and wander, and hardly sleep all that time, and I think now I really am a goner. Then I see some hills, way off in the distance, which look like they draw on the map. I went up to those hills and see far over there a creek. I went to the creek and it was running the wrong way. I say to myself: "My God, this creek is wrong." Then I don't know what to do. I wander all over some more, and finally I find myself on the river. Then I think I will not leave this any more. I keep follow it up all around big bends and points, but I'm scared to leave. Finally on the third day, I come to mouth of big creek, and there is Tom, all comfortable in camp.

We work all summer long. In the fall we come down from Twelvemile Creek, no gold after all. But we were going to get good clothes and go down to see town at Bettles. We got down to our cache and we couldn't find it. It had been a very dry summer, and the swamp had dried up, and the whole country was on fire, and our cache had all burned up. We couldn't find anything but a few burned blue dishes. That was all right, we couldn't help it. We go down to Bettles, as flat broke as could be.

Then the South Fork fellows come down. They have pretty good blowout. We drink that squareface gin. I didn't know that stuff. It look like water but it did not taste like water. They drag several fellows home on sleighs. By and by my partner fall on floor, off counter. The fellows say, "Let him lay there, he'll sleep good there." But just when

Knute Ellingson:
He struck the first real money in the Koyukuk in 1899.

JESSE ALLEN, AUTHOR, AND NUTIRWIK AT CANYON CREEK CAMP.

I leave, Pat Judge, he say, "Come, Carl, let's bring your partner home." So we took him home, he's nice and loose and limber, and I think he will be fine in the morning. Then he was sleeping to beat the deuce. After an hour I came away, he was still sleeping good.

Sunday morning I look out of my cabin. The sun was shining so nicely on the new snow, and I stretch my arms over my head, and think this is a great world. All at once I see Pat Judge run like the dickens. I run out, and shout, "What's the matter?" He say: "Tow Dowd is dead."

We bury him then. Israel make a speech. He mean it good, but it sound pretty funny. He says: "We're living here in a cold country, and if we take a drink we mean it well. It wasn't your business, God, to get sore at poor old Tom." Then we all start to sing a song, *Nearer, my God, to Thee,* or what was it they sing.

The history of the upper Koyukuk since 1898 may be told succinctly in the three parallel columns of the following table. The white population, the gold production, and the prostitutes all reached approximately simultaneous peaks in two different periods. The first occurred from 1900 to 1903 when successive stampedes were on to numerous creeks, and nearly $800,000 in "sunburned" gold was recovered from the shallow gravels of their valleys. The second was from 1908 through 1916 when the deeply buried bedrock on Nolan Creek and Hammond River was being mined.

Year	Permanent White Population	Gold Production in Thousand Dollars	Prostitutes
1898........	200	...	0
1899........	120	...	0
1900........	270	107	2
1901........	320	173	6

Year	Permanent White Population	Gold Production in Thousand Dollars	Prostitutes
1902	350	200	10
1903	300	301	7
1904	210	200	0
1905	220	165	1
1906	160	165	0
1907	120	100	0
1908	240	220	6
1909	230	420	5
1910	190	160	8
1911	160	130	5
1912	230	216	9
1913	250	368	8
1914	270	260	13
1915	300	290	14
1916	250	320	12
1917	200	250	7
1918	150	150	2
1919	130	110	2
1920	119	90	0
1921	107	78	0
1922	101	132	0
1923	97	37	0
1924	92	54	0
1925	88	50	0
1926	93	68	0
1927	98	78	0
1928	90	46	0
1929	83	32	0
1930	77	31	0
1931	71	27	0
Total	...	5,028	...

The first streams to yield gold in large quantities were Myrtle Creek, Emma Creek, and Gold Creek, all discovered in 1899 and 1900. They were located between sixty and eighty miles from the store at Bettles, and consequently it became necessary for a trading center to spring up a great deal closer to the hub of mining activity. As early as 1899 the town of Slate Creek was started at the mouth of the creek which bears that name. In the summer of 1900 one of the waves of green stampeders got as far up the Koyukuk as this point, then got cold feet, turned around, and departed. This incident was enough to change the first, unromantic appellation of the settlement to Coldfoot. The real boom in Coldfoot did not come until the next year when both the Northern Commercial Company, the great trading organization for all Alaska, and William Plummer opened stores. At the same time other essential concomitants of a frontier civilization had commenced to function, so that when the peak was reached in 1902 Coldfoot boasted one gambling hole, two road-houses, two stores, seven saloons, and ten prostitutes. But there were no churches, and indeed to this day no house of worship has ever appeared north of Allakaket.

The diggings on Myrtle Creek and Emma Creek were only a few miles from Coldfoot, so the men who were mining there paid frequent visits to town in quest of hilarity. Twice a year, in the spring and fall, there was a general reunion when the men came down from the more distant creeks to haul back their summer's or winter's supplies. In the normal celebrating which ensued some of the fellows became pretty wild. Fred Swift, one of the worst dare-devils, tried one night to enter the house of Lydia, fairest of all the prostitutes. Lydia was having a brief spasm of living steadily with another miner at the time, and she did not want to let Swift in. She locked the door, and Swift tried to break it down. He employed such energy that she became frightened and blazed away with her revolver, right through the door. The shot missed its mark, and Swift said in an ordinary, conversational voice: "A little more to the right, Lydia." Then he jumped to the left. Lydia fired according to his new direction and Swift said calmly: "A little more to the left, Lydia," and jumped to the right. After repeating this several times he tired of it, and built a bonfire on her front porch. Finally, in frantic desperation at the thought of losing her house, Lydia allowed him to enter.

In the spring of 1905 there was a large crowd of impatient miners waiting in Bettles for the first grub boats, that they might get provisions to outfit for the big stampede which was going up John River that season. The first boat brought no food but considerable dynamite. The exasperated miners broke into some of the boxes and took out the sticks. To these they attached cap and fuse, then ignited the latter, and chased each other around town with the blazing sticks of dynamite. Just before they exploded they would toss them over the bank into the river. Miraculously nobody was hurt, but there was a noise like a battle all through the night.

Nevertheless, in spite of such riotous antics, it was never a camp of desperados. "It was too hard for the really tough guys to come so far from comforts," one of the veterans of those early days once told me. Argo Bill had the reputation of being the bad man of the Koyukuk. He would bluster, and aim his gun at people, and growl that if they wouldn't do whatever he might desire he would blow out their brains. Finally a mild-mannered Austrian called his bluff, and subsequently Argo Bill became as docile as any one in camp. After the first few years nobody carried guns any more, except to go hunting.

It is truly remarkable that in this period there was almost

no trouble between the white people and the natives. It must have required an amazing amount of tolerance and consideration to bring about that happy state of affairs. The first contact had not been so propitious, for the whites had been very careless with their fires as well as their sexual activities, and the Indians had grounds to be incensed. The murder of John Bremner may be attributed to such early friction. The Eskimos, who commenced to migrate to the Koyukuk from the North at the same time that the big stampede of 1898 populated the country from the South, never had had any difficulty at all. There is not even a single instance, in the thirty-four year history of contact between these two races, of any serious physical injury being administered by a member of the one race to a member of the other.

Although there was still a great amount of gold being taken out of the ground after 1903, the number of people in the Koyukuk commenced to decline. This was largely because the cost of living was so high. In 1905 some exaggerated rumors of a bonanza on the John River brought probably 400 transient prospectors to the Koyukuk, of whom several dozen remained, but aside from this brief boom the population diminished steadily. In 1906 there was a big stampede to the adjacent Chandalar country, and this made such a marked depletion in the ranks of the Koyukuk that within two years its population was cut in half.

In the autumn of 1907 three Swedes, John and Louis Olson and John Anderson, were given a strip of ground 300 feet wide on Nolan Creek. They were supposed to prospect this ground and find if there was any gold deep down below the surface. If there was gold in paying quantities on this narrow sample then it would be worth the owners' while to mine the adjacent claims. Actually there was almost unbelievable fortune. The three Swedes took out $100,000 the first winter. In three years they recovered over a quarter of a million dollars from their narrow strip. No piece of ground in the whole country ever yielded so richly. The news of fortune, even with the slow communication of those days, speedily traveled all over Alaska. By the spring of 1908 there were over two hundred new men rushing into the Koyukuk, and half of them stayed. The lonesome valley of Nolan Creek throbbed with activity. Fifteen or twenty different outfits were sinking holes, and a dozen boilers chugged away, day and night. Responding promptly to the stimulus of gold, half a dozen prostitutes had arrived before the end of the summer. A new boom was on in earnest.

More gold was recovered from Nolan Creek and its tributaries in four years than had been taken from the entire Koyukuk in all the years before that. Then, just as the riches of Nolan Creek commenced to wane, Verne Watts finally located the deep channel of Hammond River in the spring of 1911. During the next five years over a million dollars came out of this valley. Food, clothing, machinery, and whisky were unloaded for both of these diggings at the site of Wright's old roadhouse at the mouth of Wiseman Creek (commemorating a transient prospector who stopped a few minutes to pan its gravels and perpetuate his own name). A new town first called Wrights, then Nolan, finally Wiseman sprang up at this point. Meanwhile Coldfoot lost ground steadily until twenty years later there were only mice and ptarmigan to hear the winds go howling down the valley of the Koyukuk.

The peak year in the Koyukuk's second boom period was reached in 1915 when over 400 tons of freight were brought in for the 300 whites and perhaps seventy-five natives living in the region. Sixty tons of booze alone came into the Koyukuk that year. Since this could not legally be sold to the natives, it made 400 pounds (including bottles and packing) for every white man, woman, and child. In some years there was as much whisky as food brought in. In fact, whisky had the priority over everything else, and "the trail never got so bad they couldn't haul whisky up here, no matter how scarce the food might be."

Some of the veterans of those days estimate that at least half of the money taken out of the ground went for booze and prostitutes. Two miners, flush with their winter's clean-up, spent $1,500 in one night on champagne. John Bowman once squandered between $10,000 and $11,000 in less than two weeks around Wiseman, most of it on a single prostitute. Half a dozen different men must have lavished at least $25,000 on the prostitutes. Of course if a person had only his sexual intercourse and a little to drink, he would not have to pay very much. There were standard prices. It cost $20 to spend the night with a prostitute, sport, hooker, floozie, or chippy (the words were used interchangeably), or $5 for a single act of copulation. But the men were easily conquered by feminine wiles. One fellow "gave a hooker $2,500 to get an education, and she knew too much for him already." A favorite trick for a prostitute was to get angry at the man who was fond of her, and refuse to have anything to do with him. If the man was sufficiently enamored he might give her a present of a thousand dollars to buy back her affections. It was far from the ends of the world, and women were few.

After 1916 three things happened. The richest claims both on Nolan Creek and Hammond River were mined. The high wages of the World War period attracted many of the most energetic men to the Outside. Prohibition went into effect, and the freely flowing whisky which had been to many such an important feature of the life in the Koyukuk was over. Consequently, population and gold production both declined almost uninterruptedly. The last prostitute left in 1919, and none has ever returned for more than a few weeks. To-day there do not remain a quarter of the white people who made the gaudy civilization which brightened the Koyukuk in the booming years when gold was coming from the ground in hundreds of thousands of dollars and fortune seemed directly within everybody's grasp.

PART II

THE PEOPLE

IV

THE WHITES

"ALWAYS, after any stampede, it's not the successes who build up the country. They go home with the stakes they made. It's the failures who stay on, decade after decade, and establish homes."

This remark of Albert Ness is one of the most fundamental things one can say about the white people of the Koyukuk. They are failures in the usually accredited sense of the term. They came to the North country to make great fortunes, and, with the exception of a minor fraction of their number, they did not. To-day more than half of them are as poor or poorer than when they set out for the North. In the entire history of the region only about twenty-five people have accumulated more than $20,000, which is a great deal more modest a fortune than many of them had expected to make in thirty weeks, let alone thirty years.

That their original purpose was to make fortunes there can be no doubt. One wanted money that he might take music lessons, another aimed to buy a ranch and settle on it with "the best-looking girl in the Methow Valley," a third wanted to go to college that he might engage in research, still another expected to make enough money to travel all over the world. Some also came for adventure, and perhaps one or two even contemplated the possibility of making

Alaska their permanent home. But certainly the overwhelming majority could echo one of their number who has not seen the outside world since he left San Francisco in 1896: "I figured if I came in the country and stayed five years and made $5,000, I'd go out and never come back again."

A typical picture of the ambitions of those days—and the realizations—might be painted in the story of Pete Haslem, who in 1898 was driving a trolley car on Coney Island. There was a store near his route which he wanted to buy that he might settle down into a life somewhat more stable than that of a trolley car motorman. Just at this time the great gold rush was on to the Klondike, and Pete would read in the papers about men making $50,000 in a few weeks, or getting quarter of a million for a season's activity. Pete was sensibly skeptical of the rumors, but he did figure that the quickest way he could raise the $2,000 necessary to buy the store was to join the rush to the North. Wages were high, work regular, and Pete spent only a small percentage of what he earned, so that within two years he had $4,500 saved up. This was over twice what he set out for, but it came so easily that Pete made up his mind he might as well wait to return until he had $10,000. That was made doubly simple when the bargain of a lifetime came his way. A man who owned a splendid new river steamer wanted to go Outside in a hurry. He would sell the boat to Pete for $4,500, not quarter its worth. Pete bought it, seeing his way clear to his $10,000 in a single summer at the prices which freight hauling was then bringing on the Yukon. He started down river, and on the first trip the boat ran on a gravel bar and was wrecked. That was thirty years ago. Pete has been in the North country ever since, and he is worth to-day about $500.

It has hardly been believable to many of these old fellows how fast the time has gone. There has been so much work, so much interest, so many happenings, such full years. "My God, the time runs away to nothing. Ain't it a corker the way the time goes? You can't accomplish anything before you're ready to be buried." It almost seems some supernatural force is holding you to the life, and you can't get away. "It's funny a person should get in a place like this and stay with it and stay with it and first thing you know a lifetime's gone."

The following table shows the number of present Koyukuk inhabitants who arrived in interior Alaska or the Yukon Territory during different five year periods:

1892-1896	1
1897-1901	41
1902-1906	9
1907-1911	11
1912-1916	5
1917-1921	4
1922-1926	4
1927-1931	2
Total	77

Of the forty-two men who came to the North over thirty years ago, more than one-third have never returned to the outside world even for a visit. Many of these have broken the last thread of connection with friends and relatives they left behind. A couple of years ago two of such old-timers died. A Koyukuk woman set herself the task of tracing their history. She found that one, an especially good friend of hers, actually had a middle-aged son living in the United States about whose existence she had not even heard a whisper. Of the relatives of the other she could find no trace, though he had occasionally spoken vaguely of sisters.

One old fellow, Hughie Boyle, came to Nome in 1900 in the great stampede which suddenly concentrated 50,000 people on a hitherto desolate coast. He left four sisters in Philadelphia with whom he expected to correspond regularly until he returned. No doubt the sisters each wrote several devoted letters, but a post office to care for 50,000 people can not be established in a moment, and besides, there were three other Hughie Boyles in Nome at the time. Whatever the cause, the letters never reached him. As for himself, he was too busy stampeding during the first few years, and after that he did not know where to begin writing. In the summer of 1930 he had not heard from his sisters in the thirty years since he left home. Then one day some one brought him a copy of the *Alaska Weekly* in which there was a letter from a woman in San Francisco who signed her name B. Boyle. She inquired whether any reader of the paper could tell her about her brother Hughie, who left for Nome in 1900 and had never been heard from since. Hughie admitted he had a sister named Bridget, all right, but he knew this couldn't be she, because the last thing any of his sisters would ever in the world do would be to go West. Nevertheless, on the urging of several of his friends, Hughie finally wrote, and sure enough, it turned out to be his sister. Furthermore, the other three had also come West with her, had married, and had numerous offspring, so that to-day "half of Frisco's related to me, between all the Boyles and MacAloones and Maguires and Quigleys."

The present white people of the Koyukuk are not only old timers in the North, they are also old residents in the Koyukuk. Over three-quarters of them have been there fifteen years or more, while a sixth have seen three decades go by since they first came to live in the Arctic. Consequently, the population is decidedly elderly. There are no pure white children (the half-breeds have been classed with the Eskimos), and only three of the seventy-seven adults are under thirty. The complete figures follow:

Age Class	Male	Female	Total
21-30	2	1	3
31-40	6	0	6
41-50	13	3	16
51-60	26	2	28
61-70	13	1	14
71-80	10	0	10
Total	70	7	77

Like all great gold rushes, the one to the North attracted people from all over the world. Some came directly from their native shores, others had been living in America for varying periods before they set out in search of gold. In consequence, all over Alaska to-day one finds a far higher proportion of foreign born people than in the United States proper. In the Koyukuk this tendency is accentuated, so that out of seventy-seven whites some thirty-two are foreign born. The countries from which they came include Ireland (5), Germany (4), Norway (3), Sweden (3), Herzogovina (3), England (2), Austria (2), Wales, The Shetland Islands, Finland, Poland, Lithuania, Dalmatia, Serbia, Montenegro, Greece, and Canada.

An even fifty of the Koyukukers had a rural upbringing, while twenty-seven were raised under urban conditions. With two exceptions, one a schoolboy and the other a gentleman of leisure, all the Koyukukers had regular jobs before coming to the North. Some had several. The following complete list of these occupations indicates one important factor which had

aided the Koyukuk's development into the self-sufficient unit
it is to-day:

Farmer	11	Cow puncher	1
Sailor	5	Horse packer	1
Logger	4	Street car motorman	1
Clerk	3	Stage driver	1
Carpenter	3	Butcher	1
Blacksmith	3	Baker	1
Cook	3	Grocer	1
Coal miner	3	Confectioner	1
Common laborer	3	Millwright	1
Gold prospector	3	Construction worker	1
Quartz miner	2	Boiler maker	1
Teacher	2	Electrician	1
Molder	2	Gas engineer	1
Storekeeper	2	Wireless operator	1
Mechanic	2	Cabinet maker	1
Prostitute	2	Interior decorator	1
Soldier	2	Tailor	1
Fisherman	2	Dressmaker	1
Copper miner	1	Business man	1
Silver miner	1	Traveling salesman	1
Lumbermill worker	1	Policeman	1
Oilfield worker	1	Missionary	1
Section worker	1	Trained nurse	1
Mule driver	1	Surveyor	1

Only four of the seventy-seven white people have ever
been to college of whom one received a bachelor's and one a
master's degree. Not more than twenty-one have even entered high school, and but eight of these completed it. At
the other extreme there are four who have never received any
formal schooling at all, and twenty who have not gone
beyond the fourth grade.

Yet in spite of this scant education I would say that as an

ERNIE JOHNSON, JESSIE ALLEN, AUTHOR, AND KENNETH HARVEY.

VETERENS OF THE NORTH: Billie Burke (33 years in the North), Ase Wilcox (31 years), Jesse Allen (30 years), Martin Slisco (28 years), Smith Wanamaker (26 years), Carl Frank (33 years), George Huey (33 years), Pete Davey (23 years), Jack Hood (33 years), Earl Workman (a visitor).

entire, self-sustaining civilization, and not just one highly cultured section of a civilization, the Koyukukers are the most intelligent people I have ever known. Unfortunately there is no other Outsider who has lived among them sufficiently to corroborate or refute my opinion. The only check available is the admittedly inadequate one of standard mental tests.

I gave the Stanford-Binet test,[1] most used of all American intelligence measures, to forty-five of the seventy-seven adults of the Koyukuk. This was not an especially selected group, but every one whom I could get to take the test (generally with very little urging). I believe these people formed a thoroughly representative sample of the intelligence of the entire community. The distribution of their marks, in comparison with the results which Terman [2] obtained for normal (i.e., not feebleminded) American adults, is shown in the following table:

Mental Age in Years and Months	Intelligence Class	Per Cent of Those Tested Falling in This Class	
		Koyu- kukers	Normal Americans
13.0-13.11	Very inferior	7	2
14.0-14.11	Inferior	7	17
15.0-16.11	Average	40	60
17.0-17.11	Superior	26	16
18.0-18.11	Very superior	20	5

Thus the percentage of the Koyukukers in the very superior intelligence class was four times as great as among normal Americans. The percentage above average was over twice as great. These marks were acquired in spite of the fact that the Koyukukers, due to the great number of years which

[1] For technical details concerning my use of the Stanford-Binet test, see Appendix II.
[2] See *The Measurement of Intelligence*, by Lewis M. Terman.

had elapsed since they had last received any formal education, were not so well prepared for this test as were the people who took it on the Outside. It is also worth noting that many institutions which give intelligence tests have found Terman's scale of ratings too high. The Judge Baker Foundation in Boston considers Terman's inferior class about average, on which basis nearly ninety per cent of the Koyukukers would be above normal.

One of the most significant features of the Stanford-Binet is the vocabulary test. Here the subject is supposed to give the meaning of 100 different words. The average number known correctly by normal American adults is only about fifty-five. Even very superior adults average but seventy-five. Yet among the Koyukukers some ninety-three per cent went normal or better, over fifty per cent equaled or surpassed the average for superior adults, while nineteen per cent knew eighty-five or more words on the list. Harry Foley and Billie Gilbert, both of whom came to the North in 1897, knew the meaning of ninety-two and one-half words, which is better than many literary people can do.

A quite different type of mental test is the Schimberg-Lowe scaled information test. Here the subject is asked the answer to twenty-five different questions covering a wide range of topics. The eight Koyukukers to whom this test was given made marks almost identical with the average for the college seniors to whom Lowe and Schimberg gave the test. The reason for such surprising knowledge is the same as the reason for such surprising vocabularies. It is the result of an amazing variety of reading superimposed on vigorous intelligences.

These vigorous intelligences are after all precisely what one would expect without the results of any formal mental tests or any opinion of my own. The men of the Koyukuk have mostly been guiding their own destinies for over thirty years. They have had to plan all their work themselves and have likewise had to execute it. The work in the Koyukuk is so varied, including as it does for most men the diverse occupations of mining, sledding, boating, hunting, trapping, fishing, gardening, and logging, that unless a man has better than normal ability he will be swamped under the casual necessities of life. Furthermore, the penalty for incompetence in the North is unusually severe. Many a man has frozen or drowned because he lacked the ingenuity to extricate himself from some unanticipated difficulty.

In general, we can say that the gold rush of 1898 attracted from the United States and Europe the more vigorous people, mentally as well as physically, because a keen-minded man is much more likely than a dull or mediocre one to have the imagination and ability necessary to venture into entirely unknown conditions such as all the stampeders of 1898 encountered. Once face to face with the severe existence of the North, there was a second weeding of the incompetent.

How thorough this double selection has been may be indicated by telling you a little about the man who is generally regarded as one of the most incapable people in the Koyukuk. This fellow had built a boat all by himself, some sixty miles from his closest neighbor. It seemed to me an amazing example of skill, but when I mentioned this to one critic I was overwhelmed by the scornful rejoinder: "Why, man alive, that boat draws more water than the battleship Texas."

It is simply taken as a matter of course in that country that every man must be his own carpenter, ship builder, mechanic, and blacksmith if experts in these lines are not available. When the aluminum ring on my camera tripod broke last winter, immediately I was going to send it to the factory. But my partner, Ernie Johnson, thought I was crazy.

"If those fellows can fix it up," he said confidently, "there's no reason in the world why I can't." That is perfectly typical of the complete assurance of the average Koyukuker in his ability to perform what on the Outside would be relegated to the expert. It is an attitude which I do not believe could occur except in people of abnormal mental capacity.

V

AN EVENING AT THE ROADHOUSE

THE REAL way to become acquainted with the people of the Koyukuk is to visit the Wiseman roadhouse some evening at the end of supper time. You stop in the stormshed in front of the main entrance and stamp the snow from your feet. Then you open the door and enter a large room in which about a dozen men, dressed in overalls and wool, are seated on common cane chairs or are sprawling over the counter of what is apparently a store.

As your eyes wander around the room you notice about two thirds of the way down its fifty foot length an old-fashioned bar, a transposed relic of the saloon days. Behind this bar is the kitchen and pantry of the roadhouse, with a large black stove, several sinks, a carving table, a safe, dishes (clean and dirty), canned goods, and an amazing assortment of junk occupying entirely inadequate space.

In front of the bar, in the center of the room, the most conspicuous object is a long table capable of seating two dozen people. It is covered with blue and white oil-cloth. At the far end four or five places are occupied by men just finishing their meal. In the center are the bowls and dishes from which all serve themselves to what they want of the roast moose, moose stew, boiled potatoes, carrots, cabbage, bread, butter, cake, blueberries, and custard pudding.

57

Away from the table one margin of the room is piled with cases of canned goods, kegs of vinegar, gunnysacks of sugar, flour, cornmeal, rice, beans. The other side has a counter running half its length, behind which are shelves covered with a variety of dry goods ranging from silk handkerchiefs to suspenders. In the front corner of the roadhouse on this side is an iron heater, on the other side an upright phonograph. The floor space at this front end of the roadhouse is relatively empty so that an area nearly the full twenty foot width of the building is available for dancing.

This floor is made of planed but unvarnished boards. The walls and ceiling are covered with a somewhat musty-looking blue oil-cloth. The ceiling is only about eight feet high, and this sometimes results in a rather heavy concentration of tobacco smoke, but saves on the fuel necessary to heat the large room. The walls show several cheap print pictures in wooden frames, and if you lift one up you notice a color beneath many shades lighter than the surrounding terrain.

The meal is over and a short, stout, bald-headed Irishman wipes his mouth with his sleeve, rises from the table, loosens his belt, and remarks in jovial ire to the roadhouse proprietor:

"Jesus Christ, I've grown six inches around the waist already since I sat down to supper. If I eat any more I'll bust, so I better quit before making a mess for you."

Quickly a short, wiry old sourdough, whom everybody calls affectionately by his first name of Verne, puts in: "You don't want to have to meet your belly in hell and have it accuse you of killing it, do you?"

I shall reproduce the remainder of the conversation in verbatim dialogue form.

Ness—The way things are Outside to-day a person's sure lucky to be living in here where he gets more than he needs to eat. I see they figure they're ten million people unemployed now—and thirteen per cent of the people own ninety per cent of all the wealth of the country.

Vaughn—Yes, and it's a lucky thing that's so. If it wasn't for John D. Rockefeller and Andrew Carnegie and the Guggenheims and men like that piling up wealth you'd be minus all the good that's come from the Rockefeller Foundation and the Carnegie Libraries and all this aviation research that the Guggenheims put up the money to do.

Verne—If them Senator bastards would cut out some of their battleships and spend the money for aviation research, we wouldn't have to finance people like the Guggenheims to give money for it.

Ness—Or make heroes of the Rockefellers because they've made a fortune starving their workers and then think everything's all right when they spend a little of it building a skyscraper church.

Rod—The Rockefellers, their motto is: "Pray as if you're going to die to-morrow, and act as if you had 500 years to live." They've gotten away with it so far. They're all right so far. But they better remember, you can peddle to the people quite a while—until they get hungry. When they start to get hungry you better watch out.

Mike—If I was young man and I have to wait in long line each day for piece of bread alongside big warehouse, I break in warehouse right away, if I die next minute. They can shoot me, put me in jail, anything before I starve. Just the same you come to my cabin, no eat for two days. You sit down and no eat? You be crazy if you do that. You come in and take what you want. Same way Outside. Poor man starve, he ought to take what he need from rich man.

Vaughn—Yes, and if you do that, what becomes of private property? There wouldn't be a thing in the whole world a man could call his own. If you want to change things you can do it peacefully by passing laws without having confiscation.

Ness—Yes, but when you try to make a peaceful change, like passing that Muscle Shoals Bill, that man in the White House goes ahead and blocks it.

Vaughn—That's all right, I think it was a damn good thing he blocked the Muscle Shoals Bill. Anything the government has ever undertaken in a business line it's done poorly. There's too much politics and graft. Look at this Alaska Railroad and the Panama Canal and the Merchant Marine and the Post Office. Private people in the same sort of work could run any one of them for half the money.

Wod—Well, they haven't. Just compare how much your parcel post and your express cost you and you'll see which is cheaper. I don't believe in socialism myself. I've been violently opposed to it ever since the MacNamaras blew up that building and all the socialists came running to their defense, but I'll be God damned if this private greed isn't ruining the country. I can't see how we can get away from socializing the utilities and natural resources, at least the way things have been running. And as for Rockefeller, what they ought to do is put him in a cannon and shoot him against a stone wall.

Verne—Yes, but instead of that they'll give the bastard all sorts of honors and degrees, and print his picture on the front page of every paper.

Martin (*the proprietor*)—Ain't that the terror, when he ought to be licked with the big stick with the long tongs on the end.

Hughie—The policy of the world to-day is to do the other fellow before he does you. That's all Rockefeller is doing.

Martin—It's my belief they could divide things right to-day so everybody have everything he need to live. When man hasn't no money, sick, too old, no work to do, everyone else should get together give him money to live. They get it back again anyway.

Harry—Yes, Jesus Christ, that's what I can't understand, how some people can be so senseless they don't see that when the poor man's given money it comes right back so everyone benefits by it. He can't save it up, he's got to put it in circulation right away. It's only the rich man who can take the money out of circulation and put it in capital which they got too damn much of as it is.

Wod—I don't believe there's any way we can clean up the mess we have in this country except through revolution. We've been too busy with what we thought was prosperity to see where we were going.

Harry—That direct turning over, putting the bottom to the top and the top to the bottom, isn't very apt to be successful. That's the trouble about Russia to-day. I think their fundamental ideas are bound to come, but they've done it too sudden. There's going to be a setback first.

Jesse—You seem to forget all about that we ever had a revolution which didn't work out so bad. But I'll bet in those days there were just as many people around the courts in France and Russia and other countries who were saying and hoping it would surely fail. We can't seem to put ourselves into the way we felt back then. But Russia to-day and us then are just the same, only the Russians have a harder job than we because the bulk of their population were peasants who did just exactly as their ancestors had been doing for generations, and any change was terrible to them. But our people were in the habit of changing, most of them or their parents or at least grandfathers had changed their whole country and their whole method of living, and it didn't seem anything out of the way to make one more change, so it wasn't very hard to stir them to revolt. No, I'd like to see all the powers give the Russians a square chance to make good. They've had hard enough obstacles of their own to overcome. And you'd think with conditions in our own country so terrible they'd be glad to have a free experiment performed for them on a different way of handling things.

Irishman (*getting up and walking toward the door*)— Jesus Christ, this bunch of Bolsheviks is no place for me to hang out. You split up all your money and you'll see pretty damn quick no one has any. It's just like if you took one of these chickens and tried to give her to all the men in camp, there wouldn't any of them be satisfied.

Rod—You don't want to do that with the chickens. You're right there. You're so slow and fat you'd never get your turn.

Irishman—Well, I'd get in ahead of you anyway. You couldn't move fast enough to keep warm with four overcoats on in July.

Rod—That's all right, you'd be surprised if you knew everything.

Vaughn—You mean astonished. Didn't you ever hear the story of Noah Webster and his wife? It seems she'd caught him kissing the hired girl one day, and she says: "Why, I'm surprised at you, Noah." He answered back, just as cool as could be: "Madame, if you had studied our great and glorious language you would know that I was surprised and you were astonished."

Poss—There's a good many men around this camp have been astonished in their day. I bet old Stanly was astonished when he caught Helen and Dave in bed together last winter.

Wod—I don't believe they did anything wrong.

Verne—No, I don't either. They were both old enough and knew how much they could stand.

Martin—I'd share anything on earth before I'd share a wife.

Harry—You couldn't help yourself if you married some women.

Martin—I know, all hell couldn't satisfy some women. It would take a whole German army to satisfy them.

Poss—When Dirty Maude married that Crocker it didn't make any more difference to her than if she'd blown her nose.

Verne—She didn't marry him. He had four or five barrels of whisky, and that's what she married.

Poss (*smiling in hazy reminiscence*)—She was a tough one all right. I've seen every hooker came into the Koyukuk for thirty years, but she beat them all.

Verne—Well, one thing you got to say for her anyway. She was the only woman I ever knew could stand flatfooted and spit over her head.

The door opens and a short man with a shock of black, bushy hair enters with a washtub under his arm.

Harry—Hello, Pete, how are you to-night?

Pete—I'm not so bad for an old man.

Martin—Pete's always pretty good, only you know he's got some little wheels in his head, and sometimes they get wound up the wrong way.

Pete—That's all right, I'm not as crazy as you yet.

Martin—More or less, every man's crazy. You can't make no people over again. If they're born bugs they're going to stay bugs. You can make bread or dogs over, but not people. Pete, he's not crazy. That's just the way he is. He's born that way and there's no use to try to make him over.

Verne—What are you going to use that tub for, to wash your conscience or clean fish?

Martin—He don't clean no fish any more. Since he raised

that big turnip he don't eat anything else at all. That turnip, I figure it change his whole life. Even he start to grow to look like it. If Pete's neck was just a little thicker his head would look just like that turnip he raised.

Pete—That's all right there. There's more substance in that eighteen pound turnip than there's ever been in your head all your life since you was born.

Martin—By Jingo, I'm afraid you're going to get reputation, Pete, if you talk that way. If you talk much more about your turnip you'll be Turnip Pete.

Pete—That's all right. I hear you're getting a reputation yourself. I hear you tried to lick Johnnie and Lester to-day.

Martin (*changing all at once from his joking mood to great disgust*)—Oh, the little bastards! They'd break anything in God's world if you let them.

Pete—I don't understand, you call these native boys *little bastards* and their sisters *little dears*. How do you account for that? They both come from the same stock.

The door opens again and a relatively young man with bright red hair enters, stamping heavily to get the snow off his moccasins.

Vaughn—What's she doing, Red; starting to snow again?

Red—Yes, there's a big storm blowing up and it's getting cold as hell.

Wod—I've looked for a cold spell all winter. It's got to average up, it's been so warm all winter. It's always worked that way so far anyway.

Hughie—Yes, I've been looking for this storm for three days now. There was a big circle around the moon Wednesday. I've never seen a circle around the moon but there was a storm after it.

Poss (*chuckling*)—Neither have I, but sometimes it took a good many weeks for the storm to start.

Martin (*stopping in front of the heater with a couple of sticks of wood on his arm*)—No, I tell you how I figure it. You've got to wait for moon to change before you get storm or get clear up. I figure this storm going to last until next Thursday when moon change again. Then we get some clear weather.

Vaughn—If you had a seven foot wheel and you started to roll it from here to Chicago, how many turns would it take to get there?

Martin (*perplexed*)—Why, I don't know.

Vaughn—Well, that's a lot more than you know about the weather.

Wod—Some day, when science gets a little farther along, we'll be able to tell all about what the weather's going to be a month or maybe a year in advance. I believe if you give it time and money science can work out anything it tackles.

Red—Sure, some day they'll be able to predict in the laboratory as soon as you're born just what you're going to do for the rest of your life.

Rod—A million people, a million ideals. How in hell are you going to predict what any person will do?

Martin—More I get to thinking more I wonder, what's it all about, what's it all about? What's all this struggling and fighting and working, what's it all about?

Harry—Yes, you and I and the rest of us without any children will keep right on wondering.

Hughie—I don't know what children have to do about it. The only way you can lengthen your life is to enjoy every damn thing you can get out of it.

Jesse—Yes, but how are you going to go about it? How can you know how to get the most out of it?

Martin—I don't know what's the reason man should come

on earth when he got to go and die so soon. People coming and going, coming and going till there's not a thing left of this earth.

Rod—Life's nothing but nonsense and dreams. You bluff half your life and sleep all of it and then first thing it's over and you're dead.

Verne—Yes, but you've had one hell of a fine time while it lasted. I don't know what more you could want. It would certainly be a hell of a lot worse if you had to look forward to living forever. How many chickens have turned you down in the last year, Rod, without having it keep up forever?

Rod (*laughingly*)—You have it right about the chickens— (*soberly*) but even so I think there's something of me left after I die. It's not all over with me. There's some spirit left.

Wod—You can die and be buried and get moldy as a caribou steak after its been kept all summer, but we all know that nothing ever really dies and disappears. A tree tumbles down and rots and then a new tree grows from the old one.

Vaughn—Yes, but your tree hasn't any feelings and consciousness when it's alive. The only thing that survives there is the chemical material of which it's made. That's a long ways different than claiming human immortality. I don't give a damn if my chemical elements last forever if what really counts, my mind and my thoughts, are ended.

Harry—Yes, but you do admit that the hydrogen in the body, the oxygen in the body, the nitrogen in the body never dies. After a person dies it just goes somewhere else. There might be a spirit the same way, something which leaves no trace we can measure, which does not die either. Of course, I don't know it's so, but neither do you know it isn't.

Wod—Take the animals, they know where to find trails which haven't been used for years. How can that be? Because they've gotten something handed down to them from their ancestors, some spirit which tells them where to go. Look how the world has jumped ahead in the last hundred years. It's because one person's spirit goes to the new born one and he gets the benefit of some of what that person knew. Take a great mind like Edison's, he must have gotten the spirit from many men. Of course the person who dies isn't conscious of any of this, but it's true just the same.

Vaughn—You've got to show me a lot more evidence before I'll believe all that line just on your say so. What do you know about what happens to anyone after death? What proof have you got, what evidence? Have you ever seen any one's spirit?

Wod—Well, I'll tell you. About twenty-five years ago, no, it must have been nearly thirty, shortly after I came to the Kobuk, I had a dream, and I saw my cousin back in Wisconsin with whom I'd been brought up as a boy. I saw him just as plainly as I see you now. He was standing beside me and we were talking together, and all of a sudden he put his hand up to his throat and started to choke, and before I could ask him what was wrong he fell over dead. Well, I was disturbed of course, but I didn't think nothing of it, only I made a note of the date, February 17 it was. Well, you know how mail was in them days, took half a year or a year or maybe two years to reach you. So in August I got a letter from this cousin's wife, and she told me how Jerry had dropped dead without any warning from a heart attack, and the day it happened was February 17.

Martin—You believe that craziness? It's like that Bill Buckney who used to be in here. He got a letter from his wife that she had a kid and he hadn't seen her in five years. But he tell everybody he have dream nine months before that he sleeping with wife and baby must have been born that way by dream.

Verne—He had to believe all that. Bill was always quite a moral advocate when it wasn't his own.

Martin—No, I tell you how I figure it. When you die you dead and nothing left only a little dust, maybe a pipeful perhaps. Heaven is the happiness and the content and the health and that you have what you craving for here on earth. Angels are good men and women, bad men and women are devils. The worst thing in my belief you can do to a man is to take away something he craves for whether he craves for liberty as much as for food.

Harry—Well, if that's the worst thing they can do to you to take away your liberty you'd better be pretty damn sure you don't go Outside.

Pete—Yes, the Ku Klux Klan would come up to you with white sheets over themselves just like a ghost, and they'd run you out of the country for being a foreigner and a Catholic and a crook besides.

Red—No, if he was enough of a crook they'd forget he wasn't one hundred per cent American. They'd take him in and put his name down in the honor roll along beside the Grand Kleagle and the other high officials.

Harry—What I can't understand is how anybody could be so God damn simple as to allow his name to be used with such an organization. I admit I might want to join them myself for some of their hilarious times but I'd never boast about it.

Ness—It wouldn't be the Ku Klux Klan only that would take away your liberty. It would be the big business men and the church and the government and everyone else in power who knows if they let you speak their side is so weak it would crumble all to pieces and drop away. The only way they can thrive is on repression. There's not a government on earth would last twenty-four hours if the people knew the truth.

ASHUWARUK, AGED 15, AND DAUGHTER OF KALHABUK.

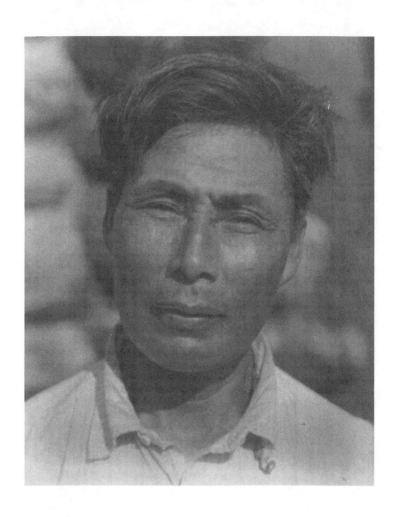

Nutirwik (Harry Snowden), Aged 46.

Harry—Repression always defeats itself. On their last legs they've got to use it, but when it starts you can be sure they're going to get licked.

Vaughn—I'd certainly hate to live in any world in which there wasn't a lot of repression. Why the anarchists and the Bolshevists would get control of everything and there'd be nothing but chaos. And if you didn't censor some of the books that are coming out to-day you couldn't bring up a child in America whose mind wouldn't be poisoned almost as soon as he could read.

Harry—That's all very nice theory, but I'll tell you how it really works. I remember one day, I couldn't have been nine years old yet, I was at church with my mother. The priest got up and he gave a sermon in which he roasted and par-boiled in hell a book that was called *Why Priests Should Wed*. I remember the name still. He said it was the most outrageous, filthy, vile thing ever written, and that it ought to be taken off sale. Well, right then I started to save my pennies and I saved them for two years until I got enough so I could buy the book. That's censorship for you.

Red—I don't believe there's a man in the world wise enough to say what books even an old stiff like me shouldn't read.

Hughie—I like to be at liberty to read everything that comes along, and I like to hear every man's story, but of course I don't always side with it.

Vaughn—Yes, but you don't understand. If you don't do something to repress pernicious theories, first thing you know they'll have control of everything.

Wod—Well, if they're really as pernicious as you claim it ought to be easy to prove them so. All you have to do is present your facts to the people. Let them judge for themselves the cause and effect and make their choice.

Vaughn—Maybe the wrong ideas are more attractive. It took thousands of years for people to realize the world was round. Perhaps some day people will understand what's right and what isn't, but why waste thousands of years just to give them the chance to haggle over it.

Ness—How else can you find out what's right? The only way you can find it is by free discussion.

A broad-shouldered, straight, dignified-looking man with white hair and rosy cheeks enters. He is seventy-five, but looks to be in the early fifties. In vivid contrast to the working clothes which all the others wear, he has on a blue serge suit, a white shirt, and a necktie. He walks the length of the room to the bar.

Verne—How are you to-night, James?

James—Fine, just fine. If I felt any better I'd have to see a doctor.

There is a pause. James walks slowly and dignifiedly back down the length of the room and goes out.

Martin—He's not all dressed up and no place to go like us poor fellows. That old fellow, he knows exactly where he wants to go.

Hughie—I'm only sorry for poor Ida. It must be a great treat for her to have that old bozo come to visit her every night.

Harry—Well, it's her own fault. She certainly don't do anything to discourage him.

Hughie—She's too polite to kick him out, and he's too dumb to take a hint.

Martin—This old fellow here's as bad as James. He's jealous, he wants to be there himself, that's his whole trouble.

Hughie (with a sly smile, showing his almost toothless gums)—Well, maybe I do.

Martin—I don't blame these old boys. She's nice girl, I

tell you. Straight, clean, orderly ways, not hard to look at, fine womanly figure.

Verne—Womanly figure? Why, God damn it, a couple of macaroni sticks would make a pair of drawers for her.

Harry—I don't mind how thin she is. Only trouble, she's too God damn moral. Why this not dancing is the most ridiculous thing I ever heard tell of. If she never does anything worse than let a man put his arm around her in a dance she'll be a virgin all her life.

Jesse—But you don't dance yourself, so you can't talk.

Harry—That's different. When I was a youngster if I so much as mentioned dance they had me going to hell on the jump, and since I've grown up I've been too busy drinking all the whisky I could get hold of to learn to dance.

At this point the conversation is permanently interrupted by the entrance of three Eskimo girls between the ages of fourteen and eighteen. As they take off their jackets and wool toques, several of the men exchange good-natured banter with them. One of the girls starts the record "Gee, but I'd like to make you happy." Three of the men arise and each taking a partner, the evening dance is on.

VI

THE ESKIMOS

THE ESKIMOS are a Mongol race, with the straight black hair, slant eyes, and dark irises which characterize that great division of the human family. They occupy a strip of country for the most part north of the Arctic Circle, extending from the East Cape of Siberia to Greenland. Their most northerly extremity is at Smith Sound in northern Greenland at about Latitude 80°, while their most southerly extension reaches into the lower Kuskokwim Valley in Alaska around Latitude 60°.

Knud Rasmussen estimates that the Eskimos total no more than 33,000 souls, which, he adds, "represents, perhaps, the outside number of persons who can gain their livelihood by hunting in a country so forbidding." These 33,000 people he subdivides into 14,000 Alaskan Eskimos, 13,000 Greenlandic Eskimos, 5,000 Canadian Eskimos, and 1,000 Siberian Eskimos. This book does not contribute to the knowledge of the original *mores* of any of these people. For this the reader is referred to the splendid studies of Rink, Boas, Thalbitzer, Stefansson, Jenness, Rasmussen, Freuchen, Hrdlicka, and others. In the Koyukuk the Eskimos without exception have been influenced by the culture of an entirely different race with which many of them have been living for over thirty years.

The fifty natives of the upper Koyukuk may be divided as follows:

Eskimo	34	Eskimo-Japanese	2
Indian	6	Eskimo-White	4
Eskimo-Indian	1	Eskimo-Japanese-White	3

For all these people I am using the group designation of *native* in contrast to *white*. Among these natives the Eskimo blood is overwhelmingly predominant. The Indians being so much in the minority, and their cultural influence being further diminished due to inter-marriage with Eskimos and whites, it seems unnecessary in this book to discuss the Indian culture except in those few places where it has influenced that of the other races.

The immigrant Eskimos of the upper Koyukuk came originally from three tribes which, in order of importance, were the Kobuk Eskimos from the Kobuk River which enters into the Arctic Ocean at Kotzebue Sound; the Arctic Eskimos who originally occupied the bleak ocean shore from Point Hope to the mouth of the Colville River; and the Selawik Eskimos from the river drainage just south of the Kobuk. Between these three tribes there were considerable cultural differences, and numerous points of linguistic variation, yet essentially they were one people with a common heritage of customs, legends, and language.

No figures of any anthropometric value can be obtained from such a small number of people as are embraced among the natives of the upper Koyukuk. Nevertheless, it is worth noting that the adult men varied in height from five feet two inches to five feet eleven inches. The women varied from an even five feet to five feet eight inches. The records for some thirteen children of all ages indicate heights and weights not appreciably different than those for white children.

All of the natives have straight, coal-black hair and dark eyes. Their complexions are in general darker than those of the whites, rather of a Spanish color, but there are some with fairer skins than almost any white person in the community. One woman has glowing red cheeks which look for all the world like those of a German house wife. The younger children, with few exceptions, have complexions as light as the average white child.

The age distribution of the natives of the upper Koyukuk is shown in the following table:

Age Class	Male	Female	Total
1-10	10	10	20
11-20	2	3	5
21-30	1	6	7
31-40	2	2	4
41-50	3	1	4
51-60	2	4	6
61-70	2	2	4
Total	22	28	50

It will be observed that in contrast to the pure blooded whites who include no children in their number, an even half of the fifty natives are under twenty-one years of age. Among the adult natives, all of those over forty-five came to live with the white men after their habits had so matured that it was impossible for them ever to adopt much of the white culture or speak better than a broken English. On the other hand, about half of those under forty-five speak almost perfect English and are closer to the white culture than the original Eskimo culture.

This brings to mind the startling fact that time, which habitually progresses in slow and dignified strides, in the

Koyukuk country takes one great jump of 10,000 years, merging in its leap the stone age and the present. For the Eskimo culture, as it existed prior to its recent contamination, belonged in all respects to the stone age, being contemporary to what flourished in Europe thousands of years before the founding of Rome. On the other hand the white culture of the Koyukuk, if not quite contemporary to the 1930 civilization of the world at large, is at least a nineteenth century rural culture. Among the Eskimos of the Koyukuk both of these extremes are found. There are still a few old Eskimos who live almost the same life as their ancestors on the tundra to the north have lived for hundreds of years. On the other hand, there are many of the younger Eskimos who live a life and think thoughts scarcely distinguishable from any unrepressed white person in the United States. Yet with all this cultural difference, the two groups are only a generation or two apart, and are actually in such close contact that the stone age and the machine age person are often living together in the same cabin or igloo.

Because of such different backgrounds it is even more difficult to discuss Eskimo than white intelligence. Perhaps the following letters will be suggestive to the reader. The first was written by a fourteen-year-old Eskimo girl who had received less than two years of schooling:

> Nolan Creek, Alaska
> May 27, 1931

DEAR FRIEND BOB MARSHALL,

I am going to spend a few minutes in droping these few lines to you.

Mother is not feeling very good this last week. I wish we were down at Bettles now. So we don't have to look at the cold snow and ice all the time can't even find the pretty flowders. Biner Wind is going down to Wiseman, in a few days from now and he well take this letter down to you.

Papa don't think he is going to work any more because there is no more water and beside Mrs. Strawbridge don't want him to work there. Because Mrs. Strawbridge told papa that the water may run on her claim. So papa stop working to-day. He was working a little yesterday and then Mrs. Strawbridge went up there and told him that. Now we don't know what to do we can't move back down. Papa said he like to get a job working on the road. If he have chance. Nothing yell's to do.

Last sunday we went and visit nearly every body.

How many times did they dance since you were up here last? did you went to every dance they had? mother is not going to go down at fourth of July and I don't think am going nether. I would like to go down and dance with you again befor you go away but I can't help it. I can't walk down by my self if I had some one to walk down with and bring me back again I well go down all right enough. Oh I guess I don't miss much if I miss one dance. You said you are going to come up and see us again in June I wish you well hole your promis and come up again. What date are you coming in? I wish you well tell me if you answer this letter.

I think this well be all for this time I may write a longer letter if you answer. Please answere this letter.

I am going to cry all day if you don't answer.

I well close with best wishes and good luck to you.

From your true friend,
Miss Jennie Kachwona Suckik.

Jennie Suckik

The second letter was written to my nephew in New York by an eight-year-old boy. Although the Eskimo language was used entirely in his home, he himself spoke good English and had been to school for three years in which time he had completed four grades.

DEAR JONATHAN:

I going to write this letter this evening. How are you feeling in the far away city so long. Why don't you come and visit this town someday. I like to see you but I can't go out of school. Some day I go out to see you. I don't know but I mite go to see the world and see the world and you. We had a storm yesterday and to-day the wind is blowing. Have you a sister I have two sisters and a brother. My sister's name is Lucy Jonas Kitty Jonas and my brother name is Harry Jonas. My sister Kitty is coming from Bettles she was down Alatna. My father Jonas is going down to take her up to Wiseman where I live in back of river. I havent seen my sister Kitty for two years I wish I could see her again. I am an Eskimo boy eight years old.

This summer I was out in the hills. I shot three caribou and one last summer. It was the first time I ever shot in my life it was last summer. My friend Joseph Hope shot more than me and my father shot the most in us three. My grandfather Big Jim shot quite a few. O about twenty or twenty one I think its twenty one.

Martin Slisco is Bobs friend and I am working with Martin Slisco. I am here alone in Bob's house writing. I am going to send something to you. Please send me a buloon. Write me back.

Your friend

OSCAR JONAS

There are some persons who require a quantitative evaluation for everything. Such people may contend that these little Eskimos, brought up as they have been with something of the white background, should be graded by scaled and scientific means. I myself am doubtful of the value of mental tests, especially when applied to children from cultural surroundings so different from those of the children for whom the tests were made. Nevertheless, for the benefit of those who require statistical measurements I have given a number of standard American intelligence tests to these Eskimo children.

The Stanford-Binet [1] test was given to eighteen out of the nineteen Eskimo children around Wiseman who were over three years. The four oldest of these had not started in school until they were between eleven and fourteen years of age. In consequence of this late beginning they were from four to eight grades behind the normal for their age. Since success in the Stanford-Binet test has considerable relationship to formal schooling, it was obvious that such children would be at a disadvantage in tests devised for High School children. It is not surprising, then, that the marks which they made were in all cases somewhat below the normal of 100, ranging from seventy to eighty-eight.

However, the fourteen younger Eskimo children between the ages of three and nine had undergone a training in most cases comparable to that which children in the United States receive. The very youngest ones were taught informally by their parents, by the older children, and by the different adults about town. All those over five went to school where they were given instruction of the same caliber as they would receive on the Outside. It is true that four of these children did come from homes where Eskimo was spoken exclusively, that one boy of five had never heard a word of English spoken until six months before I gave him the test, and that all of these Eskimos lacked several features which were commonplace in the everyday lives of those children for whom these tests were devised. These handicaps were partially offset by the *rapport* between myself and the children who were never given the tests until they had come to make my cabin a regular playground, and had ridden piggyback hundreds

[1] For technical details concerning my use of the Stanford-Binet test, see Appendix II.

of yards on my shoulders. The following table shows how the distribution of intelligence among these Eskimos compares with the normal which Terman found in calibrating this test and which the Lynds reported in Middletown: [2]

		Per Cent of Children Tested Falling in This Class		
Intelligence Quotient	Intelligence Class	Eskimo	Normal American	Middle-town
0-69	Feebleminded	0	1	5
70-79	Borderline	0	5	8
80-89	Dull	14	10	21
90-109	Average	50	64	52
110-119	Superior	14	13	10
120-139	Very superior	22	7	4

This startling record shows these little Eskimos to far better advantage than normal American white children. Other tests give a similar impression. Of the five children who were old enough to take the Schimberg-Lowe scaled information test, three went above the normal for their age and two went below. All went far above the normal for their grade. One of the younger children thought that George Washington was president and one said that the Pilgrims came to this country to fight, but these do not seem very serious blunders for children fresh from the tundra where the founding fathers are far less important than the route of the caribou.

Florence L. Goodenough at the University of Minnesota has devised a picture drawing intelligence test. The child is asked to draw a man, and he is marked on some fifty-one different points which an accurate picture should have, including the presence of all important members of the body,

[2] See *The Measurement of Intelligence*, by Lewis M. Terman, and *Middletown*, by Robert S. and Helen Merrell Lynd.

proper connection of parts, and approximately accurate proportions. It is not a test so much of artistic ability as of accurate observation. All six of the younger children made marks better than the normal of 100, ranging from 106 to 150. The older children were about normal except for the fourteen-year-old Jennie Suckik about whose drawing Dr. Goodenough wrote: "above the highest standard."

The Wallin Peg Board test and the Pink Tower test are designed to measure manual coördination. In the former the children must place different shaped pegs in holes, in the latter build a tower out of five pink blocks. The marks are in speed of performance. On all but one of twenty-three trials the Eskimos varied from slightly faster than the normal for white children of the same age to three times as fast.

In concluding this discussion, it seems appropriate to mention the views of teachers in regard to the intelligence of the Eskimo children. Both the present Wiseman teacher and her predecessor agreed that the Eskimo children were on the average brighter than the white children they had taught Outside. The mission teacher at Allakaket had a similar viewpoint. Given a nine months school year, she was certain that she could teach both Eskimos and Indians as much as the average white children.

When the intelligence of adults is considered, the problem becomes a great deal more difficult. Standard intelligence tests are certainly meaningless with grown people who have in most cases great language difficulties and in all cases an entirely different background than the people for whom the examinations were intended. One must form opinions entirely on impression based on evidence which might be given several interpretations.

It is interesting to observe that while all but three of the twenty adult Koyukuk Eskimos speak the white language passably, only one of the seventy-seven whites can speak the Eskimo language at all. All of the Eskimos who attended the white man's school before they were twenty speak as good English as the average white man anywhere. But I have never heard of a white man who speaks as good Eskimo as the average person of that race.

The Eskimos seem to have a special facility in drawing maps. Ekok once sketched for me the first fifteen miles of the Alatna River, a stream which is nothing but bends in this lower portion, and she had them all plotted from memory almost as accurately as the instrumentally constructed Geological Survey map. Big Charlie has drawn me dozens of maps which never fail to check splendidly. Philip Smith, head of the Alaska Branch of the United States Geological Survey, has written me:

"During my contacts with the Eskimo of northwestern Alaska, I have always been impressed with their almost universal ability to represent graphically the tracts of country with which they are familiar and their capacity to interpret correctly cartographic information shown on our maps. Although some of their sketches show weakness in scale and orientation, especially in those parts depicting remote regions, the fidelity of their portrayal of the significant features makes their drawings extremely instructive and helpful. Their ability to read understandingly, with a minimum amount of explanation, the rather intricate schemes of representing relief by contours adopted for our maps was rather astonishing and seemed to me to be superior to that from average college students to whom I have tried to explain the same subject."

As I mentioned in the introduction, one of the purposes of my sojourn in the Arctic was to make a study of tree growth at northern timberline. In connection with this investigation I had a number of instruments set up on the hillside back of Wiseman. These included not only the standard rain gauge, maximum and minimum thermometers, and anemometer of any normal weather station, but also two other types of instrument, much more difficult to handle. The one consisted of five Livingston atmometers for measuring evaporation. The water evaporated from each of these atmometers had to be replaced daily and measured by burette to the tenth part of a cubic centimeter. The other instrument was a dendrograph designed to record tree growth so delicately that one can see how the tree grows during the night and shrinks during the day. During the summer I was away from Wiseman for a couple of months. I arranged for Ekok to run my scientific station during my absence, and after three lessons this Eskimo girl with only a fifth grade mission school education took over the entire work and ran the instruments faithfully and accurately for fifty days. She had to leave before I returned, so she broke in another Eskimo girl, Dishoo, who also did an excellent piece of work. On one occasion one of the atmometers was blown over by the wind, and the water all spilled out. It is such a complicated task to set up one of these instruments, involving the complete elimination of all air bubbles, that I had not dared to explain the process to Ekok. Nevertheless, she used her own ingenuity, and after considerable experimentation had the atmometer working again so well that when I returned it was checking perfectly with the instruments which had not been upset. I might add that I have seen more than one college student who was unable to run satisfactorily a far simpler weather station than this one. The splendid performance of these two women on the scientific assignment entrusted to them seems to me to furnish a most eloquent testimonial to the potentialities of Eskimo intelligence.

AN EVENING AT BIG JIM'S

THE TIME is now ripe to introduce you to a few of my Eskimo friends. The place to begin is at the cabin of Big Jim and Nakuchluk, for this is the center, social, spiritual, and economic, of the native population of Wiseman. I think the economic is the most important, for Big Jim, due to his great energy and experience, has generally had more food and more worldly wealth than any of the other natives. With the prevalent Eskimo custom of "potlatching," dividing up whenever one has more than the others, Big Jim has sometimes been the chief support of the entire Eskimo community. In addition every one admires him for his cool-headed courage which about five years ago enabled him to kill a bear near Coldfoot with an ax. Furthermore, Jim is wise, kind, and without favoritism, so it is quite natural that he should be the leader, and his large, clean cabin the communal center of the Eskimos of Wiseman.

Perhaps some night, after supper and half an hour of chatting around the roadhouse, I decide to pay Big Jim a visit. I start down the main street and across the Wiseman Creek bridge, with yellow light pouring out on the snow from a couple of cabins to my right, and moonlight flooding the whole frozen valley of the river to my left. At the store I turn and cut diagonally back from the river, passing more

83

snowcovered cabins with cheery lamplight in the windows, and also several deserted ones, looking even by moonlight very black and cold. All the while the bright waves of the aurora flicker overhead, and the stars twinkle in the thirty below air like sputtering magnesium powder.

I open the door to Jim's cache, a shed in front of the cabin which serves for the storage of all non-perishables as well as for a vestibule, and then open the inner door and enter the house. Jim smiles cordially and says a hearty *konnowitbitch* [how are you?], and of course I reply *nakurunga* [I am fine]. Nakuchluk laughs, says *alapah* [it's cold], and I say *alapah apie apie* [it's too cold]. Then everybody laughs, they all continue with what they were talking about when I entered, and I seat myself beside Kupuk.

At one end of the single room of the cabin, which measures 14 x 32 feet, all the women are seated on the floor. Nakuchluk is working on some skins, scraping them thin with an amazing collection of homemade implements, some iron, some bone, some obsidian. She sits with her legs straight out in front of her, her body bent forward, her head bowed over the skin on which she is working. She is a little, dried up old woman, wrinkles all over her face, but with the sweetest childish smile. All the while she works she hums, except when she breaks into the conversation, which is frequently.

Beside her, smoking an eighteen-inch-long pipe, with legs also straight in front of her, sits old Utoyak, most elderly woman in camp. She is probably almost seventy. She is very quiet, seldom smiles, seldom even sings. Although she has lived intermittently among the whites for a dozen years, I have never heard her speak even one word of English. I think she is entering dotage, and I imagine that her mind strays most of the time over the windswept tundra to the north where she wandered for more than half a century. She is the

OSCAR JONAS, AGED 8: "This summer I was out in the hills. I shot three caribou and one last summer."

KAPUK, AGED 3$^{1}/_{2}$: She showed an intelligence quotient of 135 on the Stanford-Binet Test, a mark attained by only one white child in 100 in the United States.

EKOK RUNNING THE AUTHOR'S SCIENTIFIC STATION: She is here shown filling
an atmometer by burette.

most tattooed woman in camp, with five blue lines running from her lower lip to the tip of her chin, whereas her closest rival, Nakuchluk, has only three to beautify this part of her face.

Beyond Utoyak sits Kalhabuk, youthful mother of four strapping Jonas children, and wife of the lazy Jonas. She is the most powerful woman I have ever known. When the store burned down four years ago, and all the people around carried out everything they could in the few minutes before they were driven out, Kalhabuk emerged several times with an hundred pound sack of flour on her shoulder and a fifty pound sack under one arm. I am sure she could beat three out of four men in Wiseman in a fight. But the test could never come off, because she is the most placid of mortals, and takes everything as it comes along in the greatest good humor, including Jonas' indolence. If you ask her why she doesn't make him work she replies vaguely: "Oh, that's all right." She exerts almost no parental authority over her children. She sits there with a cynical smile on her face, unless she is laughing or yawning, and peacefully smokes her pipe.

Between me and Kalhabuk sits Kupuk. She is about twenty-six. She married Louis Sackett, a native from Alatna, who soon after deserted her and left for the Kobuk. Her face is homely, her back deformed, her temper rather fiery, so the poor girl has had a hard time finding another man with whom to live. This she wants above all else, and she is often terribly depressed by her enforced celibacy which is only occasionally relieved by sporadic intercourse which fails to give her the companionship of her longing. Nevertheless, externally she keeps up a jolly appearance, and is the most uproarious mimic in camp. As I sit beside her she jokes, and nudges me, and whispers about licentious dreams.

In the center of the room, facing the women, Big Jim,

Oxadak, and Itashluk sit on chairs. Big Jim is about sixty-five. He has closely cropped gray hair, bright eyes, a protruding jaw with a little stubble on it. On either side of his mouth are holes into which he used to insert ivory labrets for ornamentation. One hole has entirely closed, but you can observe soup oozing through the other when he eats. His clearly enunciated voice is always dominant in the conversation.

Oxadak is several years older. He is Utoyak's husband. He speaks hardly any English either, but is much jollier than his wife. He has a deep, bass voice, in striking contrast to the high-pitched voices of the other Eskimos.

Itashluk, his adopted son, is a surly-looking native of perhaps thirty-five years. He seems solemn and morose, and this impression is accentuated by his very dark skin, the other Eskimos being as light as dark complexioned Whites. He dresses exquisitely, mostly in furs, and seems to take great pride in his personal appearance. About ten years ago he brought his wife, Louise, from the Arctic, and she refused to go back with him. This November he came in with another wife, Annie Kayak.

I sit beside Kupuk and watch them all: Big Jim and Oxadak conversing in loud, guttural voices; Nakuchluk working; Utoyak smoking her pipe; Kalhabuk smiling across at me; Kupuk whispering about the dream she had last night; all the women, now chattering together, now singing in low voices, now breaking into the conversation of the men. Very frequently everybody in the room rocks with laughter. Sometimes Big Jim tells me in English what the joke was about. Here is one typical story, in the exact words which he used to explain it, which caused everybody to roar, made Big Jim break down laughing before he could finish it, and almost compelled Nakuchluk to choke.

"Long time ago, me young man, six men go hunt. Take him along fish, take him along seal oil, pack them over. Pretty soon no more grub, all gone, he no last long, somebody get him little bit of flour from ship. No steamboat. Ship.

"Make camp, old man get him over close to fire all time, no one else get close. Take off parky, all time close fire. Turn one side to fire, turn other side to fire, no keep him warm. Young man fix it up, mix him flour, in frying pan, no grease in it, put him on fire. Says, 'Here, old man. You all time too close fire, you hold him pan'. Old man says he no savvy make hot cake. Young fellow give it to him right away, says: 'You hold it.'

"Pretty soon hot cake burn him on bottom. Young fellow says: 'You turn him, Move him.' Hot cake no cook him on top at all. Old man shake him little bit higher, little bit higher, little more up, up, up, up, up above him head, [all the while Jim talks his whole attention is concentrated in acting out what he is telling, the old man shaking the frying pan and gradually raising it until it is high above his head, and at the same time nervously uncertain of how he should flap the hot cake over] pretty soon throw him up, pretty soon [hot cake] fall, hit him over head, old man turn head round, pretty soon he [hot cake] roll him down back of head. Hot cake stick him there on neck behind, no parky, no nothing. Everybody laugh then, old man roll down in snow, take him out. Old man no mad, he laugh too."

Late in the evening Jim brings in the bass drum, while Oxadak and Itashluk take the little ones, and then every one joins in singing until the rafters fairly ring to the stirring music of *Atowachii-unga* and *Ah Yay Yah E-Jah*.

VIII

ESKIMO BIOGRAPHIES

ONE NIGHT when I was over alone with Big Jim, learning to sing, there was a frenzied knocking at the door. Jim opened it, and there were Bessie and her daughter Jennie, almost choked with crying.

"My Charlie dying," Bessie wailed. "He coughed up blood, he's bleeding from the lungs, come quick."

Then she and Jennie started back on the run to their tiny cabin, about fifty yards away, and Jim and I followed. On the way, Jim made a very practical division of labor. He said: "Me make praying business, you give him medicine."

And so it was arranged. As soon as we got inside the cabin Jim dropped on his knees, and, with bowed head, commenced an earnest Christian prayer for Charlie's recovery. Charlie was sitting at the edge of his bed, bent over an old butter can which was used as a cuspidor, and now and then spitting out a little blood. It was a slight hemorrhage, and on the spur of the moment I could think of no medicine except to make him lie down, as quietly as possible, and to loosen everything tight about his clothing, which was almost nothing. When these simple performances were completed I joined Jim on the floor, and helped with the "Amen" in which Jennie also chorused, but Bessie shook so with sobbing she could not enunciate a sound.

I have never seen such a picture of complete, woebegone misery as Bessie presented. You would have thought she was watching her husband and daughter being burned at the stake. No, it was worse than that, for in such an event she would perhaps have mercifully fainted. Now all she could do was stand and howl and shake, with a look like a woman of ninety on a face which chronologically was only thirty-three years old. After a while, when the bleeding had stopped, she managed to splutter out a few phrases.

"Oh, my poor Charlie—why did I ever come to Wiseman? —if Charlie dies I rather be dead—that's how I lost my two little children already—Marie was sitting right beside me sewing—all of a sudden she started choking—whole lot of blood come up, just like this—in a few minutes she was dead —I wish I was never born—I wish I was in Bettles—oh, my poor, poor Charlie—"

Then she would lay her head on Charlie's chest and sob again, until I would have to impress on her that it was essential that Charlie be kept quiet.

Meanwhile Charlie took the whole matter with stoical indifference. He was not the least bit excited about the blood, assured Bessie that he felt a whole lot better since he had coughed it up, that the cold which had been bothering him for two months would now be cured in no time. He said to me, with philosophical resignation: "Funny thing, my Bessie. Me get sick, she act just like crazy. She love me too much, I guess. Funny thing."

And Bessie, with great heaving of her breasts, sobbed out: "I can't helps it."

After that evening I became on exceptionally intimate terms with the Suckiks, as they call themselves, for that is Big Charlie's Eskimo name, and the last name which the whole family has adopted. Bit by bit, I picked up their biographies and their philosophy.

Big Charlie was a native of the Kobuk country, where as a boy he grew up largely on caribou, seal oil, berries, and fish. In 1898, when he was sixteen, he and his father set out on an all summer's hunt to the Koyukuk. It was here that they met the first white men they had ever seen. I will let Charlie tell the story.

"First white man I ever saw down below Bettles, '98. Me and old man come over from Kobuk down head of John River. We see white thing like smoke against hill, and we go see what it is. Pretty soon we see man, look different any man I ever see. He say: 'Hello!' I don't even savvy *hello*. He give me tobacco, and I smoke that fine. Pretty soon he motion like this [making beckoning motion]. Then me and old man follow. Then he walk a little ways and motion again, and we follow some more. Pretty soon I say to old man: 'Maybe he want us to go with him.'

"Then we follow him, and pretty soon we see big boat in slough. We never see anything like that, white smoke coming out and everything, and we scared. But he go on board over gangplank, and pretty soon he go down in cabin, and come out with tobacco, and throw it at us. We know that. When he motion some more we think he all right, so we come on over gangplank. Then he take us down to cabin and make motion, and long time we no savvy nothing. But then old man says to me: 'Maybe he wants us fetch him caribou skins, he give us tobacco.'

"Then he take us to other cabin, and we set down at table. I never see him table before. Funny thing. Then man comes in and bring all sort of grub, set him on table. I know nothing about that sort of grub. I don't know nothing about use him fork, I no savvy plate. I no know which way to hold knife and fork. Pretty soon I eat bread and tea, I know that

all right. Pretty soon white man put something yellow [but-
ter] on bread. Pretty soon I swallow it, pretty soon it go
down just like strong whiskey. I feel it go all the way down
to stomach, it burn like fire in stomach. My papa all scared,
he try doctor me up this way with hands, blow on me. Pretty
soon I all better."

The year before Charlie came over from the Arctic, Bessie
was born somewhere down the river near the mouth of the
South Fork. When she was still a baby her father, Big William, had taken pity on his brother, Betas, who had just lost
his only child, and he gave Bessie to him and his wife to
raise. At eleven she went to work at the roadhouse in Bettles,
and for five years she stayed there, waiting on tables, helping in the kitchen, dancing all night long, drinking heavily,
smoking, and giving the men who stopped there frequent
sexual gratification. She learned there both the white language and the white customs.

Meanwhile Big Charlie had prospered exceedingly well
in the Koyukuk. He was strong, energetic, intelligent, lucky.
He made good money at mining in the summer and at trapping, hunting, and freighting in the winter. He was scrupulously honest, and the old Northern Commercial Company
often trusted him with the transportation of several thousand
dollars in gold. At one time he had over $2,000 deposited at
the Northern Commercial store, which was something absolutely unprecedented among the natives. He made his home
in Bettles, living next door to Bessie's home.

In the spring of 1913, shortly after the breakup, Charlie
was starting out for a summer up the John River. As he was
about to shove his boat off, Bessie came down to say good-by.
She had liked him very well for years, had come to think of
him as a big brother, in fact called him *brother*. When she

came down this morning Charlie said jokingly: "Don't you want to come along with me up John River?"

"Sure," she said instantly. She went right home to get her things, and left with him that day. They must have spent a very joyful summer together, judging by their frequent fond recollections of little incidents. They returned in the autumn by way of the North Fork and Wiseman, where they were officially married in the white manner.

During the next four years they wandered all over, mining, hunting, trapping. Three children were born to them, and they were very happy. But in the spring of 1919 all of their children developed severe colds, and the oldest and youngest died within a few weeks.

This broke them completely. For months they did nothing but lie around and moan over their misfortune. They never regained their old energy, and to-day they have the reputation of being a very lazy couple. As a matter of fact this is largely unjust. Neither of them is in good health. Consequently, they are just as saving as possible on labor, and cheerfully accept any offerings which the whites who are fond of them may care to make. But when necessity arises they set out for the hills, and Charlie is such a splendid hunter that I have never known him to come back empty-handed.

Charlie says: "My Bessie and me just like two kids together. Have good time together all the time, never fight." Bessie reciprocates with: "I think Charlie's the most wonderful man in the world. He's always good natured, never gets angry about anything." Both agree that "happiest time of all is when we're alone together with Jennie, away from all other people."

Both parents are passionately proud of this pretty Jennie who is fourteen years old. Bessie shows me the magnificent beadwork she can already do; Charlie points with pride to some drawings she has made. Both stress what a very good girl she is. Both delight in telling stories of her precocious remarks, just like any white parents. For example, when she was five she had asked her papa: "What make ptarmigans so wild? Do you think maybe little mice chase them all the time?"

Charlie asked amazedly: "Who told you that?"

To which Jennie replied saucily: "Don't ask too much question."

After nine years they still are made happy, just by recounting that tale.

In connection with Jennie they frequently discuss their attitude toward child education which Bessie summarized in one short remark.

"I never punish Jennie," she said. "Charlie and I never spank her in our lives. If she do something wrong I just tell her it's not nice and she don't do it any more. Punishing children all the time is no good. It just makes them mean."

They like to philosophize about many other things besides education: about life and death and reality and the ways of man. Charlie, for instance, believes very strongly in the essential sameness of the human race. He says: "All over just the same. Some people fine, some people no good, some people just like dog, no heart at all. Native, White, Arctic, Koyukuk, Yukon, Outside, all over, all the same. Long time ago, maybe one man meet other man in woods, kill him with bow and arrow, long time ago. To-day some man all same, only maybe they scared to kill because marshal arrest them, otherwise all same."

But their conversation is not all or even mostly philosophical. They love to joke better than almost anything else. One time Bessie cautioned me with a very solemn look on her face: "Bob, when you go down to Alatna you must look out when you dance with the chickens that you can't get your beard in their hair, otherwise you might get koomik in your oomik [lice in your whiskers]." Another time I was taking a picture of Jennie, focusing through the ground glass of my camera with a shirt over my head to keep out the light. Bessie shouted: "Quick, Jennie, get a picture of Bob so I can send it to my cousins on the South Fork and tell them that's how white man makes medicine."

This brief biography may well be concluded with Bessie's account of one of the near tragedies she faced which ultimately cemented her love for Charlie more firmly than ever.

"One time, back in 1921, Charlie set out with a white man who was in Bettles. He says he was only going to be gone eight days, they was just going up John River a little ways, and in eight days they was going to be all back here again. But they wasn't back in eight days, and they wasn't back in eight weeks or five months neither. I thought my Charlie had drownded sure. I cried all summer long. I couldn't hardly stand to eat nothing or do nothing, I feel so bad. Just mostly I sit around and cry and wished that I could be dead. I jump up every morning, look out of the window, don't see my Charlie, and go right back to bed. I cry all night and howl, and that makes Jennie cry and howl too.

"One morning about one o'clock some one started to knock on door. I was been asleep, and I just wake up, and I'm too scared to answer. He knocked on door some more, knocked on door harder, seemed he was going to break my door down. I don't like any one to break my door down at one o'clock in the morning, so I says, as mean as I can: 'Who's that?'

" 'Me,' Charlie says.

"Then I recognizes my Charlie's voice, but I couldn't believe it.

" 'You?' I says. 'You still alive? Why, you're drown.'

"Then I started to cry, and I open the door. I cried a whole lot more when I kiss him. I wake up Jennie and she cry too, but she was scared. It was so long since he went away she does not know him, and besides he had long hair below his ears, and smells all like seal oil.

"Next morning Mamma says to me: 'You cry all summer, pretty nearly drive me crazy. Now you got Charlie back, don't you ever angry at Charlie again.' Sometimes now I get a little mad, but I do as she say, and I don't think I ever really angry at Charlie again."

When Ekok was eighteen she was by far the most beautiful of all the native girls around Alatna. It was, to be sure, not a delicate loveliness, but the beauty of vivacity and life and splendid physical development. Most of the boys around there were ardently wooing her, and her parents constantly urged her to marry one of them, but she steadfastly refused because she had never felt the slightest desire for marriage.

That summer the Episcopal Archdeacon from Nenana paid a visit to the mission at Alatna and brought in his party a half-breed Indian boy known as Isaac. As soon as ever she saw him Ekok fell madly in love. She could think of nothing but Isaac, night and day. But being a girl she knew she could never win him by pursuit, that her only hope lay in waiting for his advances. But no advances came, after two weeks the Archdeacon's party left, and Ekok bitterly had to reconcile herself to the realization that the one man she had ever loved was gone. Meanwhile her parents kept urging her to marry, and the young fellows, many of whom she loathed, continued their active pursuit, until finally the strain of resistance became too great for her. She married the least objectionable, a sturdy Eskimo named Unakserak. Ten years later when Isaac returned for another visit she discovered that he had been as much in love with her as she had been with him, but that he had been scared to press a courtship which he imagined was hopeless.

Ten years later also, when her youth was gone and the fresh beauty of her face had been replaced by lines of suffering and power, Ekok summarized that decade with these resigned words: "No, we didn't get along so awfully nice I admit, but we got to make the best of it, that's all. It seems to me a person can't live without bumping into troubles and things like that unexpectedly. You dream when you're a child that everything is going to be sunlight, and then when you're too full of real things to dream any more you see the sun doesn't shine very many days in the year. But what can you do?"

The first cloud came as soon as Ekok was married when she realized that when you love one man overpoweringly the second best is no substitute at all. The second cloud was not delayed many weeks when she found that Unakserak was frightfully jealous, unlike all other Eskimos would not permit her to talk with the man with whom she danced, and insisted when each of her first three children were born with light complexions that some white man was their father. The last two were almost as dark as negroes, and Ekok jokingly remarked that even Unakserak was satisfied with them.

She had five children in eight years. This was enough to exhaust her, but to make matters worse Unakserak, who was a splendid worker, acquired from the whites a great fondness for whisky and poker, and threw away most of the money he had earned. As a result she and the children were often half starved for weeks on end. Through much of the time when she was pregnant with her first child she had virtually nothing to eat. The baby girl was very sickly from birth, but just because of her need for special attention Ekok seemed to love this child more than any of the others. Last spring, when the girl started to fail very rapidly, and it became obvious that the only chance to save her life was to send her to the hospital at Tanana, Ekok was broken hearted. But for the child's sake she never cried once in her presence and bore her misery with the most indomitable courage. It was not until the plane had flown away and her child was gone, as it proved, forever, that she broke down. But even then she would not indulge in any useless introspection. "Forget your misery is the only thing to do," so she went over to the dance which was being held especially to distract her sorrow. When I asked her to waltz with me her remark was: "Sure! It's no use sitting here hating myself." She wept bitterly all through the dance.

But life has not been all sadness, and she herself would be the last one to waste time on self-commiseration. She has a sparkling sense of humor, and gets much laughter out of the ridiculous phases of life as it passes by. She is the best ball player among all the Eskimos, and revels in a sort of a "saluchi" which the natives play. She is also the best dancer in the Koyukuk, and in the rhythm of a waltz everything else in life can be forgotten. Artistically she does lovely beadwork from which she derives a true artist's joy in creating the beautiful. She enjoys especially talking with friends, and her conversation ranges from pure gossip to the deeply philosophical. Some day she hopes to write an English-Eskimo dictionary, just for the fun of it.

At this moment I can picture Ekok, somewhere out in the wilderness of the North. She is hooded and cloaked in a great fur parky, and she strides competently along on snowshoes, breaking trail for the sled driven by her husband in which her children are warmly bundled. The wind blows fiercely into her face, and sharp pains tingle in her nose as the frost nips it. It is bitter traveling, and maybe as she stops a moment to get her breath she wonders what all her hardships are for, what good comes from all the suffering and misery and futility of life. But if so it can only be for an instant. Reasons are only for children who have time to dodge actuality with philosophical diversion. Here is snow and wind and freezing in the storm-filled sky. Here is life and the Arctic and the great, instinctive surge to live. She bends her head a little lower and pushes forward once more into the blizzard.

PART III

THE ECONOMIC LIFE

IX

LABOR

THE FIRST question, I suppose, that interests the normal person in connection with the economic life of a civilization is: What do the people do to make a living? There are two fundamental methods of making a living. It may be made directly from nature, as the so-called primitive races have chiefly done, or it may be made indirectly from nature, as the so-called civilized peoples have customarily arranged it. In the latter case some system of exchange, commonly money, is required, and the chief object in making a living is not to acquire directly the thing you need but to acquire the thing with which you can buy the thing you need.

In the Koyukuk the direct and the indirect method of making a living are intermingled. On the whole the natives are more inclined to the former and the whites to the latter method. But there is not an adult native in the upper Koyukuk who has not been paid hundreds of dollars in cash for work he has done, and there is not a white person who has not many times made his living directly by hunting, trapping, fishing, gardening, berrying, and cutting his own fuel wood. Thus at the start it is necessary to emphasize that nobody makes his living in only one way.

Consequently, in listing the occupations of the region there is some confusion. Among the Eskimos most of the people had at least two major fields of work so that the total occupations number nearly double the adults. The twenty-five Eskimo grown-ups divided their energies among the following activities:

Hunter, trapper, fisherman	17	Freighter	4
Housewife	14	Gold miner	4
Clothesmaker	6	Laundress	2

It is important to point out in connection with the occupation of housewife that the Alaskan Eskimo woman has complete economic equality with the man. In general the women do the cooking, making of clothing, and weaving of fish-nets. The men are the chief hunters, trappers, woodcutters, makers of houses, sleds, and snowshoes. There is no real preference between these two sets of activities, and even if there were any choice this would be largely nullified by the fact that the tasks are frequently reversed. Further, in the very important matter of deciding on movements of camp the women have usually more to say than the men, and they are certainly the masters in the home.

For the whites it is possible to list a single primary job. The following occupations took up the greater share of the time of each member of this race:

Gold miner	55	Gas engineer on scow	1
Freighter	3	Odd jobs man	1
Housewife	3	Cook	1
Farmer	2	Dressmaker	1
Storekeeper	2	Bootlegger	1
Roadhouse proprietor	2	U. S. Marshal	1
Teamster	1	Wireless operator	1
Hunter and trapper	1	Teacher	1

In addition to these principal activities, five men listed above did sporadic carpentry, blacksmithing, and mechanical work. At least a dozen used many hours of their spare time in farming. Most of the men cut the wood for their own use at least, and six people cut small quantities of additional wood to sell to the store, roadhouse, and occasional private purchasers. Four men spent a month or two in freighting, an average of six were constantly engaged during the summer months on improving the dog sled roads, while forty did a certain amount of hunting.

The more important activities on these two lists will be discussed in greater detail in subsequent chapters. At this place it is merely important to point out that all of these are essentially individual tasks which require in their most complex form only a few men working together, and consequently they do not necessitate any very elaborate economic configuration.

As a result the economic system which has evolved in the Koyukuk is a simple one. In general each person receives directly the profits which accrue from his labor. If several men are working together as partners then the profits are divided among them in proportion to the work which each has done. This is the old-fashioned rugged individualism of the frontier, but emphatically not the "rugged individualism" which received so much attention in the Republican Party propaganda of 1928. Concerning that type, one of these true individualists of the Arctic remarked: "This rugged individualism they're all talking about Outside, it's ninety-nine individuals do the work and one individual gets all the profits."

Now let us see how this Arctic individualism actually works in practice. Suppose there is a man who owns a mining claim. He feels he cannot work it efficiently himself so he gets three men to join him in a partnership for the winter's work. Each partner has an equal voice in directing the operation, but financially there is not quite equality. The agreement which the partners will make, generally verbally, will be something of this nature. From the gold which is recovered the expenses which the operation has incurred are first deducted. Then each man is to be paid ten dollars for every day's work he has done, or if less than that amount is recovered then he receives his proportional share of the total. If, after these equal wages are paid, there should still remain a balance, twenty-five per cent is given to the man who owned the claim and the remainder is divided equally among the four. As the wages and expenses of a four man outfit, working say six months, would amount to six or seven thousand dollars, and as very few outfits have taken out that amount of money during the past fifteen years, the actual income derived from ownership is very insignificant compared to that which comes directly from labor. During 1931 about $27,000 in gold was recovered, of which only $1,200 was paid in royalties to the claim owners. About $1,200 additional went for equipment expenses. But labor actually received more than ninety per cent of the gross income for its own share.

It is thus apparent that while most people depend on owning or renting property for their livelihood, the great bulk of their income comes directly from the work they do and not from their ownership as such. When, as it occasionally happens, the owner sells the privilege of operating his claim, the rent which he is paid is small. The one transaction of this sort during my year in the Koyukuk returned the owner just twelve and one-half per cent of the net profits.

Sometimes the partners on a claim, if they are in rich diggings, will hire men to work for them. This does not usually happen during the entire length of an operation, but generally occurs near the end of the winter or the summer mining season when there is a rush to finish work before either the thawing of the ground in spring or the freezing of the creeks in autumn make further operations impossible. With the scarcity of richly paying claims during the past fifteen years and the high wage scale of $10 a day, it is actually true that if a man worked for wages all winter long he would be better off than a partner in nine cases out of ten.

Thus we find in the Koyukuk this remarkable situation. A wage worker is just as well off financially as an owner. Furthermore, physically both men do exactly the same type of work under the same conditions. Socially there is not the slightest stigma attached to wage work. Finally, there isn't any real wage class as opposed to an owner class anyway, for the man who is in a rich pay streak and is hiring labor this year may be working for the man he hired next. Just within my year in the Koyukuk there were four cases of this reversal of status. As a result we discover that the capitalist and the working class have become thoroughly merged in the Koyukuk.

This fact is realized alike by the employers of labor and the employed. One of the former remarked: "You take any man in here who's hired for labor, he's just practically like a partner, not like a workingman at all." On the other side, one young fellow who has done practically nothing but wage work since his arrival in the Koyukuk says: "You'll find it's different working for a man in this country than it is for a big corporation Outside. Here, even if the man who hires you is nominally the boss, you're friends and practically partners. You don't care how hard or how many hours you work then. Why I've put in three days without sleep for Jack White on the river which I'd never do for ten times the money from a corporation which didn't seem like a personal friend to me."

As a matter of fact, the number of wage workers in the Koyukuk is very small. Only six of the 102 adults spent more than half the year working for wages, and three of these were the government paid marshal, wireless operator, and school teacher, who, being so far removed from their directors, were virtually their own bosses. Two storekeepers and a teamster made up the balance of those who spent over half their time working for wages. Almost two-thirds of the adults did not work for wages at all, as indicated in the following table:

Amount of Time Working for Wages	Men	Women	Both Sexes
Over 6 months	5	1	6
4 to 6 months	3	1	4
2 to 4 months	6	0	6
A few days to 2 months	22	0	22
Not at all	44	20	64
Total	80	22	102

As a result of this absence of a hired class, work in the Koyukuk is done on a much more leisurely basis than Outside. If a man feels like resting for a few minutes, whether he is working alone or is one of a group of partners or is a temporary wage worker, nobody objects. If a friend comes along to pay a visit everybody may stop and chat with him for half an hour, or in certain special cases they may even take off the remainder of the day. If there is a big dance in town, if some interesting person comes into the Koyukuk by plane, if fresh moose tracks are seen near the cabin, if any one is sick and needs help, a day or even a week may be lost from work. There is no regular schedule to which one must adhere, and so any distraction of great enough importance may take the precedence over work.

It is interesting to observe the enthusiasm which is taken in doing a job well merely for the satisfaction which a neat piece of workmanship brings. It is the old delight which the craftsman used to take in a splendidly executed product before the era of mass production. An elderly lady comments: "One thing I have found remarkable in here is how conscientiously the people all work, even without any boss watching over them. That's because they're used to being their own boss so much of the time. When Henry fixes up something which I'd do any old way, just in a hurry to get it done, Henry must do it just so, and I simply can't hurry him." I remember one November evening, when three of us were camped near the head of the Dietrich River. Kenneth Harvey was skinning a wolverine which he had trapped that day and doing a magnificent job. We were making fun of him because of his excessively painstaking work on such a commonplace pelt, to which he replied with entire honesty: "I like to do a good job anyway. I hate just as much to cut a $20 fur as a $200 one."

X

CAPITAL

THE CHIEF money-making activities of the Koyukuk are peculiar in that none of them brings a steady income, but instead all receive their returns once or at most twice during the year. If you are a miner you reap practically all of your reward at the spring and the fall cleanup. If you are hauling freight you are very apt to be paid only at the end of the season. If you have furs to sell you generally send them to the Seattle Fur Exchange at the close of trapping and receive in return one lump sum check. Your garden, your fish, your berries all come seasonally, and actually the only economic activity capable of bringing a year around return is hunting. But even in hunting there are often unexpected periods of several months when nobody can bring in any game.

As a result of this irregularity of income some credit system is needed. This system is supplied by the store and the roadhouses. It should be mentioned that the two roadhouses in the Koyukuk, in addition to serving the meals and shelter which constitute the normal functions of a roadhouse, also go into competition with the store by selling food and clothing. It is probably the most ticklish function of both the storekeeper and the roadhouse proprietor to know how much credit it is safe to advance. Knowledge is necessary of the borrower's integrity, energy, and above all of his prospects.

If a man is working on a piece of ground which it seems certain will produce a large amount of gold, then it is safe to advance him a substantial amount of credit. Sometimes, however, the storekeeper will misjudge the ground, and advance credit on what proves to be worthless. The Bettles branch of the store lost nearly a thousand dollars in this way a couple of years ago. This loss, of course, is passed on at least partially to the whole community which must pay in increased prices for the poor guesses or the dishonesty of a few of its members. That this is no insignificant matter is indicated by the fact that the store which made a profit of $3,208.59 in 1930 had $10,937 outstanding in credits at the close of the year.

The problem of slap-her-down [1] becomes additionally complicated by the entirely different economic background of the Eskimos. From time immemorial they had entertained no conception of money, profits, loans, or credit. In the nomadic life which they led there was nothing of any value which they could accumulate except extra skins, a few simple trinkets, ornaments, and charms, and the equipment which they were constantly using. Otherwise, everything which a man acquired he divided with his neighbors, or "potlatched" it as the local vernacular has it. This was a very rational thing to do. If a man had just shot a dozen caribou it was more meat than he could possibly use himself before it would spoil or he would travel, so why not divide it among his friends, thus avoiding useless waste and bringing himself the reputation of being a great hunter. It was probably from such psy-

[1] It is interesting to note that in the vocabulary of the Koyukuk the actual term *credit* is seldom used. Instead people talk about *slap-her-down*. This derives from the fact that when men ordered things at the store and did not want to pay cash, they would say: "Slap her down," meaning "Write it down in the ledger and I'll settle for it later." Thus *credit* became *slap-her-down*.

chological reasons that the custom of potlatch originated. This
developed into a great social event among the Eskimos. Periodically they would all gather and each one would contribute
to a common coffer in proportion to his possessions. The more
one contributed the greater the honor of course, but every
one, no matter how poor, had to contribute something. Then
it was all redivided equally, and if anything was left over
it was given to the feeblest people. In this way the problem
of the poor was solved without rewarding the rich with
anything more than popularity. The people who had bene-
fited by the potlatch had no conception of paying back what
they received, and the rich men, or the *oomallik* as they were
called, never even dreamed of asking anything in return for
their donations. It was simply a normal part of life. Consequently, with such a background, it is easy to see why the
Eskimos found it hard to understand the white man's system
of credit. The storekeepers were simply the *oomalliks* with
greater wealth than the common run of people, and it was
merely fitting that they should divide this wealth with those
with fewer riches.

So, between the white men who use the food they obtain
on credit to nourish them while they sink holes from which
there is no return, and the Eskimos who can not sincerely
see how credit advanced to them while they are impoverished
constitutes a just debt, the life of the store owners and roadhouse proprietors in the Koyukuk has not been an altogether
happy one. If they do finally refuse further credit, or become too insistent about the payment of credit long overdue,
then they are cursed through all the rounds of perdition. It
must be admitted, however, that several of them have also
contributed just grounds for unpopularity. The absentee
owner of the two stores in the upper Koyukuk is an exceptionally inefficient man, and the Koyukukers appreciate that

they have to pay for all his blunders. Furthermore, the fact that he charges from twenty to fifty per cent profit on everything he sells seems exorbitant. Finally, he has been a very vindictive man, and many of his petty acts of revenge have blotted out the recollection of some splendid acts of generosity. The general dislike for this man has one peculiar social advantage. In most regions where a group of people gather among whom there is some sort of strained relationship there is nothing to talk about except the weather. In the Koyukuk there is one subject which makes all men kin, for the worst enemies can become almost friendly in the cursing of Abe Makin.

Nevertheless, the Koyukukers do not heap their criticisms indiscriminately on all traders. Jack Dodds, the Bettles roadhouse man, is universally popular. He is more or less of an invalid, suffering badly from asthma, and he has no personal ambitions except to live as comfortably as possible. Everything above his meager living expenses he gives away in the form of credit which half the time he never gets back. He is especially generous to the natives around Bettles, and one of the big features of the year is a tremendous free dinner which he serves to all of them every Christmas.

In addition to what is purchased in the store and roadhouse, quite a number of people order their goods directly from the Outside. By cutting out the middleman's profits it materially reduces expenses. The Stanich brothers found they could lower their annual cost of living from $2,100 to $1,800 by ordering directly from Montgomery-Ward, instead of buying locally. However, trading with mail order houses requires money in advance, and this few Koyukukers have, especially since orders must go in at the poorest time of year, just before the spring cleanups, in order that the goods may be shipped for the brief season of water transportation.

In view of the fact that such a great reduction in cost of living is possible by ordering supplies directly from the Outside, it may seem strange that people do not borrow money for their orders. The reason why this is so seldom done is that the interest rate for commercial transactions is fixed by custom at the high rate of one per cent a month or ten per cent a year. This, however, does not apply at all to loans to individuals who are penniless and require money for the immediate purchase of the essentials of life. Such loans are made without either interest or security, but merely as acts of neighborly assistance. The store, in advancing credit, charges no direct interest, but the high profit which it exacts on all sales virtually means that every one has to pay the interest on whatever credit is granted.

It is not only the interest rate which is set by custom, but also most of the locally controlled prices. Thus the price of meat, berries, and garden truck are standardized by tradition, quite regardless of the supply and demand. Even when there is a scarcity of meat in camp and certain well-to-do people might be willing to pay as much as a dollar a pound for moose meat, no hunter would have the temerity to raise the long-established price of thirty-three and a third cents a pound. To do so would be taking advantage of a communal misfortune for one's own aggrandisement, and this would be considered the most indefensible sort of avarice. Similarly, freight rates have remained constant for many years. When the camp commenced its very rapid decline after 1916, and the facilities for hauling freight for 400 people had only to meet the requirements of a third of that number, there was no competitive price cutting. Most of the freighters left the region in preference to depending on a rate-cutting war for their means of livelihood. Wage workers, too, have refused to work for less than the standard rates of ten dollars a day without board or six dollars a day with board. Most men greatly desire occasional wage work to help finance unprofitable mining ventures, but they would not think of getting a job by the expedient of underbidding one of their friends.

Closely associated with this desire for occasional wage work, is the belief of many people that the greatest need of the camp to-day is the introduction of Outside capital to finance prospecting and to develop some of the known claims which cannot be worked without a large initial outlay of money. It is a significant fact that in the whole history of the region there has only been one instance of Outside capital being invested in the Koyukuk. In 1926 a fly-by-night promoter brought in some $50,000 which he so grossly mismanaged during the next four years that scarcely any gold ever came out of the ground for all the money put in, although the cash did temporarily enliven the whole economic life of the community. Nevertheless, if Outside money were to come into the Koyukuk in any large amount and absentee ownership be established as the rule instead of the exception, most of the unique freedom and independence which distinguishes the individualistic economic system of the Koyukuk would disappear. The thing has happened before. The rugged individualism of the United States pioneer has vanished before capitalized industrialism, and it would take a hardy man indeed to say that the change has been for greater happiness.

Partly because there was no Outside capital invested any more in the region, partly because the only things the Koyukukers sold on the markets of the outside world were gold, which still brought the standard price of $20.67 for each pure ounce, and fur, which for biological reasons was in the midst of one of its regular periods of scarcity, the great depression of 1930 and 1931 had practically no tangible repercussion in the Koyukuk. People read about it with the same abstract interest that they read Malinowski's description of cross-cousin marriage in the Trobriand Islands. There were no frozen assets, no bank failures, and no unemployment to make the people miserable. They went about their mining, their freight hauling, their hunting, their fishing, their trapping, their gardening, their berrying, their wood chopping the same as ever. And they genuinely felt, as old George Huey remarked, that "nothing Outside affects us seriously here. We're interested, of course, but it doesn't really matter. We've got our own country and we fight our own way and we're just as aloof from the rest of the world as if we were on Mars."

This typical view is not entirely realistic, for the welfare of the Koyukuk obviously hinges on the worldwide status of gold. If the United States, for instance, went off the gold standard the purchasing power of the Koyukukers would be tremendously depleted because of the rise in all prices while the monetary value of gold remained unchanged. On the other hand, the present decrease in Outside prices should theoretically increase the purchasing power of the Koyukukers, although actually up to the close of 1931 the store owner had not passed on this cheaper cost of goods to his customers.

It is also true that if all contact with the outside world were cut off, the present civilization on the Koyukuk could not long survive. There are not more than half a dozen of the whites who could live entirely off the country, and even many of the natives would have a hard time subsisting without some of the store goods to which they have become as thoroughly accustomed as the whites. Without ammunition every one would fare still worse, for very few could survive an abrupt transition back to the bow and arrow culture. Nevertheless, under favorable conditions, with no early frost to ruin the gardens and plenty of game around, I believe that the entire civilization could continue at least two years without any intercourse with the outside world.

This chapter seems to be the appropriate place to discuss the subject of the money used in the Koyukuk. Probably eighty per cent of the total volume of financial transactions is carried out with gold. This gold is measured by weighing, so that a gold scales becomes as much the normal equipment of every miner in the Koyukuk as a check book is for a person with any capital in the outside world. Again, analogous to the pocketbook of the Outside is the poke, or leather sack, in which a man carries his gold.

Pure gold, as has been already mentioned, is worth always the standard price of $20.67 to the ounce. That is what any mint in the United States will pay for it. However, gold as it comes in nature is never pure. No matter how carefully you clean away the dirt, you cannot clean out the quartz rock which is always fused with the gold. Consequently, the purest gold ever recovered from the Koyukuk was worth an even $20 to the ounce. It came from the Nolan Creek drainage. As one goes down the Koyukuk River the purity is lower, until at Myrtle Creek it runs just about $18 an ounce. Nevertheless, despite the fact that the mean value probably runs around $19, the stores and roadhouses have adopted the standard value of $18 an ounce, regardless of the creek on which the gold originated. This sets the scale for a general value, and all through the Koyukuk gold is passed as currency at the standard rate of $18 to the ounce. Scales are calibrated in terms of those values, and the weights are marked not in fractions of an ounce but in dollars and cents.

The smallest weight is the two-bit or twenty-five cent one. From this fact it develops that no amount of money less than twenty-five cents is recognized in the Koyukuk. A dime or a nickel is worthless. Most of the people have not seen such coins in years. Bills are always balanced to the nearest two-bits.

The white man's system of money was not at once apparent to the Eskimos. Big Charlie has told me his first impression. He had just sold a tanned skin to a trader, and the man had given him a five dollar bill. "I no savvy money. I ask native boy: 'What good this dirty thing?' Native boy say: 'See that tent? You get anything you want there for that money.' 'Crazy,' I think, but I go over and get coffee, flour, sugar, lots of things for little dirty piece of paper. Then I savvy white man's money, want money all the time since then."

XI

TRANSPORTATION

IN A community as remote from the centers of trade as is Wiseman, the problem of getting in supplies is a particularly complicated one. It involves a long and diverse series of conveyances before the transportation of the goods finally terminates at the frontier destination. Suppose a miner on Nolan Creek orders a pair of Bergman shoes to be sent by freight from Portland, Oregon. First the shoes would bump along for 200 miles over the tracks of the Northern Pacific Railroad before they would come to a halt in the depot in Seattle. From here they would be hauled by truck across the city to Pier No. 2 where they would be loaded into the hold of an Alaska Steamship Company vessel. Then would ensue 1,850 miles of an ocean journey to Seward, where the shoes would be transferred to one of the freight cars of the Alaska Railroad. After 400 miles around the hairpin bends of this route there would be a third reloading at Nenana, and this time the shoes would find themselves in a steamboat, booked for about 600 miles down the broad channels of the Tanana and Yukon Rivers. Just below the mouth of the Koyukuk the much traveled footwear would stop again, this time at Nulato, where they would await the arrival of the leisurely, gasoline-propelled Koyukuk boat which would carry them against the current of this river some 565 miles further to Bettles. Here they would be unloaded once more to await the horse drawn scow which would negotiate the last eighty-five miles of the upper Koyukuk to Wiseman. This short link in the journey would require a greater human energy output than all the others combined, but finally the shoes would arrive in Wiseman where the owner would receive them and pack them on his back to his home some six miles further at Nolan Creek. Thus we find these shoes would have a total journey of some 3,700 miles by train, truck, steamer, train, steamboat, gasoline boat, horse drawn scow, and back packing before they would reach the feet of their owner.

The cost of this long journey is seven cents a pound all the way into Bettles. From Bettles to Wiseman it is seven cents a pound additional in summer and eight cents in winter. Once the freight is in Wiseman the standard charge for hauling it to Nolan Creek or Hammond River is two cents a pound by sled in winter and six cents a pound by wagon in summer. To some of the more remote mining centers as much as ten cents a pound may be charged. It will be seen, then, that on top of the normal price which people in the United States must pay for what they buy there is added to the bills of the miners of the Koyukuk from fifteen to twenty-five cents for every pound they get. In the case of clothing this is not so very important, but in the case of food staples, where the freight from the West Coast may be from half to four times the purchase price, the effect of transportation on the cost of living is tremendous.

The methods of transportation within the Koyukuk alter completely with the two principal seasons. During the seven months of winter, from the time the rivers freeze between the first and twentieth of October, until ice crossing stops and the snow melts in the valleys between the first and twentieth of May, there is one very definite form of transportation, by dog team. During the three months of summer, from the time the flood crest of the river has passed during the early part of June until the freezing source streams make the rivers too shallow for navigation some time in September, there are several quite different forms of transportation. During the single month transition seasons of spring and autumn there is no transportation at all if a person has even the rudimentary vestiges of sanity.

Dogs certainly are the chief beasts of burden and the primary motive power of the upper Koyukuk. There were 185 dogs distributed among seventy-eight of the 102 adults in that region during the winter of 1930-31. A great deal has been written about the dogs of the North, much of it nonsense. When I first came to the Koyukuk one of the sourdoughs told me: "If you've read any of those books by James Oliver Curwood and Rex Beach, well, they paint a picture of dog teams like a fellow might dream about, but they don't actually come that way. Dogs is dogs, and a fellow don't want to expect too much of them."

"Dogs is dogs," and they have to be cared and cooked for, day in, day out. They frequently fight, repeatedly have worms which require eradication, and constantly disturb the peace of the Arctic night with their barking. Their judgment is often faulty, and the leaders do not unerringly choose the ideal route. It is a tedious nuisance to have to hitch them into the harness every morning, and frequently an agony to unhitch them with numb fingers at night time. They often play out just when you yourself are feeling most tired, and thus they necessitate your auxiliary efforts to replace their fagged energies.

Yet withal, there is nothing in the Arctic as valuable, and in many ways as admirable, as a good dog. The amount of freight these animals have hauled is staggering. I know of a team of four strong malemutes (the type of dog used in the Koyukuk) which hauled a load of 1,100 pounds a distance of sixty-four miles in three days. If they do lay down on the job when they can get away with it, their faithful performance with a good driver in the face of hardships which would kill any other animal is nothing short of marvelous. As for companionship to lonely men, far from the nearest human being, there is nothing like them in all the world.

It follows logically that the affection which some of the old sourdoughs lavish on their dogs replaces part of the affection which ordinary people extend to their children. One of them remarks proudly: "There's one God damn thing sure, I've got four dogs that welcome me when I come home. I ain't got no women to keep so I can afford dogs, and by God, I'm a-telling you, there's mighty few women I've ever met in seventy years of ramming around whom I'd take ahead of them dogs." Another says: "I've been too drunk to do almost anything you can mention, but that's one thing, I've never got too drunk to feed the dogs."

The feeding of the dogs is really a serious problem. A man cannot go anywhere or do anything without making provision for having his dogs fed. There are a great many different recipes for dog feed. Most commonly they are given a mulligan consisting of boiled cereal, salmon, and tallow. However, meat is an excellent substitute for the fish. Many of the natives feed their dogs on it exclusively. The cereals used are chiefly cornmeal, rice, flour, and rolled oats. Some people who have substantial gardens use turnips and potatoes in place of the cereal. Everybody uses what scraps of food are left over from his own meals, so that the dog bucket replaces the garbage can in the Koyukuk.

The estimated cost of feeding dogs varies from ten to fifty cents a day. A fair average for a man who does not augment the dog feed with meat which he has shot would probably be about twenty-five cents a day. One man has kept the following itemized record of costs for feeding his four dog team for a month while it was doing fairly hard work:

30 lbs. of cornmeal @ 20 cents a lb.	$ 6.00
25 lbs. of flour @ 22 cents a lb.	5.50
30 lbs. of rice @ 25 cents a lb.	7.50
15 lbs. of tallow @ thirty-five cents a lb. ..	5.25
45 lbs. of salmon @ twenty-eight cents a lb.	12.60
Total	$36.85

The cost of feeding horses is of course immensely higher than dogs. The price of hay shipped into the Koyukuk from Outside is $360 a ton. Local grown oat hay brings $120 to $140 a ton, while wild hay is sold for $100 a ton. At these rates, unless you raise your own hay, it costs about $3,000 a year to feed a team of horses. It costs just about the same whether you use local or Outside grown hay because the latter is so much more nourishing. Of course horses are a great convenience, both in hauling freight and in hauling wood. They can pull far more than the biggest team of dogs. But nearly ten dollars a day is an exorbitant price for the feed of a single team which only has intermittent work. Perhaps that is why there are but two teams of horses left in the Koyukuk, and why the owners of both are broke.

Before going on to the subject of sledding, it seems desirable to complete the survey of domestic animals in the Koyukuk. The remainder consists of a solitary cat of doubtful age, sex, and utility, which affords a few children considerable amusement and occasionally catches a mouse.

The sleds of the Koyukuk are of two sorts, the Yukon sled and the basket sled. Both types were invented by the natives, though the whites have added iron runner shoes and brakes. Both sleds are similar in construction. They consist of a spruce wood platform built about a foot above the birch runners which are turned up in front. In the Yukon sled there is nothing above this platform. In the basket sled there are basketlike sides rising above the platform, about six inches high at the front end and perhaps twenty-four inches high in the rear. The rear runners of the basket sled extend a foot or more behind the main body, and there are handle bars projecting from the top of the basket part, so that a person, if he has a light load and a good trail, can stand on the rear runners and be pulled by the dogs, merely jumping off now and then to steer by pushing on the handle bars. With the Yukon sled there is no place to ride except on top of the load. In most cases a person does not have a well-broken trail, so he will usually snowshoe ahead of his sled, steering by pressure on a pole extending forward and upward from the right side of the front end. This is known as the gee-pole.

People often ask how far a person can travel with dogs in a day. Actually there can be no categorical answer. It depends on the dogs, the load, and above all the condition of the trail. I recall one time when we had to break trail every foot of the way where eight miles was an exhausting day's journey. But four days later, on a well-traveled trail, with exactly the same dogs and a slightly heavier load, we made fifty-three miles and scarcely noticed the effort.

The fundamental factor behind this great contrast in trail conditions is the peculiar snow of the Arctic which is far lighter than any snow of temperate regions. This is both because the Arctic air is so cold that there is a minimum of moisture in each flake, and because the snow on the ground never thaws all winter long, and thus remains as fluffy as when it was fresh. Consequently, a dog will often sink out of sight in untraveled snow, making it necessary to tramp ahead of one's team, often two or three times, to pack the snow sufficiently firmly that the dogs can get a foothold. This is exceptionally arduous work. But once a route has been traversed, the pressure of the passing weight will slightly melt the snow, which refreezes into a solid ice pavement. Even after a subsequent storm the "bottom" remains, so that no matter how bad the blizzard, a trail already broken out is easier traveling than one through the untrodden snow.

The rivers are generally the easiest routes for winter travel because they always have solid ice underneath, because they are windswept, and because the overflows reduce the amount of snow. On the other hand overflows also make the rivers the most hazardous traveling. When it gets very cold the streams at places freeze to the bottom, and this dams the water which is flowing under the ice all winter. The water is backed up until it finds an outlet by way of some crack or air hole and flows out over the top of the ice. The colder it is, the more the river freezes to the bottom, and consequently the more it overflows. The fresh water surface soon glazes over so that unless one watches very carefully it looks like good ice until one breaks through. Of course the moccasin-clad feet immediately become soaked, and then one has to build a fire and dry out as fast as possible.

In spite of the hard labor and the frequent danger involved, winter travel, or mushing as it is generally called, is one of the genuine joys in the life of most of the Koyukukers, and nearly a fifth of all the white people actually claim that they get their greatest pleasure in being on the trail. As Ike Spinks has told me: "It's so attractive you just can't get away from it. There's a fascination to it, you know yourself, you couldn't buy for any price. And you've got it all the time here when you're traveling without paying a cent for it."

This sense of fascination, which is built of both a delight in the beauty and the adventure, is shared by Eskimos and whites alike. Perhaps I can give you some slight idea of it by describing an actual mushing trip of my own. Jesse Allen and Kenneth Harvey had invited me to join them to help haul back the sheep which they had shot and cached in the autumn near the head of the Middle Fork, sixty-two miles from Wiseman. It was a sparkling clear morning in early November that Jesse and I set out on the trail to Hammond River where we were to meet Harv. The sleds were nearly empty so we made good time, Jesse with five dogs to pull him, I with four. We stood on the rear runners, holding the handle bars for support, and though we only averaged seven or eight miles an hour, with perhaps a maximum of fifteen miles when we struck the downhill stretches in a spray of dry snow, so close were we to the ground that we seemed to be hurtling over the trail. We tore down long aisles between dark green spruce trees, were brushed by the willow branches and the evergreen leaves of the Alaska Tea, followed the rhythm of the legs of the huskies as they beat on the pathway, had time to look up at the mountaintops and note the constantly changing outlines they cut against the deep blue sky, and felt ourselves to be a part of the world through which we were traveling. It was in complete contrast to riding in an auto, where you are you and the landscape is the landscape and never is there any merging of the two.

The next morning at eight o'clock, before the first streak of dawn, we set out up the Middle Fork, following the course of the river. Our three teams followed each other in single file, Jesse and Harv as the experienced mushers breaking trail, and I as the greenhorn bringing up the rear. In spite

"If he has a light load and a good trail, a person can stand on the rear
runners and be pulled by the dogs."

EASY TRAVELLING: The well broken trail from Bettles to Wiseman on the last mile into Wiseman.

HARD TRAVELLING: It took us all day to break out eight miles of trail through this soft snow.

of the hard going and the softness of the dogs we covered over twenty miles that day, and pulled up by 2:30 in the afternoon at a little cabin just below the mouth of Bettles River. Straight across the Middle Fork, scarcely a mile away, was a horned pinnacle which jutted more than 3,000 feet into the air. Beyond the mouth of Bettles River was an even loftier mountain with a precipice wall several miles long and over 1,500 feet sheer.

Next morning we were up shortly after five to start breakfast, and by 8:30, still before the first daylight, we were once more on the move. It was a day spent alternately running along in front of the dogs on the easy stretches, helping them pull on the hard ones, and detouring cautiously around the frequent overflows on the river. Shortly after two the sun disappeared behind the high limestone crags to the west, and the temperature dropped so rapidly that we commenced to think about camp. We were beyond the zone of cabins, and had to set up a tent and chop spruce bows to cover the snow. But we had a good stove, and we could make the inside of the tent as warm as any steamheated apartment if one of us would spend an hour or two cutting wood. By the time we had everything done—dogs tied, tent set, boughs cut and spread, stove blocked up and stove-pipe pieced together, wood cut, ten gallons of water melted, our supper cooked, our supper eaten, the dishes washed, the dogfeed cooked, cooled, and given out, clothing brushed off and hung up to dry, holes and tears sewed—four or five hours of steady hustling were consumed. We left the stove full of wood when we crawled into our sleeping bags around ten o'clock, but the fire was burned out in a couple of hours, so that by morning the tent was as cold as the outside air.

It took quite a dash of fortitude to crawl out of the warm bed and start the fire, but once it was going the tent speedily

warmed. A couple of hours sufficed to cook and eat breakfast, break camp, pack the sleds, hitch up the dogs, and be
on the way. The weather was perfect, the going was good,
and we could observe the whole pageant of a midwinter
Arctic morning growing out of a midwinter Arctic night. It
was full starlight when we started, heading straight on the
course toward Polaris. After half an hour the black sky commenced to turn gray, and the unbelievable brightness of the
stars slowly faded. The gray became faintly blue and then
a single snowy peak in the northwest showed a tip of pink.
So gradually that you could hardly notice it advancing, the
pink spread from peak to peak until all the summits to the
north and west were colored. The pink kept creeping down
the slopes, changing imperceptibly in color, until all at once
you noticed that it had vanished, and the whole mountainsides were bathed in a golden spray—craggy peaks, snow-
fields, dark spruce timber, everything. And then suddenly,
after a whole morning of shadow, there was a wide bend in
the river, and at high noon we drove out into the sunlight.

We reached our destination at the Upper Forks that afternoon shortly after one. The sheep had not been disturbed,
and they were ready to be loaded for the downstream journey on the morrow. It was getting constantly colder, and we
could not work hard enough to keep warm while setting up
camp. We had to stop frequently and thaw our feet and
hands by the fire where the cornmeal was cooking for the
dogs. But by 5:30 all the chores were completed, and we
retired to the well-heated tent for supper and relaxation.
The thermometer dropped that night to forty below zero,
but this merely seemed to accentuate the snugness of our
solitary habitation in thousands of square miles of freezing
wilderness.

The most important summer freight hauling is along the main Koyukuk River from Bettles to Wiseman. This is done chiefly by large scows capable of carrying fifteen or twenty tons of goods. They are moved for the most part by genuine horse power in the form of teams of from two to four horses which actually pull these clumsy crafts up most of the eighty-five mile stretch of river which separates the two communities of the upper Koyukuk. They also are equipped with motors which may be used in occasional deep stretches, and are invaluable in crossing the river when the gravel bars along which the horses must walk change sides. By means of a capstan and cable attached firmly to shore, the scows sometimes pull themselves up the river. But motor power is distinctly secondary to horse power.

When business was at its height back in 1915 there were six scows plying on this stretch of river. To-day there is only one. It is manned by a crew of six, among whom the most highly skilled job is that of the sweepman who steers the boat from the rear by means of a huge oar. It is interesting to note that the three best sweepmen on the Koyukuk are all Eskimos.

The journey upstream is a tedious drudgery. The record time is five and one-half days for a trip, but it sometimes takes a month to cover the eighty-five miles which separate Bettles and Wiseman. The current of from four to six miles an hour is continually running over shallow riffles with only a few inches of water, so that brute force alone can work the heavy load over these places. The deepest channel changes, day by day, and no successive trips follow the same route. At best there is constant, backbreaking labor and repeated soakings in the river which even in mid-summer is only a few degrees above freezing. At worst there is always the danger of swamping the boat and losing all the precious freight, not to mention the hazard of drowning.

The journey down the river is a very different matter. Aside from the sweepman, who must be constantly on the alert to avoid swamping the craft on some hidden rock, cut bank, or tree trunk lying horizontally on the river, the rest of the crew can relax. The entire journey is customarily made in a single day.

The most common boat on the rivers of the North is the poling boat which penetrates where the larger vessels could not go. Typically the poling boat is from ten to twenty feet long, from three to five feet wide on top, and has a narrow bottom from eighteen to thirty inches wide. It has a nose shaped something like a shovel which is raised high above the water so that it does not bury in the current. As the name implies, the principal motive power is obtained by shoving against the bottom with a pole. An expert poler can make about fifteen miles against a four mile current in a single day. Sometimes the current is too swift and shallow, so you jump overboard, grab the boat by the nose, and pull it over the shallow place by brute force. At other times you neck the boat up the river, that is, walk along the river bar some distance ahead of the boat, tugging against a rope which is attached on one end to the bow and the other to the stern. By lengthening or shortening these two segments you can keep the boat straight with the current, and by endless perseverance and straining you can make some progress. When there are two men one may pull with the rope and the other help with the pole. Sometimes both pull. Sometimes you harness up your dogs and let them pull the boat. The most primitive method is to pull the boat upstream by grasping bushes along the shore. This is known as "milking the bushes."

Coming downstream the current furnishes the motive

power. This is much easier and faster than going upstream, but also more dangerous. In a four to eight mile current you have to think and act very quickly. If you cannot read water at a glance you continually run aground, and that always means a danger of tipping. Especially you must be careful of sweepers. The rivers are geologically very young and physically very turbulent, and in their constant change of course they frequently undercut the banks of the stream. As the banks are undercut the trees growing on the edge fall over, but often their roots still cling to the shore. Thus, all up and down the rivers of the North you find trees leaning horizontally over the water, sometimes dipping into the river, sometimes a foot or two above the surface. Any boat or raft passing under one of these, if it is not swamped outright, will have any loose objects including the passengers swept overboard. More than one Koyukuk navigator, either on raft or poling boat, has lost his life through such sweepers.

The raft is the most primitive of river crafts. It is of course only useful for floating downstream. It is usually helped along by a pair of oars or by poles, and is steered by a large oar. Two men can build a small raft in a few hours if they have a couple of axes and rope to tie the logs together, but in an emergency willows will take the place of ropes. Rafting is the slowest and most dangerous of all methods of river travel, but when a man wants to cross an unfordable river or has a heavy load to carry downstream and no boat he has only one choice.

A great deal of the summer travel is done simply by backpacking over land. This is not particularly different from backpacking in any other part of the world, except for the stupendous scenery, the fact that one often travels hundreds of miles without seeing a human being, the constant necessity of wearing nets over the head and gloves on the hands for mosquito protection, and niggerheads. A nigger-head, I suppose, among all the gifts of bountiful nature, ranks as the most cursed. It starts as a little clump of sedge, and over a long period of years gradually builds upward and outward into a great, mushroom shaped, sodlike mass. The end product is from two to four feet high, perhaps a foot thick at the base, and double that size on the top. So close together do these niggerheads grow that it is impossible to walk between them, while if you try to step over them you become exhausted in no time. So what you attempt is to bal-ance upon their tottering tops as you walk along. This works splendidly if you happen to step on the very middle, but the niggerheads are so overbalanced that on the frequent occa-sions when you miss the center of gravity, over they flop, and down you go into the mud beneath. Occurring once this merely provokes profanity. Occurring fifty or a hundred times to the mile it is likewise exhausting.

Dogs are also used as beasts of burden in the summer. They have canvas packsacks harnessed on their backs in which from twenty-five to forty pounds may be loaded. These bur-dens the dogs carry very nicely unless they suddenly have a notion to tear through the brush after a ptarmigan or swim a river, in which cases the cargo may become somewhat scat-tered or damp.

Closely associated with the matter cf freighting is the haul-ing of mail. There are eleven mails in the Koyukuk during the year. Seven mails in winter are carried 380 miles by sled from Nenana to Wiseman. Four mails in summer are brought around 1,250 miles of river from Nenana by steamer, gas boat, and scow. The summer mails bring all the parcel post which costs twelve cents a pound from any point in the United States to any point in Alaska. The winter mail is much the more regular, however, because sled trips, unless there is an exceptional blizzard, can be carried out pretty much on schedule. But in the summer there is nothing regular about river transportation. In 1930 the first summer mail did not get into Wiseman until August 11, the last winter mail having come on April 20.

Since 1912 there have been wires connecting Wiseman, Nolan Creek, and Hammond River. This is a great convenience for telling the people on the creeks about prospective dances, the arrival of the mail, and the general gossip of the region, and for receiving from the miners information about gold discoveries, supplies required, or the need for help in case of sickness or accident. This publically used telephone system was installed by a miner on Nolan Creek primarily for his own convenience. The small fees he has obtained from those with phones in their houses has never been sufficient to pay for the upkeep of line, let alone the original investment for its installation.

XII

THE ADVENT OF THE MECHANICAL

ONE OF the great events in Koyukuk history occurred on
May 11, 1925. But I will allow Dishoo, an Eskimo girl who
witnessed it, to describe the happening.

"They had wired the plane was coming in here, and we
were all sitting out in front of the old store waiting for it.
The fellows was mostly all down from the creeks, and they
had been staying around town two weeks waiting for it. It
just seemed as if they thought there wouldn't ever be another plane in here.

"Suddenly Martin jumped up like he was crazy, and he
shouted: 'I see it! I see it!' We all looked the way he was
pointing, but we couldn't any of us see it. After a while we
saw something way down the river, looked like a mosquito
hawk. Then it looked like a bird, and we told Martin it was
nothing but a bird he saw. Finally it got as big as a raven
and then we heard it and knew it was the plane.

"It flew over the town up toward the roadhouse, and we
all ran up toward the roadhouse. Then it started to circle
around, and we all ran around back of the roadhouse. Then
it came back again in front, and then it flew back, and then
it flew front, and then it flew back again, and we all following it. Never to lose sight of that plane for an instant was
all we could think of. We ran around and around in the
snow. Somebody knocked me down three times in the snow,

SUMMER TRAVEL BY WATER: Ernie Johnson, on his way up the Alatna by poling boat, stopping for lunch.

SUMMER TRAVEL BY LAND: The best road in the Koyukuk. There are six miles of this splendid boulevard between Wiseman and Nolan Creek.

but I picked myself up and ran some more. Everybody was running, old men, old women, little children. Seemed like they were all crazy.

"Then the airplane came right down toward the road-house, and Ed Marsan was afraid it would knock down the roadhouse. It started to come right toward us, and Nakuchluk and Kaypuk made an awful scream, and tried to hide in Jack White's cabin near the roadhouse. It circled around and came lower and lower, and all of a sudden it landed out there in the bar in the river.

"There was about two feet of water in the slough between the roadhouse and the bar. I ran into the slough until the water came up to the top of my boots. Then I looked around to see if any one was coming, and they was all coming after me. Green was just behind, and he had little low shoes just up to his ankles, and I thought if he could run across in those I could. So I ran as hard as I could, and behind me I heard every one in camp splashing in the water. Jimmie Tobuk and I were the first to reach the plane, but everybody else was right behind, never nobody stopped. Martin kept shouting, 'I saw it first, I saw it first, I saw it first,' just as if it made him own the plane. Some of the old natives, they just shook their head, didn't seem to know what to make of it."

The whites didn't either. They got not only the normal emotional reaction which any one received seeing his first airplane, but also they had the exceedingly practical sensation that civilization in an emergency was no longer three weeks to three months away, but only a matter of two or three hours. Notions set by nearly thirty years' experience were turned topsy-turvy in a moment. Small wonder then that they should feel as one old sourdough, especially not given to superlatives, expressed it: "I think it was the most wonderful sight—well anyway, I got the greatest thrill from it of anything I've ever seen." Small wonder that they should regard Noel Wien, the first aviator to land in the Arctic, as one of the greatest heroes in the world, and that the adulation which they conspicuously withhold from the more advertised explorers should be given to this modest pilot and his colleagues, Ed Young, Joe Crosson, and Robby Robbins.

To-day, because of the great saving in time and effort, the people of the Koyukuk have become exceedingly air conscious. This is in spite of the high one-way fare of $150 for the 200 mile journey. During the past year the number of white people who entered and left the Koyukuk by plane was greater than the combined total of those who journed by boat and sled, and there was an airplane into Wiseman almost every month.

The airplane freight rate was forty cents a pound. This was so high that the plane was normally used for carrying goods only when a person was in a great rush for something, or when the article to be shipped was very light. When the store ran out of bacon, butter, eggs, and milk these were so greatly desired that the people were willing to pay the high toll. But mostly food stuffs were too heavy to ship by plane, and the river remained the chief highway for freighting.

For travel entirely within the limits of the upper Koyukuk region, airplane transportation is virtually unused. There are only two flying fields, one at Wiseman and one at Bettles, so that landings at other localities in the region are perilous and often impossible. Furthermore, the expense of getting a plane all the way from Fairbanks to transport a man from one point to another within the upper Koyukuk would be prohibitive. It is only when a plane happens to be in the country already that a person may take it occasionally from one community to the other. But it is practically true to say that intra-regional travel is still by the time-honored methods of sled, boat, and backpacking.

A few months before the first airplane arrived the government established a wireless station in Wiseman. This was almost essential to make the use of the airplane practical, for without some method of communication with Fairbanks it would be impossible to order a plane when it was needed. The wireless is also used for sending weather reports, for ordering goods from Fairbanks, and occasionally to get medical advice from the doctors at Fairbanks, Tanana, or Fort Yukon. In spite of the success of this public station, no private radios have ever appeared in the Koyukuk. The cost of getting a good receiving set into the region would be more than most people have any desire to spend. The presence of unusual static and the absence of advance programs are also drawbacks. Finally, the phonograph and the magazines give, far more satisfactorily than the radio, the best that is to be had of music and information.

In the winter of 1929-1930 another important mechanical contrivance made its début in the Koyukuk. It was a caterpillar tractor, always referred to as *the cat*, brought in by the store owner to transport his freight from Bettles to Wiseman. The first winter it was laid up most of the time, waiting for spare parts to replace the ones which were broken. The second winter it was a tremendous success, for there was very little snow and far better knowledge of how to run it. As a result it was possible to reduce the freight rates between Wiseman and Bettles from eight to six cents a pound. But in spite of this apparent saving, the tractor actually was a detriment to the economic welfare of the Koyukuk. Formerly all of the eight cents a pound paid for hauling freight was expended right in the region, being given directly to the local people who did the work, while now at least four of the six cents goes Outside for gasoline, oil, and extra parts, and is lost entirely from the coffers of the Koyukuk. It was simply another instance of a mechanical improvement which was a technological triumph but an economic injury.

The third type of mechanical vehicle reached the Koyukuk on July 3, 1931. This was nothing less than an automobile. On second thought it was considerably less, and I think it was best described by Floyd Hyde, a young mechanic in the Koyukuk, who said: "You know sometimes you buy a third hand Ford for about twenty-five dollars and they throw in a very much older car for extra parts. Well, this is about like the extra parts car." Nevertheless, the wireless operator paid $150 freight to have this extra parts car shipped in by boat. Before it got working properly almost every important old part had to be replaced. Furthermore, there were just six and one-quarter miles of passable road for it to travel, six miles to Nolan Creek and quarter of a mile to the flying field back of town. The possible season when the roads were open enough that even these few miles could be followed was not more than four months. Nevertheless, the owner claimed it was worth its cost for the ease with which it permitted the hauling of freight to and from the landing field.

It was interesting to observe the reactions of the people toward this unexpected innovation. Only three of all the natives, those who had been out to Fairbanks, had ever seen an automobile, while there were still five whites left, men who had not been south of the Yukon since the turn of the century, who were unacquainted with this type of vehicle. There was a big crowd in town the evening it arrived—people who had congregated for the Fourth of July celebration. But there were fewer people to watch it being assembled than usually hung around to watch the mailboat leave. One of the old whites who had never seen an auto did not even come down to look at it, and the other one who was in town left to dance before it was put together. Only the two owners, four other adults, and most of the children stayed to see it reassembled. When, in the full daylight of eleven o'clock, it finally raced by the roadhouse, all the people came running to the door, but soon returned to the dance. The next time it passed they looked out of the window at it. After that they did not bother to even look around when it went by. It was merely the event of the day, but no long-remembered thrill. Of course the reason was that the airplane and the tractor had made the automobile an anti-climax.

A few of the remarks overheard might be of interest as giving a cross section of the reactions of the community.

Bob MacIntyre—Why, if the roads were in good shape he could run the six miles to Nolan in half an hour.

Kenneth Harvey—It doesn't give me any kick at all seeing it like that first airplane.

Vaughn Green (facetiously)—Now when the cat comes down they can have a race for Fourth of July.

Kaaruk (disappointedly)—Is that an automobile? I thought it was something great to look at, not a shabby old thing like that.

Nutirwik (realistically, after he had ridden in it on its first trip)—Bump all time. Bump up and down awful. Pretty soon stop in hole, jump out, push him, bump some more, stop, push him some more again.

XIII

FOOD

IT IS really surprising, considering the totally different backgrounds of the whites and Eskimos, that their present diets should be so much alike. The white people were brought up to eat the same food that any normal American of the late Nineteenth Century was accustomed to consume. The Kobuk diet, on the other hand, would have driven the normal American to suicide. It included:

(1) Dried fish without any salt. This was sometimes prepared by boiling and sometimes rotted in the ground. A hole about four or five feet deep was dug, and the bottom was covered with grass and willows. Then the uncleaned fish were piled in until the hole was full. After several months of this curing the fish were removed. In the words of one of my informants: "Fish on top no good, give him to dog. Fish on bottom not so rotten, not so bad him smell him, no need him cook, eat him up."

(2) Land game, seal, and fowl.

(3) Berries.

(4) The roots and leaves of various wild plants.

(5) The inner bark of willows, birches, and alders.

(6) Seal oil, whale oil, fish oil, and bear oil to flavor everything, including berries as well as meat.

One of the most luscious of all the Eskimo dishes is what

they themselves jovially refer to as Eskimo ice cream, due to its resemblance to vanilla ice cream. It is made by extracting the marrow from caribou or sheep bones, mixing this with a great deal of fat and a few blueberries, melting them all together, removing the molten liquid from the fire and beating it much as you would whip cream, and finally allowing it to solidify into a beautiful, white substance, somewhat speckled by darker blotches. My estimate after eating some of this titbit is that it consists of about seventy per cent pure fat, ten per cent blueberries, ten per cent lean meat, and ten per cent animal hair.

Nevertheless, the average present day Eskimo of the Koyukuk lives on fundamentally the same food as the whites, the chief difference being in degree, for most of the Eskimos eat more meat and fish and fewer store products than the whites. Some of the younger Eskimos abhor the most prized dishes of their ancestors. One boy of eight says: "When I even smell seal oil I feel like I want to throw up. It tastes like a mouse." As far as cooking utensils are concerned, the Eskimos have entirely adopted the white equipment which is no different from that which any rural housewife would use in a district without electricity.

The continuous low temperatures from October through April eliminates the necessity of any cold storage facilities, so that meat shot in the latter part of September may still be eaten in May. The frozen meat is also easy to transport, for there are no dripping juices. Similarly stewed fruit or any other partly liquid foods may be carried on the sled in a frozen condition without danger of spilling. But the cold also has its disadvantages, for eggs are injured and many of the canned goods ruined if they are frozen. Thus a person with such foods in his cabin can not leave it for more than twenty-four hours without a fire.

The food consumed in the Koyukuk falls into two classes, that imported from the Outside and that procured from the local resources. The details of living off the country will be discussed in a subsequent chapter, so that at this place I shall only cover the subject of living off the store. It is not my intention to record each of the 120 food products which the store carries. I do think, however, that it would be interesting to list those things which the majority of the Koyukukers consume, together with a comparison of their retail cost in December, 1930, both in Wiseman and in a typical American city such as Baltimore.

Product	Wiseman Cost	Baltimore Cost
Sugar (granulated)	25c lb.	5c lb.
Butter (canned)	$1 lb.	48c lb.
Milk (canned)	33⅓c can	10c can
American cheese	65c lb.	33c lb.
Lard	44c lb.	14c lb.
Eggs	$1 doz.	43c doz.
Olive Oil (Map of Italy)..	$3.75 ½ gal.	$1.50 ½ gal.
Coffee (Hills)	87½c lb.	35c lb.
Tea (Liptons)	$1.50 lb.	71c lb.
Chocolate (ground)	75c lb.	35c lb.
Baking powder	$1 12 oz.	35c lb.
Flour	22c lb.	4c lb.
Corn flakes	33⅓c pkg.	8c pkg.
Jersey cream crackers	50c lb.	20c lb.
Vegetables (No. 2 can) ...	62½c can	16c can
Corn meal	20c lb.	4c lb.
Rolled oats	22c lb.	8c lb.
Rice (polished and brown)	25c lb.	9c lb.
Boston beans	30c lb.	9c lb.
Lima beans	32c lb.	9c lb.
Split peas	30c lb.	10c lb.

Product	Wiseman Cost	Baltimore Cost
Prunes and figs (dried) . .	44c lb.	12c lb.
Apples and apricots (dried)	60c lb.	15c lb.
Onions (fresh)	33⅓c lb.	4c lb.
Macaroni	36c lb.	18c lb.
Ham (Swift's Premium) . .	75c lb.	30c lb.
Bacon (Swift's Premium) . .	75c lb.	35c lb.
Cornbeef (canned)	62½c can	20c can
Soup (Campbell's)	30c can	10c can
Fruit (No. 3 can)	75c can	30c can

Transposing the tabular to the general, the people of Wiseman have to pay from two to eight times as much for their food staples as they would have to pay for the same products in the United States.

In the line of food luxuries, the first boat up the river in the spring brought both fresh apples and fresh oranges. The former sold for $1.50 and the latter for $1.75 a dozen. The store also carried regularly canned crab, lobster, shrimp, and asparagus for those who had particular tastes and plenty of money.

A few people use powdered instead of canned milk, but there has never been any fresh milk in the Koyukuk. Beef cattle were driven into the region all the way from Fairbanks during the boom years, but the cost was prohibitive. Chickens have been tried, but the peculiar light conditions of the far North, the expense of feeding when garbage is consumed by the dogs, and the ease with which ptarmigan can be procured as a substitute all contributed to make the experiment a failure.

Closely allied to foods are the materials necessary for smoking. Pipes are most used, and include both the types common to the outside world and the long stemmed pipes of the Eskimos. Cigarettes are about equally divided between the manufactured and rolled varieties. It is interesting to note that even before the advent of the white men the natives used as tobacco some variety of big leaves which grew in Canada. These leaves were sewed up in caribou skin sacks with as much as 100 pounds to the sack. The Canadian Indians prepared this tobacco, and it passed westward from tribe to tribe by barter. Perhaps it is this long-standing use of tobacco which makes smoking fully as common among the natives as among whites. Out of twenty-five adult natives there were some twenty smokers, while out of seventy-seven whites sixty used tobacco. It is worth observing that only one of the seven white women smoked, whereas all but four of the fifteen native ladies puffed pipes or cigarettes.

Without exception, every adult in the Koyukuk has been a cook at times, and most of them cook for themselves regularly. Having eaten with the majority of the white people, I would certainly say that they rank far above the average bachelor cook of the Outside. Perhaps this is a case of survival of the fittest, for the strain on digestion and temperament which thirty years of the usual bachelor's bill of fare would impose might be more than could be borne under the adverse conditions of the Arctic. At any rate, one finds surprisingly few men living on a fried diet, and many abhor this method of cooking as they would the plague. I have one friend who prepares regularly and deliciously such delicacies as creamed crab flakes on toast, an elaborate clam chowder, and ptarmigan a la king. I recall one dinner in a cabin more than fifty miles from any store where we had roast lamb *Bordelaise* and chocolate eclairs, but that particular man had been a professional cook.

With every one a cook, it is a little surprising how seldom

one hears recipes exchanged. Perhaps all that was done years ago. At any rate, I only recall three expositions on cooking technique during all my stay in the Koyukuk. One was for blueberry cold jam, one was for that sheep meat *Bordelaise*, and one was for cooking a porcupine. The last went as follows: "Place the porcupine and a rock in some boiling water. Cook until you can shove a fork into the rock. Then throw out the porcupine and eat the rock."

CLOTHING

PEOPLE seem inclined to think of the Arctic as a region where one piles on endless garments, yet old Utoyak who has bucked the northern blizzards for nearly seventy years concentrates her entire clothing into two pieces. From the waist down one garment of caribou fur is made to take the place of what in the well-dressed American woman would be the step-ins, slip, dress, stockings, and shoes. The second garment is a tunic of caribou fur replacing the shirt, dress, coat, hat, and scarf. When she is out on the trail she does have to add moccasins as a sort of overshoe, and gloves to protect her hands. But practically all she has to do when she gets dressed is to jump into the lower garment and pull the upper one over her head.

This upper garment is really the most important piece of apparel among all the clothing of the Arctic. It is not particularly associated with race, sex, or age, for it is worn by every Eskimo and white, every man and woman, every adult and child in the entire region. It is called the *parky*.[1]

The parky is a loose-fitting garment which is slipped over the head and comes down about to the knees. It has the dual advantage over most white clothing that there are no open-

---

[1] This word is usually spelled *parka*, but I am spelling it the way it is always pronounced.

ings between buttons through which the wind can blow, and that there is no tightness of fit. Thus it furnishes almost perfect insulation to the body without impeding the circulation. On the top of the parky there is attached a hood which not only covers the entire head, but can also be pulled far out in front of the face to break the wind. The margin of the hood is trimmed with wolverine which seems to be the only fur of the region which will not become frosted in very cold weather when it is breathed upon. Parkies for men and women are similarly designed, but the women have fancier trimmings to their apparel. It is customary to dangle the tails of various small animals all over the back and the sleeves of the woman's parky, as well as to make the bottom gay with a patchwork of different colored skins. But fundamentally there is no difference between what men and women or what Eskimos and whites wear.

The parky has one peculiar utility. I recollect an evening last November when I entered the roadhouse where they were holding a dance, and observed two new Eskimos, Riluk and Selina, who had just come to town with their children from a summer of hunting in the caribou hills. They were all dressed in their heavy furs. Almost immediately I observed that poor Selina was extremely hunchbacked, and I felt very badly, for I realized the tremendous handicap which a cripple must face in a nomadic existence. A short time later the phonograph was started, and every woman on the floor was promptly chosen as a partner except Selina. This made me sympathize all the more, so I promptly asked Selina for the dance. After a momentary hesitation she accepted. In spite of her crippled condition she fox-trotted beautifully, and we really had a splendid dance together. After it was over I took her to her chair, and then seated myself on the counter. A moment later I nearly fell over backwards, for Selina's back burst out crying. And that was my first introduction to the way the Eskimo mothers always carry their babies, in between their backs and their parkies, and held up by a girdle around the waist. The pressure of the legs against the mothers' bodies makes almost all Eskimo babies bowlegged, but if the infant was not always carried around by the mother in this warm manner there would be grave danger that he might freeze to death. Bowlegs may not look so nicely, but, after all, who would not prefer a bowlegged baby to a frozen one?

It is interesting to note that the parky was contributed to the present fused culture of the Koyukuk by the Eskimos. The whites have made no modifications in the design, though they did bring in a heavy cloth drilling which is utilized by both races in the making of parkies for only moderately cold weather. The Indians had parkies of their own, but they omitted the invaluable attribute of the hood.

Another article of clothing which the natives contributed to the common culture is the mooseskin moccasin. This is the footwear used almost exclusively by all three races in the winter, unless it happens to be very cold, when a fur boot made of caribou or sheepskin is worn. This may have the fur side faced in or out, but in either case it is an Eskimo contribution.

It is not the making of the moccasin itself which is the time-consuming task in preparing footwear, but rather the preliminary tanning of the mooseskin, which must precede the actual shoemaking. All the mooseskins are tanned by natives, and this tanning is both a delicate art and a tedious labor. The entire involved process, in thirty-three different steps, has been dictated to me by Ekok, who is one of the best tanners in the Koyukuk. Her first step was, logically enough, to shoot the moose.

Aside from a few old Eskimos like Utoyak, who still wear

only fur and leather garments, the two races have practically the same sort of clothing. This differs radically, however, between the winter and summer. Before describing the winter clothing, it is desirable to mention a few general principles which govern its selection. First, there must be something which will insulate the body and keep the heat in. Second, there must be something, either leather or closely woven cloth, which will keep the wind out. Third, everything must be loose fitting, especially footwear, so as not to impede the circulation of the blood. And most important, a person must be sure not to wear so much that he perspires, for the most disastrous thing of all is to get wet. The majority of the people who have frozen to death in this north country have first gotten wet, either by breaking through overflows or sweating. Wetness in very cold weather means ice in short order, and no matter how much clothing one wears it is impossible to warm up with a coat of ice against the body. The only thing to do is build a fire as soon as one gets damp, and dry out before it is too late.

Specifically, the normal winter clothing for the trail might consist of a suit of medium weight woolen underwear, an ordinary flannel shirt, a pair of light woolen pants, a pair of cotton overalls outside of these to break the wind and keep the snow from sticking to the wool, a sleeveless sweater, a lumberjacket or heavy cloth jumper, and over everything a parky, either drill or fur, depending on the temperature. On the head one might wear a fur cap, a woolen toque, or a woolen cap with fur-lined earlaps. The feet would be protected by two or three pairs of woolen socks, covered by loose-fitting moccasins with eight-inch tops and felt inner soles. The snow of the Arctic winter is so very dry that you can walk all day in moccasins without having them get wet. It is only in the fall and the spring that the snow is soggy, and in those seasons shoepacks with rubber bottoms and leather uppers replace the moccasins. In very cold weather fur boots coming to the knee are worn. For walking through water one uses mukluks, a high boot made out of sealskin, with the fur side in and the well-oiled meat side out. These boots combine both warmth and waterproofing, and are virtually the only thing you can wear if you have to go through an overflow in really cold weather. To keep the hands warm one may use anything from canvas gloves to fur-lined mooseskin mittens with woolen mittens inside. It all depends on the temperature and the condition of one's circulation.

The woman's winter clothing is not much different from the man's, except that a heavy dress replaces the shirt and trousers. Children, too, wear the same general costume. But in summer both the Eskimos and whites wear clothing distinctive of their sexes. In fact the summer costumes of the Koyukuk are almost what any rural people might wear in the United States. Perhaps an exception should be made in regard to foot and head wear. The usual summer foot wear consists of shoepacks, although the people traveling on the river use rubber boots. In town ordinary leather shoes are worn, but the summer trails are so wet that most people do not like them. A few of the Eskimos wear moccasins all summer, and sneakers have become quite popular among them. Broad-brimmed hats are in greater vogue in the Koyukuk than Outside because the wide rims are well adapted for holding the mosquito netting away from the face. The only other unusual feature of the summer costume of the Koyukuk is the wearing of canvas gloves for protection from mosquitoes.

But what do the Koyukuk people wear when they are dressed up? How do they clothe themselves at their most fashionable social functions? The women wear brightly colored and freshly laundered print dresses, or somewhat more

ESKIMO MEN IN WINTER ATTIRE: Nutirwik, Riluk, Suckik, Oxadak, Itashluk, Saukluk.

ESKIMO WOMEN IN WINTER ATTIRE: Kalhabuk, Distklinnah, Kaypuk, Selina, Kayak, Utoyak, Nakuchluk.

MEN'S FORMAL DRESS IN THE KOYUKUK: Albert Ness (aged 63), George Eaton (aged 70), Billie Burke (aged 57), and Verne Watts (aged 60) recuperating from 13 consecutive hours of dancing.

WOMEN'S FORMAL DRESS IN THE KOYUKUK: Kaaruk, Ekok, Ashagak, and Dishoo taking life easy after an all night dance.

sedate serge garments. One girl even had a velvet dress, but at the other end of the scale old Utoyak wore her parky to all social functions. I once made the mistake when she was visiting in my cabin of asking her politely if she did not want to take it off. I was mirthfully informed that there was only nature's garment beneath. Most of the Eskimo women and a few of the white ones wear splendidly beaded mooseskin moccasins, the remainder wear high-heeled pumps. The stockings may be rayon or wool, tightly pulled or wrinkled, depending on the wearer. In winter they come to the dances cloaked in beautiful parkies, though it is amusing to note that several of the younger Eskimos are quite proud of tawdry looking overcoats which they feel are much more stylish than their magnificent furs.

I kept detailed account at one of the biggest dances of what clothing each of the thirty-three men wore. About a quarter had on business suits. The remainder wore overalls, heavy woolen trousers, light khaki pants, or breeches below, and a variety of old coats, jumpers, and sweaters above, though a third of all those present were in their shirt sleeves. Of the shirts, nineteen were flannel, eight colored cotton, and but six white. Only ten of the thirty-three men wore neckties, and none had stiff collars.

There is a general sentiment in the Koyukuk that "good clothes are the cheapest in the long run." Nevertheless, clothing wears out rapidly due to the hard use to which it is put. It may also be partly due to the rough treatment it receives in laundering, for practically every man who is not married or living in Wiseman (where two of the Eskimo women take in laundry) has to do his own washing. It is not a task tackled with much enthusiasm. "It doesn't take me very long to wash them once I get started," says old Poss Postlethwaite, "but it's just the thought of bending over that old board that gets me."

Most of the older Eskimos are not very enthusiastic about laundering either, but the younger ones are scrupulously energetic about washing and ironing. Since most of them sleep in their dresses, frequent laundering is almost essential if they wish to remain neat enough to attract the men. And neat and clean they certainly always do look at the dances. If you meet an Eskimo girl in the morning she may look a little bit frowsy, but in the evening her attire, simple though it is, will be immaculate.

SHELTER

THE KOYUKUK boasts three skyscrapers. Splendidly these massive edifices rear themselves out of the all-abounding willows and alders, magnificently they tower above the lesser huts and hovels of the Arctic. Each one is two stories high.

All of the remainder of the 180 houses which were occupied during at least part of my year in the Koyukuk are one story structures. Dividing these occupied buildings according to more fundamental architectural principles, 176 were cabins and four were igloos. From a functional standpoint, the following were the uses to which these houses were put:

Dwelling cabins	109	Social hall	1
Trail cabins	39	Schoolhouse	1
Barns	10	Post Office	1
Storehouses	9	Wireless station	1
Workshops	3	Jail	1
Stores	2	Tractor house	1
Roadhouses	2		

The cabins of the Koyukuk are constructed of spruce logs laid horizontally on the four sides of the building. Where the logs of adjacent sides come together in the corner they are locked by simple notching. Spaces for windows and the door are either sawed out after the logs are in place, or the log lengths are shortened before they are laid. The walls are chinked chiefly with sphagnum moss. The floors of the cabins near town are usually of boards made by the tedious process of whipsawing, but in the cabins along the trails and on the more remote creeks spruce boughs are spread directly on the bare ground. The roof consists of logs covered with dirt and sods. It may be either ridged or flat. Some twenty-two of the cabins are luxuriously roofed with tin, which is really a great convenience in summer, for in the dirt-covered buildings, during heavy rains, one frequently is sprayed by a shower of muddy water. But in winter the dirt provides much better insulation than does the tin.

Out of the 109 dwelling cabins, some eighty-two are one-room affairs, twenty-four have two rooms, only three boast the luxury of three rooms, while more than that are unknown. The size of the buildings varies from the twenty by sixty-five foot roadhouse in Wiseman to some of the trail cabins which are as small as seven by eight feet.

These trail shelters are an important adjunct to winter travel, as they make it unnecessary for persons following the main routes to take along tents. A quickly started fire in the stove of one of these cabins has saved the life of many an old sourdough. Because of the vital importance which sometimes attaches to getting a fire to blaze immediately it is probably the most urgent of any of the unwritten laws of the Koyukuk that a person in leaving a cabin must always provide shavings and enough wood for at least one fire. There are few breaches of social etiquette which cause so much disapproval as failure to obey this custom.

It is interesting to observe that windows in the Arctic are meant for light and not air. No one ever opens them in winter, and only a few highbrows do so in summer after they have first put up screens. Ventilation is obtained either

A Typical Prospector's Cabin.

AN IGLOO IN SUMMER.

through an unattached stovepipe leading directly from the top of the room to the outside air, or by a small rectangular opening on the upper wall which may be covered with a lid. Some of the cabins on the trail have gunny sacks, canvas, or cloth for windows.

In front of most dwelling cabins in the Koyukuk is what is known as a cache. This is really a vestibule, enclosed by canvas or lathing, which serves as a storm shed so that when a person enters the cabin in a blizzard he is not accompanied by a shower of snow. Not being heated, the cache also provides cold storage, and one can there keep meat which would spoil, snowshoes which would crack, and gasoline which would involve a fire hazard in the heat of the cabin. Miscellaneous trash which would be in the way in the cabin is also stored in the cache, for the neatness of which one feels no responsibility. On the more remote creeks and even near several of the cabins in town a different type of cache is built of logs set on top of poles. Here the animals can do no damage.

But it is time to leave the cabins and speak a little bit about the product of that other Koyukuk school of architecture, the igloo. If you were raised, as I was, to picture an igloo as a house of pure snow blocks you will be dreadfully disappointed to learn that the Alaskan Eskimos have never built snow houses. Indeed it is only the Canadian Eskimos, numbering but five thousand souls in all, who have gone in for the romantic type of shelter generally associated with their race.

The igloo of the Kobuk Eskimos had a circle of logs, either from green trees or driftwood, as a foundation. Next to these logs, all the way around the igloo, they set the longest willows which they could find. They laid moss against these willows, gradually bending the stems inward at the same time until they almost met, forming a beehive or dome-shaped structure. When all of the willows were bent over and well covered with moss, they piled on an outside coating of dirt and sods. Right where the willows would have come together at the apex of the dome they left an opening to serve as a window, ventilator, and smokehole. Beneath this opening in the center of the igloo they put up a rock wall, eight or ten inches high, for a fireplace. One narrow entrance was left in the side of the willows, a skin serving as a door. Sometimes skins were used instead of moss to cover the willows and always they were used to cover the ground. In winter snow was piled over and around the structure to keep it warmer.

The present day igloos of the Koyukuk show numerous changes. They all have iron stoves and stove pipes. Most of them even have glass windows set in their sloping sides, one has a board floor, and all have wooden doors. Spruce poles have replaced the willow framework. But essentially they have the old-fashioned architecture and appearance. In winter they look like great mounds of snow, but in summer they are simply glorified mudpies.

The furnishings of both cabin and igloo are much alike today, so that the following remarks about the fixtures which the Wiseman people have in their homes apply to all the dwellings. There are no carpets or linoleum, but a few of the homes have small rugs. Shades are unknown. Curtains are found on the windows of three white women's homes, but almost every one else considers them a decided detriment in winter because of the light which they exclude. Almost every cabin has a calendar, and most have cheap pictures on the walls. These walls are generally covered with canvas or oilcloth, but not unfrequently show the bare logs. Oilcloth is almost always used to cover the dining table which generally also serves as a writing desk, card table, and magazine rack. Tablecloths and napkins are unknown except in the houses of a few of the white women. The beds in about three-quarters of the cases are wooden bunks, either single- or double-decker, with straw ticks. The remainder are spring beds, most of them relics of the old houses of prostitution. Every one knows their pedigrees.

Cooking is always done on iron stoves. Many cabins also have large iron heaters above which wooden racks are placed so that the clothes may be dried. Whether one is in a cabin, igloo, tent, or just sleeping in the open, the one fuel universally adopted for heat is wood. Spruce wood is preferred, birch and cottonwood are also used, but if a person penetrates beyond the northern timberline he must depend on willow. For sleeping out in the open, or "siwashing" as it is called, rotten cottonwood is especially good because it holds the fire so long.

Light is obtained from candles, coal oil lamps, and gasoline lanterns. The latter give by far the best light; in fact their illumination is as good as electricity, but they are also the most expensive to operate. The gasoline which they burn costs $1.80 a gallon. A man living alone might burn about ten or twelve gallons a year. Coal oil also costs $1.80 a gallon in Wiseman, but it goes much further. Candles are generally used only by people who are on the trail, or in very remote localities, or too poor to afford anything better.

Every cabin has for washing purposes a small table with a wash basin, mirror, water bucket, and slop pail. Baths are taken in the large washtubs which are used for laundering. In summer the necessary water is carried directly from some nearby creek, but in winter a large wooden barrel must be kept filled with snow which melts in the heat of the house. A few people have pumps which can be used the year round. The toilet facilities are provided by outhouses which are less uncomfortable than I had imagined even at fifty below.

THE QUEST FOR GOLD

THERE were two classes of men who came to the North in quest of gold. The prospectors would set out for undeveloped creeks where, by panning the surface gravels or by sinking trial holes to the bedrock of the valley, they would sample the ground for evidence of valuable deposits. This prospecting might yield them occasional good-sized nuggets and a small quantity of fine gold, but in its net results it always cost, merely in food and equipment, far more than a man ever regained. It was only after rich ground was discovered by prospecting that the money-making activity, the mining which actually developed the ground, was possible. The natural course was for a man to be first a prospector and then a miner, but many of the latter waited until some one else had done the fatiguing prospecting. On the other hand there were those who abhorred the steady grind of mining, and preferred to be roaming the hills in quest of something just a little richer than any one had ever found before.

"This prospecting's a funny game," Albert Ness once told me while we were reclining after a strenuous day in a lonely little cabin on the upper Middle Fork. "You never can tell for sure whether you're at the edge of a fortune or just a sucker. Look at old Harper. He worked his bench for four years without getting hardly anything. He told Poss he was going to sink one more hole and then give up. He got pretty good color in that hole, so he continued for two more years and found the deep channel, and then he took out nearly $100,000 in a few years. But other times you see a color and you may think there's something very rich ahead and spend years prospecting it and in the end you may not get enough to pay for the overalls you wore out. Knute and Billie spent several thousand dollars sinking holes on Minnie Creek one winter and panned out seventy-five cents. But if you aren't likely to make a fortune, look at the fun you have. It's a funny thing, but take a man like old Pingel. He can't do any work any more and he knows it. He's got enough money for him and the old lady to live luxuriously for the rest of their lives. But still he wants to come back and mine. It's not the money he's after at all. There's just something about this gold game that fascinates."

This notion that there is a delight in hunting for gold, quite apart from any financial return, is shared by most of the Koyukukers. The oldest prospector in point of service in the whole region thinks that it is because "every damned proposition you come against is different, so you don't ever get tired meeting the same old problem over and over again." Another man who has been mining continuously since 1898 has an esthetic explanation. He says: "There's something about gold you have to love too, just like you might love a picture or a statue. I tell you, there's something beautiful about a bunch of nuggets." A third man feels that "gold mining is the cleanest living you can make. You're not robbing any one or hurting any one to get it. You're just taking it clean from nature."

I recollect one afternoon when I was working underground with some friends on Hammond River. I was removing small boulders from the bedrock, when all at once under one which I lifted I ran into a regular nest of nuggets. In a few minutes I had picked up nearly eighty dollars' worth of gold. Now none of this money belonged to me, nor did it represent any sensational fortune for my friends. Nevertheless, I confess a thrill such as I have rarely experienced, just in finding that virgin gold, a joy in picking it pure from the bedrock, a delight in the unique pattern which every nugget assumed. After that incident I could always understand the enthusiasm which men who have been finding gold for a third of a century still manifest whenever they discover another nugget.

But I never was quite able to fathom the indomitable courage with which these old miners meet the most devastating disappointments. Complete failures after months of tireless activity are taken as a matter of course. Old Poss Postlethwaite, seventy-eight years old and going blind, could still say after an entire winter which yielded four partners a total of $181, "Discouraged? Christopher, no! I couldn't have survived thirty-two winters in the Koyukuk if I got discouraged that easy. In this country a man doesn't think nothing of working all winter and getting nothing at all."

The following was remarked very complacently to me by a man the day after the ground water had flooded into the tunnel in which he was working and had completely ruined the fruits of three months' labor: "I ain't the least bit discouraged. Heavens, the chances are just as good as ever. It's just one of the risks you've got to take in this mining game."

Another man, who after a whole winter's work was penniless, sick, and half starving, said to me: "Tide always turns, and it's the same with man if he keeps on long enough."

As a prelude to any description of the technological methods of mining it is first essential to explain a little about gold

geology. Gold originally occurs in quartz veins, chiefly running through the schist rocks. As these rocks weather, par-
ticles of gold break off and are washed down the steep mountainsides into the streams which run through the valleys.
These soon become too sluggish to carry the gold farther,
so it settles to the bottom. Now gold is a very heavy mineral,
and consequently it keeps working downward through the
lighter sediments in which it has been deposited until most
of it ultimately rests on bedrock. Some of the gold may be
scattered for several feet through the dirt and gravel, but
most of it rests upon and especially among the crevices of the
solid rock. Thus the great object of all placer mining, as that
mining done for loose gold is called, is to get down to the
bedrock where all the valuable deposits occur.

During the geologic ages when this gold was being deposited, the streams which carried it have wandered back and
forth across the entire valleys in which they are located. Consequently, the gold deposits are not a bit more likely to occur
where the streams are to-day than where they have wandered
at any time during their past history. As a result, in prospecting a creek it is useless merely to sample the bedrock under
the present watercourse. It is necessary to sink holes across
the entire width of the valley before it is possible to say
whether a drainage has any gold.

The actual process of mining has two totally different
phases. The one is the phase of winter mining, which consists in underground mining or *drifting*, as it is called. The
other is the phase of summer mining, which consists of washing the dirt away from the bedrock. This is known as *open
cut work*. Drifting is sometimes attempted in summer, but
open cut work, which demands flowing water, can never be
used in winter.

The first step in drifting is to sink a shaft down to the bedrock. This may only be a distance of a few feet, but it may also be several hundred. One hole put down years ago in Wiseman Creek went 370 feet without reaching bedrock. Last winter the major operations in the Koyukuk had to sink from seventy-five to 100 feet. In view of the fact that the ground is solidly frozen this would be a most laborious task, involving the constant use of dynamite, if it were not for an ingenious expedient that was developed in the Klondike days. Hollow iron pipes, six feet long, are driven into the frozen gravel and steam is relayed to them through rubber hose from the boiler house, which furnishes the power for the operation. This steam makes the dirt around the pipes as loose as any gravel bank. But all around the six by six foot shaft, where the dirt has not been thawed, it has all the advantageous qualities of solid rock, with the freedom from the necessity of bracing which that implies.

Once the shaft or hole is down the next step is to uncover as much of the bedrock as possible. Primary tunnels are run in several directions from the hole, and subsidiary tunnels branch from the main underground ways. In this operation the ground is also made workable by steam thawing, while the frozen sides and ceiling of the tunnel remain almost as solid as rock. The size of the tunnels vary in height and width. If a man is just prospecting he will make the tunnel only big enough that he can move about. If he is in "good money" the tunnel may be about six feet high and six to eight feet wide. Where he runs into especially rich ground he will work laterally from the main tunnel.

The dirt which must be removed in making these tunnels is shoveled into a wheelbarrow, and then it is wheeled to the main shaft. Here the dirt is dumped into a steel bucket holding about three wheelbarrow loads. The bucket is hoisted up and down the shaft by means of steel cables which wind and

SLUICING.

THE CLEANUP: Kenneth Harvey, Verne Watts, and Victor Neck, with $2000 in gold at the bottom of the pan. This represented about thirty per cent of their winter's gold recovery.

unwind on a drum. The drum is located in the boiler house, perhaps a hundred feet from the hole, and it is driven by steam power generated by wood fires. It is one man's constant duty to operate this machinery and keep the boiler stoked.

After the bucket has been raised to the surface of the ground it hitches into a trolley. The winding cable proceeds to pull this trolley laterally along another cable, which extends from the mouth of the hole upward to a tall spar known as the gin pole. This may be from thirty to fifty feet high. A simple device trips the bucket at whatever point is desired. The "pay dirt" which comes from the crevices of bedrock and the gravel immediately above is customarily dumped near the gin pole, while the "waste dirt" from the upper part of the tunnel and from the shaft is deposited nearer the hole.

This same drifting operation is sometimes worked much more primitively without any boiler or cables. A wooden bucket is hauled up and down the shaft by a hand-turned windlass. Thawing is done with wood fires. Such an operation may be carried out by a single man, and it is consequently often used by prospectors alone in the hills.

In the latter part of May or early June, as soon as the melting snow swells the streams, the pay dump near the gin pole is sluiced. A series of wooden boxes, twelve feet long by about a foot wide by a foot deep, are set up with end overlapping end to form a long trough. To these boxes water is brought from some nearby creek by means of an irrigation ditch ending in a dam. At the dam the water flows into an eight-inch canvas hose. The amount of water necessary to fill this hose is called a sluicehead of water. One always hears the volume of the creeks in this North country measured in terms of sluiceheads. A man won't say that Goldbottom is running so many gallons per second but instead that "she's got about four sluiceheads of water." The hose carries the water to the upper end of the trough of boxes, and these are tilted at such a grade that the water flows through them with a strong current. Into this swiftly moving stream the pay dump is shoveled. The light dirt is washed away, but the much heavier gold sinks almost immediately to the bottom where it is trapped between wooden corrugations known as riffles. After the dirt has all been shoveled into the boxes, the riffles can be removed and the gold swept into a pan. Careful blowing will separate the small amount of heavy dirt mixed with it, leaving a residue of almost pure gold.

Summer mining or open cut work involves washing away the dirt which covers the bedrock. The water is led to a small dam from some neighboring creek by a ditch with a grade of about two inches to the 100 feet. From here it is fed into canvas hose with a one- to three-inch nozzle from which the water is bombarded against the dirt which is to be washed away. Before this bombardment begins the sphagnum moss which covers the entire surface of the ground must be peeled off.

Two things are essential to make open cut work possible. First, there must be enough water for sluicing. The water problem is an exceptionally serious one, for most of the creeks near the better open cut grounds in the Koyukuk are small, and their volume has been further decreased by forest devastation. Consequently, during the brief period that sluicing water does last, from late May until early July, the people with summer claims work at top speed. A twenty-four-hour shift is usually maintained by staggering the available labor, it being at this season of course perfectly broad daylight at midnight. It is not uncommon for a man to put in eighteen hours a day, though the usual mining hours at other times are only eight. But there is so little adequate water that every use possible must be gotten from it. Sometimes this first snow water is augmented by summer rains, but many years the bulk of the summer work is over by Fourth of July. The second prerequisite for open cut work is that there must be sufficient grade between the lower edge of the area worked and the main valley floor for the tailings (the dirt and bowlders which are washed away) to be carried off. In order to get this grade, the ground worked is either on some steeply pitched side creek or more commonly on a bench above the main valley. Obviously it is not possible, when you have to wash away all the overburden, to work as deep ground as by drifting. In fact thirty or forty feet seems to be the greatest depth of dirt it has been found practical to remove by water. Once bedrock is attained all the water which flows over it is diverted into a series of sluice boxes and here again the lighter dirt washes through and the heavy gold settles to the bottom. It is also necessary in this type of mining to clean the bedrock, that is, remove the dirt from the crevices where the richest deposits of gold are found.

I have here merely outlined the major steps in mining. To go into all the essential details, to discuss the numerous devices which have been adopted to overcome the abnormal Arctic conditions, would make a technological book in itself. But the successful miner in the Koyukuk must be thoroughly familiar with all these practices, and he must have the ingenuity to think up new ones when these fail.

He must be at the same time a carpenter, a construction expert, a mechanic, a blacksmith, a cable splicer, a boiler maker, a steam engineer, an hydraulic expert, a logger, a geologist, and an economist. During his off hours he is supposed to be also a hunter, dog musher, cook, baker, and laundryman. Of course there are miners in the Koyukuk who do not qualify in every one of these capacities, but most of the best can do at least a tolerable job in all these diverse trades.

XVII

LIVING OFF THE COUNTRY

IF IT were not for living off the country, civilization on the Koyukuk could not survive to-day. The $27,000 in gold taken out of the ground during the past year would obviously be insufficient to support the 127 people with the high prices they have to pay, were it not for the additional subsistence provided by the animal and plant life of the region. These biological resources are made available through hunting, trapping, fishing, berrying, logging, and gardening.

HUNTING

Hunting is at the same time one of the major occupations and one of the chief sports in the Koyukuk. It is more seriously depended upon for a living by the fifty Eskimos than are any of the other activities. It is pursued by over half of the whites as an important means of filling the larder. Yet to both races, with a few disgruntled exceptions, it is a labor anticipated and performed with the greatest joy. I know one fellow who made over $2,000 last winter in his mining, but great as was the thrill of his successful venture, it paled beside three weeks of an autumn hunting trip in which he and his partner killed a dozen sheep. I recall three other men who returned to Wiseman after a week of autumn hunting without a single animal to show for their efforts. They had trav-

eled with the lightest possible equipment, taking no tent and
insufficient blankets for the season. Consequently, they had
gotten very little sleep: But despite the hard work and the
failure and the fact that each had been going on similar expeditions for years, they were as elated as children who had
just been on their first overnight outing.

Hunting in the Koyukuk may have such dangers as are inevitable in midwinter traveling and in merely existing fifty or
100 miles from the nearest human being. But it is free from
that common danger of Outside hunting—being killed by
some other hunter. In the thirty-four years that the whites
have been living in the Koyukuk not a single person has ever
even been wounded by another man.

There are five different species of big game in the Koyukuk. Of these, the moose is by far the largest animal. The
average moose probably dresses 500 or 600 pounds, while it
is not uncommon to shoot animals weighing 800, 900, and
1,000 pounds even after the head, lower legs, and entrails
have been removed. The largest moose on record in the region is one which weighed 1,039 pounds. In winter it is easy
to carry such masses of meat by dogsled, but under summer
conditions the transportation is quite another matter. Consequently the Eskimos, when they kill a large moose in summer, do not try to pack it to their camp. Instead they move
camp, which probably only weighs two or three hundred
pounds, to the moose. Then they live by this moose until he is
all eaten up or rotten, when they go and shoot another moose
and live by that moose.

The caribou, though it is a much smaller animal than the
moose, never exceeding 400 pounds dressed and averaging
not more than half of that, probably furnishes more of the
total meat supply of the Koyukuk than any other animal. The
reason is that this American species of the reindeer travels in

great bunches, often with tens of thousands of animals in a single herd. In such a crowd even a poor hunter can readily shoot all the meat he requires, which is quite different from hunting the moose, which seldom travels with more than a bull, cow, and calf together. Good caribou hunters, by dropping certain key animals, stampede the herd in just the right way for it to keep milling back and forth instead of running straight away. Consequently, one successful hunt sometimes yields an Eskimo a winter's food supply for himself, his family, and his dogs.

Because the caribou migration usually passes through the Koyukuk or the adjacent Chandalar country in summer, the Eskimos who depend especially on this source of food spend most of the summer months in the hills along the route of migration. They shoot away at the caribou continually until the rutting season, which commences early in October, gives the bull's meat such a sickening, rotten flavor that even the dogs will not eat it. But prior to that time the Eskimos build smoke houses where they dry and cure prodigious quantities of meat for winter use. They also hold great feasts, and altogether have a very jovial time. When they leave town for the hills in May or June or July their food supply has generally run pretty low, and they are looking rather lean or "poor" as they would say. But when they return in the autumn "the wrinkles are all out of their bellies," as one old sourdough wrote me.

Thus this annual summer caribou hunt divides the Eskimos' year into two contrasted segments. In the winter season they live virtually as the white people do, dwelling for the most part in log cabins in the heart of town, buying from the store, sending their children to school, joining in all the dances, and mixing thoroughly and very prominently in the social life of the whites. In the summer they live out in the hills virtually as their fathers did, dwelling in igloos, moss huts, or tents, depending almost entirely on a meat diet, only seeing white people on rare encounters with transient hunters. Which season they like best depends on individuals. The majority of the older ones prefer the hills while most of the younger ones like the towns better, but few there are who would be really satisfied without both lives.

The meat of the mountain sheep is the favorite of all meats to most of both the natives and the whites. The sheep is generally the hardest animal to get because its chief habitat is among the rugged mountains near the Arctic Divide, fifty to 100 miles from either of the towns. The sheep are found in groups ranging from two or three sheep to upwards of 100. A normal sheep will average about ninety pounds dressed, but occasionally an old ram will be found which weighs 200 pounds.

Neither the black bear nor the grizzly bear is highly prized for its meat, but all of the Eskimos and probably half of the whites willingly eat them when nothing else is available. These bears do not become very large in the Koyukuk, the black bear seldom dressing over 250 pounds and the grizzly never exceeding 400 pounds. Nevertheless, with their heavy fur, they appear a great deal more massive than these figures would indicate. According to Ernie Johnson, the black bear hibernates some time from September 20 to October 10, and emerges between April 25 and May 10. The grizzly goes into hibernation during the first twenty days of October, and he comes out between May 5 and May 20. The black bear generally dens on the lower, south-facing slope. The grizzly, on the other hand, usually dens on the north slope, well up in the hills. This difference in the locus of hibernation probably accounts for the earlier emergence of the black bear.

In spite of the terrifying position the bear occupies in outdoor literature, the fact remains that no Koyukuker has ever been even mildly injured by one of these animals. The most experienced of all the white hunters says: "There is no question that a bear will sometimes attack a man, just like there are occasional humans who will do the same thing, but it happens so rarely that it's not worth thinking about. I've run around Alaska as much as most men, and I've never yet seen a bear that did anything except run away from me."

Rabbits and ptarmigan are sometimes hunted, but they are generally caught in snares. The ducks stop in the Koyukuk in late May and early June on their way to the Arctic Ocean, and again in late August and early September on their return. A few of them are killed at these seasons, but in general they are classed as luxury food. The geese in their migrations fly so high that they are out of range. A few spruce hens and golden plover are shot, and these complete the list of animals and birds killed for food.

While most of the meat shot is used directly by the hunter and his family or friends, several thousand pounds of meat are sold annually to those who do not hunt. The standard price of meat is thirty-three and one-third cents a pound for moose, caribou, and bear, and fifty cents a pound for sheep. The choicest morsels from these animals, including the heart, tongue, liver, brain, and moose nose, are never sold, but are often given away to special friends. Among the older Eskimos, the bum gut or large intestine is especially prized, but most of the younger generation, as well as the whites, show a striking apathy toward it.

Hunting in the Koyukuk for both whites and Eskimos depends entirely on guns. Bows and arrows are extinct, even among the most unaltered natives. A great variety of rifles are used of which the .30-.30 and the .30 government seem to be the favorites. For rabbits and ptarmigan .22's are chiefly employed, while double barrel shotguns are also used against the ptarmigan as well as against the other fowl.

In spite of more than thirty years of virtually uncontrolled hunting by an average population of 250 or 300 people, the game supply of the upper Koyukuk apparently has increased. Moose are very much more abundant than they were when the first white people came to the region, no doubt due to migration from more settled parts. The caribou were fairly plentiful in the Koyukuk prior to 1902 when they changed their route of migration and disappeared from the country. For years only an occasional straggler was ever seen. Then, without any advance indications, they suddenly thronged into the Koyukuk in unprecedented numbers in 1919 and have returned either there or to the Chandalar country every year since. Only sheep, of all the big game animals, show any observable decrease, and that has been due not to the killing of approximately 100 sheep a year by hunters, but to the slaughter of many hundreds of them by wolves. Prior to 1919 there were scarcely any wolves in the Koyukuk, but when the caribou came back that year the wolves came as a parasitical concomitant. Apparently, like the humans, they preferred sheep meat, for they have since remained to prey on that smaller but juicier animal.

TRAPPING

The story of trapping in the Koyukuk centers about snowshoe rabbits because most of the fur-bearing animals depend to a large extent for their food on this species of hare. Now the rabbits of the North are most transient creatures. Their numbers vary in cycles of about ten years, so that at the crest the whole country may be overrun with rabbits, it being considered nothing to see fifty on a hillside at one time, while in the trough one may go a couple of years without seeing a single rabbit. Nobody knows for certain the cause of this amazing difference. Since the whites first came to the Koyukuk there have been three major troughs when nowhere in the whole region could any rabbits be found. These depressions occurred in 1909 and 1910, in 1918 and 1919, and in 1930 and 1931, and in each case there was a parallel decimation among the fur-bearing animals.

The last virtual disappearance of the fur bearers covered the year of my visit to the Koyukuk. As a consequence the total amount of money brought into the region from the sale of furs was only about $1,200, in contrast to fifteen or twenty times that amount in peak years. In the winter of 1928-1929, when fur was at its maximum, two partners made more than $5,000 on a single winter's catch, while the year before a lone trapper made over $3,000.

The furs which are obtained in the Koyukuk are either sold to the store or roadhouse, or they are sent out to the Seattle Fur Exchange. In the latter case the furs are sold at auction, the trapper receiving the full price of sale minus a five per cent fee to the Exchange. But when the furs are sold at one of the local trade centers the proprietor offers the minimum price he thinks he can get away with. Last winter the roadhouse man paid $493.50 for thirteen pelts and sold them in the spring for $560. Even including a ten dollar fur dealer's license, this represented a ten per cent profit on a three months' investment.

The method of trapping among both whites and Eskimos is virtually the same. It is carried out in winter, the legal trapping season and the period when the fur is prime practically coinciding from November 15 to March 1. Steel traps are used, sometimes with bait and sometimes merely laid along runways. Many people set scattered traps here and there in the vicinity of where they are working and attend to them incidentally. But if a person centers his winter's work on trapping he generally sets a line of traps over a large expanse of territory. It may take him a week or more to make the rounds of these traps. He may have cabins set at convenient intervals along his trapline, but mostly he will depend for his night's shelter on a tent carried on his sled. As he makes his circuit he will stop at each trap. If nothing has disturbed it he will pass on, but if an animal is caught he will kill it, if it is not dead already, and load it on the sled. Then he will reset the trap and continue on his rounds. At night in his heated shelter he will skin the animal, and after getting back to his base camp he will stretch the pelt on specially designed racks.

The animals which are trapped in the Koyukuk include red fox, silver fox, cross fox, lynx, mink, marten, beaver, wolf, muskrat, marmot, ground squirrel, ermine, wolverine, coyote, and otter. The last two are rare. Wolverine is used entirely locally, being especially valuable for parky trimming. The muskrat, marmot, ground squirrel, and ermine are also seldom shipped Outside, but are in much demand for parkies. The other pelts bring prices ranging from five dollars to almost $1000, but no general level can be quoted because this varies so much with the size, primeness, color, and condition of the fur, and with the state of the market. As a rule the most valuable furs are those from the cross and silver foxes.

Rabbits are chiefly snared with ordinary number three picture wire. The wire is made into a noose with the free end attached to a willow or some other substantial shrub. The rabbit, not seeing the noose, runs into it and pulls it tight. After a few futile tugs he chokes to death. In good rabbit years it is easy to snare fifty rabbits this way in a day, while thousands will be caught during the course of a winter. This materially reduces the cost of living, not so much because they are excellent eating for man, but because dogs may be fed almost entirely on them. In good rabbit years the price of feeding dogs is not half that of barren years. Ptarmigan are snared in a similar manner, and even the larger fur-bearing animals such as fox and mink may be caught with a number six wire snare.

There was just one experiment in fur farming ever attempted in the Koyukuk. Two brothers started a fox ranch in 1914 at a location about seventeen miles above Bettles. After ten years they decided that the financial returns were too negligible and the isolation too great, so they abandoned their project, which has never been resumed.

FISHING

Practically every Koyukuker has frequently enriched his summer diet by dinners of delicious grayling or brook trout, freshly caught from some deep hole with the aid of a black hackle fly in the spring, or a brown hackle fly in the summer, and a little trout line and a willow stick at both seasons. There are several large bodies of water in the region where lake trout sometimes weighing as much as fifty pounds may be caught by trolling or by fishing through the ice. Whitefish are found in the main rivers, being much prized for their splendid flavor, while pickerel occur in several of the smaller ponds. But from a professional standpoint there is only one fish and that is the salmon.

Occasional adventuresome salmon come up the Koyukuk River as far as Wiseman, but in large numbers they are not found more than fifty miles by river beyond the Arctic Circle. However, in this extreme southern margin of the Arctic region the river banks in summer show fish camps every ten

LAYING IN A MEAT SUPPLY: Al Retzlaf with two sheep which he had just killed.

BOBBIE JONES: "I'm perfectly happy. That's all I care for. That's all life is."

or fifteen miles where countless salmon are caught in gill nets. Great quantities are sun-dried and smoked for year round preservation. These fish become a major item in the diet of both the natives and their dogs, and they are also sold for dog feed to the white men further up the river.

BERRYING

Berries are gathered in the Koyukuk chiefly for personal consumption, though there are some small sales. The two important kinds of berry are the blueberry and the cranberry. The former retails for two dollars a gallon, the latter for one dollar. Both ripen some time in August, but the cranberry has the unusual quality of remaining edible all winter, and it is often picked by the Eskimos when the snow goes off in the spring. Among herbs those chiefly eaten are lamb's quarters and the first tender shoots of the fireweed.

LOGGING

Logging operations supply both the fuel for home consumption and for running the boilers used in mining. The felling is done by saw and ax. The wood cut is almost entirely spruce, which never exceeds twenty inches in diameter at breast height, and does not average more than eight inches. The transportation of the wood from the timber operation to the place of use had always been by horses or dogs, but starting last winter the caterpillar tractor did the major hauling. The original light stands of timber around Wiseman have not been sufficient to outlast nearly a quarter of a century of exploitation, so that wood to-day must usually be cut five or ten miles from where it is needed, and it costs $15 to $18 a cord.

The present scarcity of wood around the major settlements is certainly augmented by the proverbial frontier carelessness with fire. The whole story was summarized by old Poss Postlethwaite who told me: "If they'd just keep the fire out they'd get all the young growth here they need. When we first came in here there was hardly any country burned. The natives were awfully careful with their fire. But as soon as the whites came, Christopher, they'd go and set the country on fire purposely just to get dry wood. And they never took the trouble to put out their camp fires. There was hardly a man in the country talked against it either. But now we're beginning to see what it means. When we first came on the creek here there wouldn't be more than one or two weeks all summer we wouldn't have a sluicehead of water. Now we always have a whole month without it at least. Oh, yes, there's no doubt that since the timber's been cut and burned we don't keep our water the way we used to."

GARDENING

It comes as a great surprise to many people that gardens flourish north of the Arctic Circle. But in the Koyukuk, though there is a frost every month and the growing season must be concentrated from mid June to early September, sufficient crops are raised to cheapen and to vary greatly the diet of the average citizen. The fact that there is no total darkness from the middle of April to late August and that there is full daylight for all but two weeks at each end of this period no doubt has a stimulating influence. In size the plants average materially greater than in the outside world. One record-breaking turnip weighed eighteen pounds and was eleven and one-quarter inches across. But if the plants are large they are also unfortunately very watery. The nickname for locally grown potatoes is "waterballs," which is quite justly descriptive. I made moisture content measurements on a number of Koyukuk potatoes and found their average solid content was only ten per cent, whereas the average potato grown in the United States has twenty-two per cent solid substance. When you bake a Koyukuk potato, nothing is left but a tough skin with a white lining. All but nineteen of the white people in the Koyukuk had some sort of garden, but there were only three native gardens. This was principally because most of the natives spent their summer nomadically. The total crops raised during the summer of 1930 for year round use amounted to about twenty-six and one-half tons. Considerable quantities of potatoes, turnips, cabbages, carrots, and beets were sold. The details of agricultural activity are shown in the following table:

Crop	Amount Raised		Price per Pound	
Potatoes	14	tons	12½	cents
Turnips	7	tons	8	cents
Cabbage	3½	tons	12	cents
Carrots	1½	tons	15	cents
Beets	500	lbs.	15	cents
Cauliflower	300	lbs.	..	....
Parsnips	150	lbs.	..	....

For merely seasonal use there was such abundant lettuce and spinach raised that every one around both Bettles and Wiseman had more than could be used from July through September, people without gardens being free to take as much as they wanted from those who had gardens. Most of the people grew swiss chard, onions, and radishes at least for their own use, and several raised celery, rhubarb, peas, and strawberries. Cucumbers and tomatoes were grown by one or two people in hothouses. Only beans, corn, squash, and pumpkins, of the common garden truck, have always proved complete failures.

XVIII

FINANCIAL SUMMARY

AFTER returning from the Arctic I gave several lantern slide lectures on civilization in the Koyukuk. These were reported in a number of different papers, and apparently stimulated people to write to me for further details. A bricklayer from Detroit, an unemployed drug clerk from Akron, a construction worker from Los Angeles, a law clerk from La Crosse, a farmer from near Burlington, Vermont, and a trapper from Juneau all sent me letters as varied as their geographical and occupational backgrounds would lead one to anticipate, but all had one common question. How much does it cost to live in Wiseman?

The answer to that question hinges on the race, financial condition, and age of the person who is doing the living. On the average it costs a white man more to live than an Eskimo, a man with a little money more to live than one who is broke, a young man more to live than an old one. The following figures, based on the annual expenses of some twenty adults, shows the range of living expenses for the white race:

| | Total Annual Cost of Living for One Adult | | |
Class	Minimum	Maximum	Average
Worth more than $500 ... (Jan. 1, 1931)	$500	$1,200	$890
Worth $500 or less	350	800	700
55 years or younger	700	1,200	930
Over 55 years old	350	1,200	680

The reason for the cheaper living costs of the old people is principally that their appetites are smaller than those of the younger people. The reason for the difference between the cost of living of those in poverty and those with money must at least be patent to the millions of unemployed in the United States. One notable difference, however, between the unemployed Outside and those without money in the Koyukuk is that the Koyukukers can always obtain with virtually no cost the meat, vegetables, and fruit that they require. They may have to eat sparingly of sugar and butter, forswear the variety offered by canned goods, dispense with eggs altogether, and attend the dances in slightly ragged clothes. But they can eat all they need for nourishment, they can dance light-heartedly, and they can live without the slightest shame of social inferiority.

It is hard to compare the living costs of the Eskimos with the whites because practically all the Eskimos lived in family groups with from one to five children. Dividing the family budget by the number of members obviously would not give at all comparable figures. It is apparent, however, that the Eskimos require considerably less money on which to live. One family of three needed only about $250 for their year's expenses, obtaining everything else directly from nature.

According to the figures of the Department of Agriculture, the average rural family in the United States, includ-

ing a husband, wife, and three children, spends between
$450 and $1,700 a year, varying greatly with the locality.[1]
There were two comparable families around Wiseman, each
with a white father and Eskimo mother, but each living according to the white man's culture. It cost the one $2,800
and the other $1,600 a year to live. This would indicate a
somewhat greater living cost than Outside, but of course the
expenses of two families are inadequate for any serious comparison.

A few itemized Koyukuk living expenses might prove interesting. The first is for a man both old and almost without
money, who lived slightly cheaper than the average for both
these classes. He buys his meat, but has a small garden and
cuts his own wood. He has no dog.

Food for himself	$400
Clothing	85
Kerosene for light	15
Living expenses for about 45 days at roadhouse	150
Total	$650

The next account is for a young man with a stake of more
than $1,000 above living costs. He kills all of his meat, cuts
his wood, but buys most of his garden products.

Food for himself	$700
Food for one dog	90
Clothing	110
Gasoline for light	30
Roadhouse expenses	110
Magazines	10
Gun and ammunition	80
Miscellaneous	70
Total	$1,200

[1] See "Standards of Living Improved by Wise Use of Income" by
Faith M. Williams in the *Yearbook of Agriculture*, 1932.

The third budget is for a married couple, about seventy years of age. The husband is the second wealthiest person in the Koyukuk, being worth between $30,000 and $40,000. The family pays for its meat and wood, but the wife raises all her vegetables, picked twenty-seven gallons of berries last year, and even makes her own soap and vinegar. The woman has kept a detailed ledger of her expenses.

Food for themselves	$962
Food for two dogs	150
Clothing	129
Kerosene and candles	40
Roadhouse expenses	15
Magazines	26
Stationery	5
Correspondence course in French	10
Photographic supplies	23
Medicines	5
Toilet articles	9
Seeds for garden	3
Wood	75
Total	$1,452

Another couple, averaging about fifty years in age and worth about $2,000, get for themselves all their wood, meat, garden truck, and berries.

Food for themselves	$1,030
Food for four dogs	365
Clothing	125
Kerosene	40
Magazines	20
Miscellaneous	20
Total	$1,600

The cost of living, however, is only one side of the ledger of any community. The income which occupies the other side is certainly of equal importance in determining the economic balance. But in a region like the Koyukuk, with individual incomes fluctuating so greatly from year to year due to the gamble of mining and trapping, the ratio between the living expenses and the income of any particular person for a single season would be meaningless. A man may be living in 1931 off the rich pocket he hit in 1929, or his luck of 1931 may have to carry him over for a couple of years in the future. In the first case the annual income would show a standard of living too low, in the second case one too high. Therefore, instead of getting entangled in the vagaries of individual bookkeeping, I shall strike a balance sheet for the entire Koyukuk. This balance sheet will show in the credit column those sources which have added to the wealth of the region, while in the debit column will be recorded the money which has left the region.

I have listed the items on the credit side of the ledger under seven headings. The returns from *gold* and *fur* have been already amply explained. *Road funds* refers to the money which the government contributes for the improvement of sled roads, construction of shelter cabins, and leveling of the airplane landing field. *Money paid by government* covers not only the wages paid the U. S. Marshal, wireless operator, and schoolteacher, but also includes their fuel expenses, and the small amount of money which the postmasters at Wiseman and Bettles received. The *summer mail contract* represents the money paid by the Post Office Department to the local man who carried the mail from Bettles to Wiseman. The winter mail contract was not included because it was awarded to a man from Tanana. The *money brought in by transients* includes what was spent in the region by the winter mail carrier and by prospectors who stayed for but a few months, living exclusively on what funds they brought from outside. *Government relief* includes two Territorial old age pensions at $360 a year, one pension to a veteran of the Indian Wars, and about $100 paid to a sick Eskimo.

Among the debit items, the *money sent outside by the stores, the roadhouses,* and *individuals* needs little explanation. These headings include all the money which left the region for the purchase of goods and for the payment of freight. They embrace not only articles of personal use, but also mining equipment and gasoline for the tractor. *Airplane passage* refers to the money spent by people for flights to and from Fairbanks. *Doctors' bills* covers the expenditures by three people who had to leave the Koyukuk temporarily for medical treatment. It also includes their living expenses while away from the region. Under *licenses and poll tax* are included special operating licenses the storekeeper and roadhouse men had to take out, and also the five dollar school tax for all men under fifty.

Of course the sums listed under each of these categories are not absolutely accurate. Nevertheless, I believe this balance sheet is not seriously in error. The following figures cover the year from October 1, 1930, through September 30, 1931:

Credit		Debit	
Gold returns	$27,000	Money sent outside by stores	$24,000
Fur returns	1,200	Money sent outside by roadhouses	6,000
Road funds	4,500	Money sent outside by individuals	18,000
Money payed by government	8,100	Airplane passage	1,900
Summer mail contract	4,000		

Credit		*Debit*	
Money brought in		Doctors' bills	$ 1,600
by transients ..	$ 3,200	Licenses and poll	
Government relief	1,500	tax	500
Total	$49,500	Total	$52,000

With approximately $52,000 leaving the Koyukuk during this year and only $49,500 coming in, it is obvious that somehow a deficit of about $2,500 must be made good. This was done by drawing on the accumulated savings of past years. In other words the Koyukukers as a group were some $2,500 poorer at the close of the year than at the beginning. Such a condition of course could not continue indefinitely, but in view of the fact that the fur shortage and an abnormally poor year in the mines made this one of the worst years on record, economically speaking, the small accrued deficit does not imply that the civilization is headed for bankruptcy.

It may seem difficult to understand how, with the high prices of the Koyukuk, 127 people could live on an outlay of $52,000, which allows only about $400 for each individual. The answer is that they did not. Much of this $52,000 performed triple and quadruple service. For example, let us assume that Roy King, who had a successful year mining, paid Harry Snowden $200 to haul freight for him. Then Harry took this $200 and bought that amount of food and clothing from Martin Slisco at the roadhouse. Then Martin paid the money to Knute Ellingson for helping build an extension on his roadhouse. Then Knute used it at the store to pay his bill. Then the storekeeper finally sent it out to the West Coast Grocery for more supplies. In the course of these events five different people possessed the purchasing power of this money, five different people figured it into their year's income. Consequently, due to this turnover the average actual income was probably at least double the $400 indicated simply by the regional balance sheet.

But even this figure did not nearly represent the total income. The game killed, the furs used locally for clothing, the fish, the berries, the wood, and the garden truck all increased the real wealth of the people, even though they were not reflected in the monetary balance. If it were possible to compute the volume of all these products consumed annually in the Koyukuk, I feel certain that their value would greatly exceed the $27,000 worth of gold which was recovered in the mining operations.

In concluding the discussion of the economics of the Koyukuk it seems that some reference should be made to the individual financial standing of the inhabitants. This is a matter more easily investigated than one might suppose, for there are plenty of veterans familiar with every sizeable stake that has ever been made in the Koyukuk as well as every one that has been thrown away. The community lives so intimately that hardly any important financial change can be hidden from general knowledge. Of course a few of the people might have had some money invested Outside which yielded unexpected dividends, but such cases would not appreciably influence the general figures. Consequently, when I asked three of the most observant old timers to estimate the approximate monetary wealth of each adult person on January 1, 1931, it was not surprising that except in ten cases there was unanimity among them. The following table may therefore be considered a very close approximation of the amount of available cash, either directly on hand or readily liquidable, which is possessed by all the people of the Koyukuk:

Number of Dollars in Wealth	*Number of People*		*Total Wealth in This Class*	
0-50	38		.....	
50-500	28	86%	$7,000	21%
500-2,500	14		21,000	
2,500-5,000	8		30,000	
5,000-10,000	6		45,000	
10,000-15,000	3		38,000	
15,000-20,000	2	14%	35,000	79%
20,000-30,000	1		25,000	
30,000-40,000	1		35,000	
40,000-50,000	1		45,000	
Total	102		$281,000	

Average wealth per capita $2,755

All the Eskimos were in the first two classes.

As in the outside world, there is a great concentration of wealth in a few hands. But there are very important differences. In the Koyukuk the man without a cent has just as good a chance to make money in the future as the one who is worth $50,000. Each must still use the same methods in his work, and each has an equal gamble for success. The possession of wealth gives a man security, a few additional luxuries, and the opportunity of a trip Outside. It does not give him the power to exact more than a very minor tribute in the form of interest, rent, or profit from the labor of the poorer man. It does not give him any control at all over the thoughts and actions of those in poverty. Nor does wealth involve any social prestige. The men who are penniless on the average rank fully as high in the community's respect and affection as the ones who are worth over $10,000.

PART IV

THE COMMUNAL LIFE

XIX

LAW AND LAW ENFORCEMENT

THE NOTION of original sin has become so intrinsically rooted in the consciousness of the average citizen of the so-called civilized lands that a general feeling has developed that unless man's evil instincts are curbed by all manner of laws, the inevitable result will be chaos. The frontiersman, on the other hand, has usually resented such a belief, and the society which he has formed has generally been characterized by a minimum of hard and fast restrictions. The Eskimos in their natural environment were even more anarchistic than the frontiersman. They had neither chiefs nor tribal councils, and the only controls of their conduct were those wrought by personal contacts with their neighbors and by various ceremonial taboos which were voluntarily enforced. It is not surprising that the civilization of the Koyukuk, built by frontiersman and Eskimos, should largely disregard the common notions of the fundamental necessity of laws, and substitute instead a strong suspicion of things legal.

The following random remarks furnish a fair sample of the attitude of the typical Koyukuker toward law. The first quotation is from an Eskimo, the remainder from whites who have spent between twenty and thirty-five years on the frontier.

"Anybody got to lie, law. You no lie, put you in jail."

"Disobedience of the law furnishes the brightest spots there are in history."

"A man isn't responsible to anything except the dictates of his conscience. If he doesn't think a thing is evil, all the laws in the world can't make it wrong for him."

"If I was on a jury I'd never vote a man guilty of a thing I do myself, no matter what the law said."

"There's no law north of the Arctic Circle. Mustn't kill nobody; mustn't steal; to hell with their other laws."

"This thing of hard and fast bound laws for 120 million people don't work. There ought to be some place where intentions should count. It seems to me the most important things there are is the exceptions, but there isn't any place for them in the laws."

Such views truthfully indicate that the citizens of the Arctic, whether white or Eskimo, are extreme individualists. Each man feels that his life is his own to lead as he will, and he resents any legal compulsions which infringe on its natural development. A few exceptionally anti-social crimes he believes should be curbed in a formal way. For the rest, he feels that right and wrong action can well enough be regulated by individual decency.

In the light of this anarchistic philosophy it is interesting to present a resumé of all the crimes which have been committed in the Koyukuk during thirty-four years practically without law. It should be observed that during this period a large amount of wealth was being produced, that it was compactly gathered in small leather pokes which would have been very simple to filch, and that many isolated people could have been murdered with weeks elapsing before any one even knew of the crime. On the other hand it is true that there were only two or three tedious routes by which one could leave the region, and the nearest crowd in which to hide was 3,500 miles away.

There have only been three murders in the Koyukuk history. One was committed when a mentally deranged man who should have been in an asylum beat out his partner's brains with a maul. The other two were committed by an old prospector when three men tried with violence to drive him off his claim. Neither of these cases required any police supervision. The insane man proceeded to dispose of himself by climbing down into an abandoned mine shaft and stabbing himself twenty-three times. The man who was repelling the claim jumpers surrendered and (unjustly, as every one felt) was later sentenced by the court in Fairbanks to serve twenty years in the penitentiary.

There has never been a large theft or robbery in the upper Koyukuk, the largest sum ever reported stolen being $150. The petty pilfering of nuggets from the mines, a practice known as highgrading, has been of rare occurrence. Occasional cheats may have passed a few brass filings for gold dust, and a number of men have tried to mix as much dirt as possible with their gold to make it weigh more than its real value. There is one man in the Koyukuk who arouses considerable mirth by the trivial swindling which has become almost a second nature to him. One of his stunts is to dip the fish which he catches into water which freezes inside them. Then he tries to sell them at so much per pound with this added weight of ice. Such fraud is so rare in the Koyukuk that people are amused rather than angered by it, and the most severe criticism I heard about this man's chicanery was the philosophical remark by one of his victims that "he's one of the low products of evolution, I guess."

There have in addition been a few cases of assault, but this seems like an inconsequential record of crime for a

thirty-four year period during which the average population of the upper Koyukuk including both whites and natives
has been about 300 people. It has been brought about in
spite of the fact that the compulsions of law have been
removed.

It is perhaps an overstatement to say absolutely that the
compulsions of law have been removed. Actually the government of the United States, which exercises a hegemony
over the affairs of its largest territory, Alaska, has felt that
America's reputation for orderly government might be im-
paired if even the most remote nook of its domain was not
supervised by some ordained official. In partitioning Alaska
for organized administration it made one district out of the
entire drainage of the upper Koyukuk as well as various
and sundry lands abutting upon it. Over this district since its
creation in 1901 some half a dozen different Deputy U. S.
Marshals have presided. The first four caused little trouble;
the fifth, who was in power during the days when Hammond
River was booming, was a most obnoxious and thoroughly
hated racketeer. The present one [1] in contrast has shown a
complete understanding of the frontier spirit, and instead of
trying to stir up trouble has gone out of his way to avoid it.
In addition he plays a splendid game of poker, so that the
surprising situation arises that the police officer of the community is also one of its most popular citizens.

It is worth studying in some detail how this man, Vaughn
Green, met the problems of law enforcement which came before him during my year in the Koyukuk. The first one arose
shortly after I arrived in the region. A fifteen-year-old
Eskimo boy climbed through a window in the school teacher's
house and stole fifty dollars from her trunk. Incontrovertible
evidence soon fixed the guilt definitely on this boy, who

[1] He died of a heart attack on February 21, 1932.

confessed his crime under cross examination. Feeling in the community ran high, for nothing like this had happened in years, and it was quite a jolt to find that this utopia where nobody ever had to lock a door (amusingly enough the school teacher was the only one who locked the house) was no longer safe from burglary. One old man even suggested hanging him by the thumbs, but scarcely meant it seriously. A few felt that the boy ought to be sentenced, but the majority certainly agreed with his father who said: "It's no good put him in jail. Maybe scare him and it make him more worse. It hurt him here (pointing to head). Make him crazy." The marshal did lock him up for a few hours to get him to tell what he had done with the money. When he insisted that he had become frightened and thrown it in the river there seemed nothing else to do but release him. The commissioner tried for several weeks to cajole a confession out of him but failed. The father paid the school teacher the fifty dollars, the boy continued in school without ever missing a single hour, and she acted in just as friendly a manner toward him as though nothing had ever happened. The matter was soon forgotten except in occasional unfavorable chatter about the boy's character and what he was coming to, and in spite of all conclusions on the necessity of punishment to keep down crime, there has not been another theft in the year and a half which has elapsed since then.

A second cause for action by the community policeman came during mid-winter. It involved a dispute over a cabin. Jack White had allowed Floyd Hyde to occupy one of his numerous houses. During the winter Hyde became drawn into a dispute in which Jack was engaged with a third party, and Jack quite naturally became embittered against Hyde for taking the other person's side in the controversy. He determined to eject Hyde from the cabin for which he was paying no rent. Hyde refused to get out. Jack paraded around, carrying a six-shooter and making ominous imprecations. The carrying of any gun except for purposes of hunting was so unusual in the Koyukuk that it alone created a great stir. When Jack proceeded to tear the roof off his own cabin while Hyde was still in bed one morning, excitement around town reached fever heat. Hyde rushed down to Vaughn Green and demanded that Jack be arrested for something or other. An officious marshal could easily have roused no end of trouble, but Vaughn, seeking only to restore the peace told Hyde that he had an extra cabin of his own and urged him to move into that building and leave Jack alone. Hyde moved and the trouble was all over.

There are two laws on the statute books which require unusually tactful handling by the marshal because they are both highly unpopular. The one is the game law and the other the prohibition law. The game law states that moose may be shot only from September 1 to December 31, sheep from August 20 to December 31, cows and calves may never be shot, and it also provides certain bag limits for both these animals as well as for the caribou. It leaves an opening, however, that a man in absolute need of food may kill whatever he requires. The marshal of the Koyukuk has had enough sense to stretch this opening to its limit, and so he has never tried, merely for the sake of principle, to enforce a law which is obviously unenforceable. Consequently the people, instead of taking delight in violating what they consider unjust, enforce as a matter of common sense and decency the one important requirement of a game law in that sparsely settled region. This requirement is never to kill except for use. A man who habitually wasted meat would be committing as much of a social blunder in the Koyukuk as would one Outside who entered a mansion of the élite and spat tobacco juice on the Persian carpet.

It is a strange fact that even before the National Prohibition Amendment was passed the people of Alaska had enacted a territorial prohibition law by a three to one majority. One sourdough who voted for it explained to me that at the time he had really imagined that with prohibition liquor would disappear and that he would no longer be tempted to indulge a habit which he genuinely desired to break. Experience has totally disillusioned him, and he now feels the prohibition law to be the most pernicious one ever enacted. The people of the Koyukuk agree with him in about a five to one ratio. Here are a few of their opinions:

"I voted for prohibition and I'd vote for it again to-day. I know it's unjust to us old soaks who've been pickled all our lives, but when they once get the graft out of prohibition and people outgrow the notion of thinking it's smart just to violate the law, it won't take many years before liquor will be as rare as dope is to-day. I've got no doubt that prohibition's a bad thing to-day, but in the long run I think it will do a tremendous lot of good."

"If an old stiff wants to drink himself to death, that's his own affair."

"There's never been a cent in camp since prohibition went in. In the old days you had to work all the time because drink kept you broke. Now you only work now and then when you've got nothing left."

"They never can enforce a law the people don't want."

"Of course if they could control prohibition it would be a good thing. Ideally it's what we want. But we've tried it and we've found it's ten times worse in every way than how it was before. I admit that I was one of them that voted for it, and all that, but I see now that it's a failure. Of course I don't believe in ever having it the way they had it before, with saloons for every one to loaf in. I believe the government should handle it entirely. I don't believe it should be put in the hands of men who want to make as many people as they can get drunk so as to make a bigger profit for themselves. But they've got to find some way that a man who craves it can get a drink."

"If the Constitution says this is a free United States, is it free if they take away my liquor when it makes me happy to drink a little? There's no real freedom if you have laws to take away a man's happiness. No, I think that was the rottenest amendment ever made to the Constitution, taking away the rights of people, costing the country millions of dollars, driving young girls who never could have thought of it to drinking, making all law a joke, making everybody into a hypocrite."

With such attitudes predominant it is obvious that no marshal would get very far in trying to enforce the prohibition law. He might stir up trouble and ill feeling, but in the end he could never get a jury to convict a man, particularly with the accused an intimate friend of all the jurors. Vaughn Green was wise enough to see this situation clearly, so he tactfully shut his eyes to what was being fermented. It was only when one moral advocate (who himself had stolen $150 from the government) threatened to send a complaint to Juneau that the marshal had to destroy one particular still.

As a matter of fact there is an economic curb to the making of intoxicating beverages in the upper Koyukuk which is far more effective than any legal one could possibly be. This is the high price of sugar. With this basic substance at twenty-five cents a pound it is a very expensive matter to make liquor. The standard price for home brewed whisky is $25 a gallon, while even the undistilled beer comes to $5 a gallon. Few people in the Koyukuk can afford to buy very much at such prices. "I haven't enough money to buy booze and grub both," said one old fellow. "I used to buy booze and never mind about the grub, but I'm different now and I need the food worse."

The most unfortunate phase of prohibition in the Koyukuk has been its effect on the Eskimos. Prior to prohibition there was a law which made it a serious offense to sell liquor to the natives. This law was generally approved because the ill effects of introducing intoxicants to a race entirely unprepared was apparent to every one. The saloon keepers were perfectly willing to adhere to the law because they could make all the money they needed selling to the whites. As a result one rarely saw a native under the influence of liquor. Since prohibition, whites and natives have become one, and in the brotherhood which a mutual restriction has placed upon them there has developed mutual coöperation in helping one another to get a drink. Further, since it is now just as much of a crime to sell liquor to a white as to a native, a person with something to sell will be impartial as to where he gets his trade. Again, with home brew replacing the bonded stuff the natives who before had never realized that they themselves could manufacture liquor now go into the business whole heartedly. The consequence has been that many of the adults, both men and women, have spent all their money in drink while their children have been half starved a goodly share of the time.

There is another side to the legal machinery of the Koyukuk—the commissioner's office. This has roughly the functions of Justice of the Peace in the outside world. The commissioner may perform weddings, conduct civil suits involving less than $1,000, decide minor criminal cases. He is supposed to record births, deaths, and marriages, and, most important, the staking of all claims.

If a person wants the use of a piece of ground for mining he must set posts at the four corners of the land which he desires. This is called staking a claim. The size of a claim is limited to twenty acres, and in general it is supposed to extend quarter of a mile up and down the valley and one-eighth of a mile across. After the claim is staked the man has to record the staking with the commissioner. He then is allowed exclusive mining privileges on the land as long as he does at least $100 worth of work on it annually. Each day's work is considered on the basis of going wage rates as being worth $10. If a man fails to accomplish this amount of assessment work the claim reverts to the government and is available for any one who desires it. Other land occupation is not recorded. In town the lots for houses and gardens are held by squatter's rights. Written agreements covering business relations are seldom made by the white men, while formal contracts among the natives are entirely unknown.

When the commissioner's office was first established in 1901 there were forty minor criminal suits and twenty-five civil suits tried in the first two years. However, the old timers who still survive those days are unanimous in their contention that most of the trouble was stirred by the Commissioner who wanted fees, and by two shysters who were later debarred. Since 1904 when Frank E. Howard, commencing a long term as commissioner, started the precedent of avoiding trouble, the lawsuits have been few. During the past ten years there have been but three cases tried in the commissioner's court. One involved a violation of the prohibition law. A second case involved a wage dispute. The third was connected with the location of a claim. Aside from these three matters, all other troubles have been settled out of court.

This voluntary settling has involved genuine self control. I know one man who gave up half a share in a claim, simply because his partner alleged the right to all of it, and "it wasn't worth picking a scrap with that son-of-a-bitch just for a half share in a bum piece of ground. Some said I should have fought him on principle, but it's a pretty bum principle that makes a man fight."

People in the Koyukuk realize that they are living together in an isolated world, sharing its work, its dangers, its joys, and its responsibilities. They recollect countless personal associations of the most intimate character imaginable. Such factors seem to furnish them with an urge to act decently which in most cases is sufficient to obviate any necessity for the more usual compulsions of law.

VOLUNTARY COMMUNAL RESPONSIBILITY

THERE is about the Koyukuk a tremendous isolation, for it is separated by 200 miles of almost uninhabited country from the most remote outpost of the Twentieth Century world. Behind this insulating zone is a vast, lonely expanse where men are so rare and exceptional that the most ordinary individual takes on an importance impossible to conceive in the outside world. He is not just one person among millions, but one of the rare human oases in the desert of the wilderness.

Thus life takes on a dignity and value which always accompanies the rare. Every person feels that he has an important rôle in the communal life, and every person feels that all the other people are likewise significant. This is clearly manifest in the great delight which the entire community feels when one of its number who has not been seen for a long time returns to town, and the genuine sadness which accompanies the departure of any member for the Outside. "When Johnny left," said one man, "I felt terribly lonesome. For about a month I felt bad all the time. It seemed as if he'd died. I'd pass his cabin at night where I'd seen the light shining out on the snow for fifteen years and it would give me a feeling like passing through a cemetery."

There are many ways in which this interest in each other

takes a more tangible form. It receives perhaps its greatest expression when any one is sick or injured. "No matter how much a man has it in for you or is sore at you, when it comes to a pinch everybody pitches in to help." It is customary to take the volunteers and divide them into continuous watches so that the sick person may have never-failing assistance. One man who was seriously ill last winter said fervently: "For the number of people in here I wouldn't have received more attention any place in the world." Another reflected: "There's only a handful of people in here, but let anything happen to one of them and everybody will stop work if necessary to help him. Outside if any one's in trouble every one walks by as quick as he can."

Whenever a death occurs in the community, all the people within a day's journey of town will give up their work to attend the funeral. There is no morbid sentimentality attached to this custom, no notion that it makes any difference whatsoever to the dead man, but simply the feeling that it is a last fitting honor to an old friend.

Sometimes if a person is very sick it becomes necessary to wire for a plane to take him to the nearest doctor at Fairbanks or Tanana or Fort Yukon. It has happened a number of times that the sick person has been in too straightened circumstances to pay the $150 fare. In such cases a collection is always taken, no matter how poverty-stricken the community may be. I know one man who borrowed five dollars last spring in order to be able to contribute to a fund raised to send a nine-year-old Eskimo girl to the hospital in Tanana. Everybody knew that the father of this girl could have had the necessary money himself if he had not drunk and gambled it away. Nevertheless, here was an immediate need, and no one tried to dodge the burden by claiming that the father should have been responsible. Similarly, a few months after I left the Koyukuk a man whose income for the past ten years had been one of the largest in the region was taken gravely ill with a heart attack. Extravagant living had left him practically penniless, so that his own resources furnished no possible hope of medical treatment. Consequently, the community considered that matters rested upon it. A collection was again taken, and a fund of $1,350 was raised to send the man to Seattle for specialists' care. To many of the contributors this definitely means lean days ahead, to one of the donors it involves giving up a contemplated trip Outside, but the man was sick, and he was one of the most splendid characters imaginable, and you certainly couldn't let him die without making a fight for his life.

Poverty brings up problems similar to sickness. A man may after several years of mining failure or following a temporary disappearance of game, find himself bankrupt. "But there's one thing about the people in this country, they'll never see a man go hungry, native or white." So some one can always be found who will loan without interest, knowing full well that he may never be paid back. It is true that a few people take advantage of this charity to indulge their laziness or extravagance, but the cases of this sort are sufficiently rare that the undeserving are usually carried right along with the unavoidably needy.

The care of the aged involves somewhat greater difficulties than sickness and poverty which are not permanent. A man, who could no longer work or take care of himself, would necessitate too great a drain on the altruism of this small community. Fortunately, the Territory of Alaska has established a Pioneer Home at Sitka where the old sourdoughs who have grown too feeble to support themselves may spend their declining years. However, if the men prefer they may receive an old-age pension of thirty dollars a month and reside anywhere they choose within the boundaries of the Territory.

The strong feeling of communal responsibility in the Koyukuk is also apparent when any member of the community has not been seen for a longer time than the people believe he intended. First some one will observe, for example, that Lawson hasn't been in town for six weeks. There will be a little concerned speculation for a few days and then some person will decide to take the six-mile snowshoe trip to Lawson's place "just to be sure everything's all right." In nine cases out of ten it will be, but there actually was a tenth case when he was found helpless with scurvy and would have died if one Victor Neck had not been willing to give up half a day to satisfy a mild anxiety.

Such acts of supererogation could be quoted almost indefinitely. I remember one day when an old man of seventy climbed 1,000 feet up a steep hillside to be sure nothing had happened to another old man, simply because when we dropped into the latter's cabin about seven in the morning there was no trace of any recent fire in the stove. "I'm sure there can't be anything the matter with old Bob," said my companion with much concern, "but you know he's got a weak heart, and it don't seem like there shouldn't be some signs of a fire in his stove if he really was here last night. You can't tell. He might have had an attack of some sort. It won't take us long to climb up there, and we can cut around the bench and come out almost at the pass without losing hardly any time."

There is a great deal of voluntary exchange of labor in the Koyukuk. If a man is sowing or harvesting his garden it is quite customary for anybody around town who may not be doing anything else at the moment to help. When the river scow was almost carried away by the ice at the breakup a couple of years ago, everybody around town got out to help the owner save it. When an unusually high spring flood inundated Bettles the same spring, the three men who were in town by most energetic efforts saved their absent neighbors many hundred dollars of damages by removing perishables from the floors of the houses about to be submerged. Of course they never were paid for it. When the mail comes to town any person down from the mining creeks will greatly burden himself on the return journey and perhaps walk several miles out of his way in order to deliver all letters and magazines as quickly as possible to his neighbors.

Although there is no civil organization in the Koyukuk, no mayor or town board or constitution, there is one fraternal order which functions as a voluntary coöperative for performing many of the tasks usually done by a local government. This fraternal order is the Pioneers of Alaska of which the Wiseman Chapter is known as Igloo (instead of Lodge) No. 8. Anybody who immigrated to Alaska prior to January 1, 1906, is eligible for membership. There is no political jobbing done by the organization, at least in Wiseman, and no member is ever favored, no non-member ever discriminated against for belonging or not belonging to the order. All its property is shared by the whole community, members and non-members alike. This includes a hall where the biggest dances are staged, a large phonograph, a library, and a fund for taking care of the destitute sick. There are certain communal tasks which cannot be efficiently handled without coöperation, so the Pioneers act as a clearing house to turn individual willingness into coördinated action. Thus they supervised the building of the airplane field, riveted the Wiseman river bank with willows to stop its continual washing away, raised funds to buy a wireless station, and protested to the Post Office Department about the abominable mail service.

When people habitually manage their communal affairs as do the Koyukukers by this voluntary system, it is almost inevitable that an unusual tolerance of each other's actions and beliefs will develop. Certain unpopular traits may be condemned, but no one is outcast for having them. It brings no personal criticism at all to entertain minority beliefs. I have already mentioned how there is a five to one sentiment against prohibition in the Koyukuk, yet that does not prevent three of those who favor it from ranking among the dozen most popular people in the region. Again there is a very prevalent sentiment in the Koyukuk in favor of sexual promiscuity, yet two of the most popular men have remained voluntarily celibate without ever bringing on themselves the criticism of being priggish. The Koyukuk people are today overwhelmingly of the opinion that the United States should never have entered the World War, yet three of the rare defenders of America's participation rank among the most highly regarded in the region.

An ex-missionary and an ex-prostitute were next door neighbors and the warmest of friends. The missionary paid this tribute to her companion:

"She's a happy-go-lucky person. A woman of that sort is the best kind for a country like this. She's so magnetic and full of friendliness she just warms up every one who comes near her. She's not a cultured woman, but the most liberal and goodhearted you could wish for. If she borrows anything she always gives you back at least half again what she got."

The other woman had this to say about her friend: "I've certainly missed Mrs. Pingel. She was the finest sort of neighbor you could ever want. She always wanted you to stop off at her place, and no matter how she was feeling she was always kind and friendly."

XXI

SICKNESS AND HEALTH

THE FUNDAMENTAL consideration in the discussion of sickness in the Koyukuk is the fact that the most accessible doctor or hospital is 200 miles away by air line. In consequence, all of the trivial ailments and a great many serious ones for which people of the outside world are accustomed to receive professional medical service are treated in the Koyukuk either by amateur doctors or by disregard. This has not always been the situation. From 1898 through 1919 there was constantly at least one trained practitioner in the Koyukuk. But in the winter of 1919 Dr. Danforth blew out his brains, and since then there has never been a doctor in the region, even to visit.

There are two persons in the upper Koyukuk to-day who are generally regarded as the closest approach to a doctor. One had been a registered nurse before she came to the North about twenty-five years before. The second, who was also the U. S. Marshal, had served for three years as a nurse and first aid man in the government hospital at Nenana. These people perform much devoted service to those of their number who are ailing, always for no compensation, and often at the expense of their own affairs. They are excellent at first aid, and they can sew up cuts, bandage sprains and wounds, and treat minor infections as well as most doctors. Their work, however, is greatly retarded by another group of people who are not usually asked to act as doctors but who are very glad to give medical advice whenever anybody is ill. Often two or three of these volunteers will visit a sick person. After the patient has heard their varied notions, usually accompanied by a severe criticism of whatever treatment he is receiving, any mental composure which may have been attained will be dissipated speedily. Occasionally the patient will permit one of these quack practitioners to work on him. One well-meaning lady made a man who had burned his legs wrap them in a raw sheep hide, thus inducing blood poisoning which almost killed him. It was a home remedy which she had learned as a girl and she could not understand why it did not work.

There are many other home remedies. One man assured me that honey is the most healing thing in the world. He said it had stopped lots of native lung hemorrhages in the Kobuk. Vinegar, he added, was fine as a gargle or antiseptic, and would kill all germs. Sage should be mixed with all medicines as it was a sort of elixir of life. Another man told me that "if you have a sore throat there's nothing like tying a strip of raw bacon around the neck. You want to cut it real thin, you know, and tie it on with cloth." Still another was spreading medical enlightenment to the natives. He confided: "I think I got a little of the idea of this scientific medicine into Big Charlie's head the other night. I explained him how we were just like a house that needed cleaning in the spring. I told him about how our blood was thick in the winter, and how it needed to be thin in the summer, and if we didn't take medicine to thin it out we'd likely get sick." There was one man who took the psychological approach. He said: "When you're real sick you don't want to pray. You want to cuss and swear and fight like hell, and if there's any chance at all you'll pull through. I think most the people who die give up cussing and start in praying too soon."

With all their lurid medicine man beliefs the Eskimos have a great deal of common sense in doctoring one another. Some of their old remedies, developed long before any contact with the whites, indicate an understanding of the same principles which influence modern medical thought. Here is the method which Big Jim learned from his father for the treatment of boils:

"I see him boiling business sickness lots. He bust, he no all come out, he grow again. You cut him, you no clean him good, bimeby he come back again. You keep him rotten all time, put on rag, put on soap, chew up sinew, put him on, keep him warm, then pretty soon he get very rotten, you clean him good knife then, no more come out."

Which in other words simply means, ripen the boil by poultices before lancing.

The Eskimo women take the matter of child birth very casually. There is generally little preparation or concern until labor pains actually commence. Then, at the very best, the mother will be put to bed while some Eskimo woman with experience in deliveries or occasionally a trained nurse will play the part of midwife. After the baby is delivered the mother may stay in bed for a week and take it easy for several more. But this would be exceptional pampering. At the other extreme I know of a pregnant woman who was walking across country with her husband and three children in the autumn of 1930. Early one afternoon labor pains commenced. The husband barely had time to erect the tent and get a fire going before the baby was born. The husband cut the cord, tied it with sinew, and washed the baby thoroughly with water, just as the Eskimos always do at child birth. After a couple of days of rest the entire family continued on the journey, the mother now packing the newborn baby on her back as she strode along over the niggerheads.

Between 1920 and 1931 a total of twenty-five babies were born within the Arctic drainage of the Koyukuk. It is interesting to note who performed the delivery in all these cases. The types of midwife and the number of babies each delivered is shown in the following table:

Midwife	Number of Babies Delivered
Some old Eskimo woman	14
The baby's father	5
The missionary nurse from Alatna	4
An ex-nurse in Wiseman	1
An Eskimo man (not the baby's father)	1
Total	25

Frontiersmen are proverbially lax in the care of their teeth. The people of the Koyukuk are no exceptions, and few of them there are who have not gone through long periods of oral neglect. Consequently, they find great need of dental treatment. This is chiefly handled by occasional, untrustworthy, peripatetic dentists who cannot meet the competition of more populated places. They talk very learnedly, make exorbitant charges, and frequently place the patient in a more miserable condition than he was before. The last dentist to visit the region left a frightful epidemic of toothaches in his wake. Yet one is situated between the devil and the deep, for without dental care teeth keep degenerating, and the resulting cavities occasion a very considerable amount of suffering. This is partially relieved by several men in the

Koyukuk who are considered good tooth pullers and who do at least as well as the professionals who visit the region. But whether one goes to quack dentists, amateur tooth pullers, or no one at all, it is inevitable that the average person of the Koyukuk will have his teeth in pretty wretched shape.

There are four white men and one Eskimo woman who wear glasses for general use. All except one of the white men had the glasses fitted by a more or less qualified oculist while visiting on the Outside. But the reading glasses which the majority of the rather elderly whites are forced to use are not usually prescribed in such an impressive manner. Both the store and the roadhouse receive what are advertised as: "Assorted spectacles for old eyes." The lenses are calculated to correct for old age sight, and they come in different strengths. The person who has been having trouble in reading tries on all the pairs of spectacles in the assortment and buys for $2.50 whichever pair leaves the print before him least blurred. That is all there is to optometry in the Koyukuk.

For general medical care many of the people keep gauze bandage, adhesive tape, iodine, unguentine, and epsom salts. With this equipment and such food items as salt, soda, and olive oil they meet all their ordinary medical and surgical needs. At Wiseman and Bettles they can buy a variety of additional equipment calculated to promote health. The medical articles with which the stores are regularly stocked include:

Unguentine	Peroxide
Mentholatum	Menthyloid kidney pills
Vaseline	Aspirin
Iodine	Bromo-quinine
Zonite	Quinine sulphate
Listerine	Eucalyptus oil

Pine tar	Boric acid
Epsom salts	Absorbent cotton
Castor oil	Gauze bandage
Cascara	Adhesive tape
Seidlitz powders	Corn plasters
Nujol	Porous plasters

This is a meager assortment compared with the medical stock of even the smallest drugstore on the Outside. Nevertheless, it seems to be sufficient to meet the ordinary needs. In the entire fifteen months I spent in the Koyukuk the only illnesses worse than a common cold or an upset stomach were several severe sore throats, one case of quinsy, one case of blood poisoning, two active cases of tuberculosis, and two or three attacks of influenza. Several of the older people had organic troubles, at least three having very bad hearts and one being much troubled by his kidneys. But the great majority of all the people were resoundingly healthy and had few requirements for any sort of medicine.

Historically, there has never been an epidemic of any disease since the whites first came to the upper Koyukuk, except that the visits of the mail carrier from the Yukon are often followed by a general outbreak of colds. There has never been a case of typhoid, small pox, diphtheria, scarlet fever, measles, or mumps. There was some scurvy in the wretchedly provisioned winter of 1898-1899, but since then only one instance of that malady. Venereal diseases have been surprisingly rare considering the promiscuous nature of the sexual intercourse, there being not a single case the effects of which were visible to the layman during my year in the Koyukuk. Tuberculosis alone among the Eskimos and Indians is of much more frequent occurrence than in the outside world, the reason for its prevalence being no doubt that the natives had no immunity to this disease when it was first introduced by the whites about three decades ago.

Communal sanitation is greatly aided by the fact that during eight months of the year the mean temperature is below freezing. There are only flies to be guarded against during June, July, and August, while the putrefying bacteria which cause unpleasant odors function for perhaps half a month additionally at either end of this period. Privies in town are treated with chloride of lime during these relatively warm months, but the rest of the year their contents remain safely frozen. Garbage is simply heaved over the bank of the river and remains frozen until the flood waters of spring carry it away. In summer the river washes away everything thrown into it. In no cases are public measures ever adopted for sanitation. However, if a man is very sloppy about the way he disposes of his waste he may be criticized. In view of the sparse population and the cold this criticism is all that seems to be required to uphold adequate communal sanitation in the Koyukuk.

Most of the white people have rather high standards of personal hygiene. They wash their hands before cooking, wash their dishes scrupulously after the meal is over, never expectorate in the promiscuous manner one is led to associate with the frontier. Their cabins may not be neat, but they are generally clean. The one or two people who keep their dogs in the cabin are objects of ridicule. A number of the people do a great deal of reading on medical hygiene and public health, while one man has made a special hobby of physical culture. The ideas which they have acquired become disseminated throughout the community and exert a considerable effect in raising the individual sanitary standards.

In concluding this chapter it might be interesting to tell the complete story of one typical case of serious sickness with all the communal ramifications which it involved. Shortly before Thanksgiving Jack White came up river with the right side of his throat so badly swollen that he could hardly swallow. His trouble was promptly diagnosed as quinsy sore throat and treated with the best medical ability available. But Jack kept getting worse and the quinsy, instead of breaking in three to seven days as the books said it should, dragged on for more than two weeks. Vaughn Green, himself suffering from heart disease, visited Jack both day and night, while Minnie Wilson temporarily dropped both her mining and her husband on Emma Creek to help in nursing Jack. It was necessary to have some one with him all the time, so practically every white man in town contributed hours to this unpleasant task as well as to cutting Jack's wood, carrying his water, caring for his horse and dogs. But still he kept getting worse. His throat had swollen so much that he could not swallow anything but ice water. No one felt competent to make an incision in his throat. He should have been sent to the hospital in Fairbanks, but the weather remained so continuously abominable that no airplane could come in. Vaughn wirelessed for advice to the doctor at Fort Yukon, and he recommended exactly what was being done.

Jack's pain was so great that for days he did not sleep for more than five minutes at a time. I remember one midnight, when Jack's groans and the beating of a fierce blizzard against the north wall of the cabin vied with each other in making the night sound dismal, how Minnie Wilson and I furtively gave Jack a dose of morphine. He got a good night's rest, which seemed to bolster his failing strength. But he was still so weak he could hardly even swear. He would repeatedly moan: "If I could only get a little sleep"; or "How many times I've laid down here in the evening, stretched out here until morning, all sleep." Sometimes he would ramble back to his childhood days, nearly fifty years before: "I remember, just in dusk of evening, when the buckwheat was flowering, how the deer used to come down to feed. . . ." "We'd go up to those wild, burnt mountains back in the Alleghenies every summer with baskets and baskets and boxes, all full of food, stews and chowders and mine pies and everything, and there'd be miles and miles just thick with blueberries, blueberries, blueberries, and we'd pick all day long and eat and laugh and have a good time all night." It was all said in a low, droning, yearning voice such as a man who had just lost a wife with whom he had lived for half a century might recall their honeymoon.

On a Wednesday at eleven in the morning, while Jack was at his worst, old Nakuchluk came in to see him. She placed her two hands on either side of his neck and then forced them towards herself, as if she were pushing a great weight. Then she blew violently on her hands. After that the process was repeated. On Thursday at the same hour she came back and went through a long prayer. Jack was so disgusted he threw a pillow over his head. That afternoon Nakuchluk met Clara Carpenter. Clara commented on how sick Jack was. Nakuchluk replied confidently: "He very sick all right, but me think he get better to-morrow."

Surely enough, the next day at exactly eleven Jack's quinsy broke inside the throat with a stench which nearly drove him and his nurses to distraction. The pus drained out rapidly, and in a week he was so much better that Mrs. Wilson went home.

But all was not over yet. The day after Mrs. Wilson departed Jack's neck started to swell on the outside. In two days there was a protruding lump about the size and color of an apple. The inflamed area extended all the way from his collar bone to his ear. We were very much afraid that in

Jack's weakened condition general blood poisoning might set in. Meanwhile the weather, which had cleared up while Jack was better, became exceptionally stormy again. With a plane now out of the question and the abscess well ripened, Vaughn determined to lance. Jack sat on the edge of the bed, so weak he could not stay up straight without support. But he never lost his nerve for an instant, and sat grimly gritting his teeth while Vaughn prepared for an operation which under amateur handling might easily have cost Jack his life. But fortune was with him. Half a plateful of pus came out in the first gush after Vaughn's deft incision, and the wound kept draining for a week. Thereafter it healed up slowly and Jack recovered his strength slowly, while the people of Wiseman, whose primary concern for several weeks had been in the sickness of Jack White, now turned again to more cheerful preoccupations.

XXII

THE HAZARDOUS KOYUKUK

THIS is the story of Oscar Johnson. He and Billie Glenn were camped together on the Twin Lakes in the autumn of 1920. One afternoon Oscar's dog took after some caribou which were feeding on the nearby hills. Oscar set out to retrieve him. He should have returned in an hour. When Oscar was not back by the next morning Billie went out looking for his partner. He was unsuccessful in his search, so he returned to Rooney's Lake for help. Several men set out together the second morning, determined to find Oscar by night. They followed his tracks for miles through the snow. It was not long before they found where he had recovered the dog, but instead of returning he had kept on traveling straight down the South Fork, had passed within a few feet of the well-known igloo on Boiler Creek, and had finally crossed the well-defined Yukon mail trail. He had apparently tied the dog to himself and the two kept on and on. Was he pursued, had he gone crazy, could he have suddenly been stricken blind?

No one will ever know the answer. They followed his tracks to a dense clump of timber on the Mosquito Fork. Then a snowstorm came up and the tracks were obliterated. That is the end of the story of Oscar Johnson.

This story was told to me by a thirty-five-year-old Eskimo who has scars to prove the authenticity of it.

"One winter when I was three years old my people was camped at the mouth of Hunts Fork. I remember one morning there was three of us children playing in the snow below a steep bank. We was carving with knives in the snow, making pictures and patterns and things like that. All of a sudden we saw a dog come across the river toward us. The other kids—they was a few year older than me—shouted: 'There's the dog we lost,' and they started whistling to him. Then he kept coming on, and suddenly the older kids see it wasn't a dog at all but a wolf. Then they holler and start up the bank, but they make it so smooth and slippery getting up that when I try I can't climb at all. I go up a little way and roll down, and then I try again and roll down, and again, and again, but still I keep slipping down, and next thing I remember is a couple of days later. I'm lying in bed, and my eye is all shut closed, and my face hurts something awful, and father asks me how I was getting on and I answered that I was going to die.

"They tell me that mother came out of the tent when she heard the kids holler. She saw me lying under the wolf, and the wolf chewing on me. She let out an awful scream and grabbed a piece of wood and ran down the bank and shouted at the wolf: 'What are you doing with my baby?' Then she grabbed me from right under the wolf's nose without ever even looking at him."

Everybody knew that Fritz Block was a miser, but it was parsimonious even for Fritz when he set out across the hills to Tanana one January with the shabbiest outfit imaginable. His clothes were nearly worn through, his snowshoes were half broken, and he had to pull his own sled in lieu of having dogs. Of course probably nothing would happen, but it was a crazy risk to take in mid-winter.

Fritz himself had no misgivings. He had been in the Far North for fifteen years without ever having experienced a single misfortune. It was true his clothes were in wretched shape, but it was mild weather, five or six days would put him in Tanana, and it would certainly be the epitome of extravagance to buy an elaborate outfit at the exorbitant Koyukuk prices when in less than a week he could make his purchases at the far lower prices on the Yukon.

The first day out was clear and warm and still. The trail was well broken, and Fritz had little trouble making the eighteen-mile cabin. The second day the temperature must have dropped forty degrees. Next morning when he awakened it was snowing hard, and the wind was howling. The well-beaten trail was badly drifted, and the easy traveling was over. But there was no use waiting for the storm to pass, especially since Fritz had not taken any excess food along. He set out into the storm, plowing along through the soft snow on his inadequate webs. He admitted to himself that he made a mistake there. He should at least have bought himself a decent pair of snowshoes.

Before he had covered many miles he began to realize he was not going to make the next cabin that night. He decided to turn around and go back to the cabin he had left. Then with the trail he had already broken to help him on the morrow he would easily make the third cabin. As he turned around he felt his fingers tingling sharply inside of his worn mittens. He had been a fool in not buying a new pair. They only cost a couple of dollars, and a man simply had to have his fingers in good shape on the trail.

He was facing squarely into the wind as he backtracked toward safety. The trail seemed to be refilling with snow almost as fast as he broke it out. Climbing a steep grade, he had to stop half a dozen times for breath, and at every rest a sickening chill started in his stomach and spread throughout his entire body. Then, all at once, he realized his fingers were no longer tingling. They were frozen stiff.

Suddenly he became panic-stricken. He left his sled and started along on a dog trot. One of his snowshoes got caught on a log and he pitched headlong into the snow. When he picked himself up there was freezing powder up his sleeves and all down his neck, and worst of all his snowshoe was ruined. He limped along painfully with one shoe for some distance, but finally discarded it and plowed along through the thigh deep drifts.

Then matters became vague and jumbled. There was only one thing clear to him, the necessity of keeping on. The cabin should have appeared around every bend, but it kept retreating. All of a sudden, just as he had given up the notion of ever seeing it, he was upon the cabin.

But now that his goal was attained he felt no elation. Rather a dim annoyance in his deadened mind that the thing he had been doing so long instinctively was now finished, and the occasion required immediately an entirely different action. He slipped his hand in his pocket, but he could feel nothing. Somehow he managed to turn his pocket inside out. A knife and some matches fell on the floor. He made a single futile attempt to pick one up, then let out a hoarse laugh, and sat down with his back against the stove. He took his left hand and tried to move the fingers of his right hand with it. Then he laughed again.

I have recorded these stories, and they are typical of dozens of others which could be told, because they illustrate the hazardous life of the Koyukuk. It is true that if everything goes perfectly, if a person is invariably deft and careful, life is a fairly safe proposition. It is easy to point out, for instance, that every man who was frozen was either careless or incompetent. Looking at matters in retrospect all of these deaths could have been avoided. A man like Ernie Johnson can set out for a winter alone in the wilderness with as absolute confidence that he will come through safely as the average New Yorker would have if he started to walk across Central Park. But Ernie is an exception, competent above all men in that North country, and it is not the exceptions which really count. It is the fate of men in general in a given environment which really measures the danger of that environment. Because Blondin could walk across the Niagara River on a tightrope with certainty does not mean that walking across the Niagara River on a tightrope is a safe occupation.

When we talk about a life being safe or dangerous we really require a statistical approach. Fortunately, it is possible to view life in the Koyukuk in such a way. I have a record of every white man who has died in the upper Koyukuk from the stampede of 1898 through the close of 1931. I also have a record of the white population of the region in every year. From these two figures it is easy to determine the death rate of the Koyukuk and compare it with the mortality rate in the outside world.

This comparison shows that the annual deaths per one thousand population tally closely in the two regions, being 11.4 in the Koyukuk for the period from 1898 through 1931, and 13.3 in the registration area of the United States for the period from 1900 through 1931.[1] However, when the

[1] The death rate figures for the registration area of the United States are weighted averages kindly furnished by Dr. Louis I. Dublin of the Metropolitan Life Insurance Company.

component parts of these general figures are analyzed, a striking difference is apparent. Nearly three-quarters of the people who have died in the upper Koyukuk, fifty of them to be precise, have met their end by accident or violence, while only eighteen have died natural deaths. The annual death rate per thousand due to natural causes has been but 3.0 in the Koyukuk as against 12.3 in the United States. But the death rate due to external causes is 8.4 per thousand people in the North country as opposed to only 1.0 per thousand in the United States. In other words the chances of meeting death due to external causes is more than eight times as great in the Koyukuk as in the United States.

But what is it that makes the life so dangerous? The following figures show the specific causes of the Koyukuk deaths due to accident and violence:

Freezing	12
Drowning	10
Mining accidents	6
Disappearing	6
Suicide	5
Freighting accidents	3
Murder	3
Burning or scalding	2
Accident due to intoxication	1
Accidental self-shooting	1
Overeating after long starvation	1
Total	50

The two main items in this list, which accounted for nearly half the deaths in the region, are causes of mortality which are almost unheard of or at least rare in the outside world. The same is true of the fourth item, disappearing. The suicide rate of one for every thousand people is more than seven times that of the United States. It is these unusual causes which have been chiefly responsible for the comparatively high accidental death rate in the Koyukuk.

The death rate due to mining accidents is not very much greater than the similar death rate in the United States. The chief cause of Koyukuk mining disaster has been the poisonous fumes of wood fires which have been used to thaw the frozen ground. Aside from the six deaths, there have been remarkably few maiming accidents. No one was ever injured so severely as to be incapacitated for further work. Even Jesse Allen who lost an arm refused to leave his beloved frontier just because of his accident, and to-day he has adapted himself so well to his deformity that he is regarded as one of the best miners, mushers, and hunters in the entire region.

It is interesting to note that the murder rate, while many times that of the United States, is still exceptionally low for the frontier. I believe Mark Twain mentions one western mining community where the first twenty-six men buried in the cemetery had met violent death. Certain it is that few successful gold mining camps in the history of the North American continent can boast of only three homicides in thirty-four years.

The low rate of natural deaths in the Koyukuk may be ascribed to three factors. First, the physically active, outdoor life is unusually conducive to health. Second, the long, cold winters are unfavorable to the development of germs and bacteria. Third and most important, the difficult life of the Arctic effected a natural selection so that only the physically fit remained in the Koyukuk.

Nevertheless, deaths due to natural causes have increased from a rate of one person in five years during the first couple of decades to eight people in the last five-year period alone.

WINTER: It is easy to understand how men can freeze to death in country like this. An idea of scale may be gained from the fact that the rock cliff on the left of the picture is about 2000 feet sheer.

This may of course be attributed to the fact that the average age of the community was not more than thirty-five years in 1901, while to-day it is at least fifty-five years.

No precise mortality records are available for the Eskimos, but it can be stated definitely that far fewer Eskimos than whites lose their lives in accidents. However, their death rate due to sickness is probably much higher. The infant mortality has been exceptionally great, but the chief scourge is tuberculosis which in certain families has been devastating.

XXIII

QUARRELS AND UNPOPULARITY

THE QUESTION was whether Bertha Badeau really did say: "I hope the son-of-a-bitch dies." I shall not attempt to pass judgment. I only know that when Jack was lying desperately sick he sent his friend Billie Burke to tear down the fence around his garden which he had permitted Bertha to use indefinitely with the one condition that her husband should get Jack as much fuel wood as there was in the fence. Two years had passed, the husband had never gotten the wood. Jack in the irritation of illness decided to avenge himself for this injustice, and consequently he sent Billie to haul the fence to his own woodpile. Bertha Badeau came running out when she saw the fence of her borrowed garden being removed by its owner's agent, and then is when she was reported by Billie to have enunciated her dire wish. Thereafter, for nearly a week, all of Wiseman was good-naturedly (except for the principals) discussing the two sides and eagerly spreading the first news of each fresh development.

Of fresh developments there were plenty. Jack White is going to dispossess the Badeaus from one of his cabins which they have been using. Ed Badeau and Billie Burke almost come to blows when Ed takes Billie to task for spreading lies. Billie says that if Ed lays hands on him he'll shoot him with no more compunction than he'd feel for shooting a mad dog. Jack White is reported to keep a revolver next to his bed. Vaughn Green serves dispossession notice on the Badeaus, requiring them to vacate the premises in ten days. Ed says he won't vacate. Floyd Hyde claims that Jack has previously sold the cabin to him, and that he will let the Badeaus stay in. Jack accuses Hyde of being a lying ingrate. Ed Badeau is going to present Jack with a bill for wages unpaid. Jack tells Ed to just try and collect it. Ed and Bertha are reported to have had a terrific brawl among themselves. Bertha is leaving for Fairbanks. Jack is leaving for Fairbanks. Won't it be swell if Bertha and Jack both go out on the same plane? Bertha is not leaving for Fairbanks. Jack is not leaving for Fairbanks. Charlie Irish, the U. S. Commissioner, attempts mediation. Ed agrees to leave the cabin in twenty days.—(Five months later) Bertha and Billie Burke spoke together to-day for the first time since last December.

This is merely one sample from some forty-three quarrels which occurred during my year at Wiseman. The following causes of these quarrels show pleasant variety:

Insult	11
Jealousy	9
Economic dispute	8
Bi-products of other fight	4
Irritation between husband and wife	3
Disapproval of other person's conduct	3
Irritations of sober person at drunken one	2
Accusation of unjust favoritism	1
Row over the school election	1
Case of insanity	1

I should at this point define what I mean by a quarrel. I have used the term to include any altercation between two people which changes their relationship for one week or more. This excludes mere hot words which are forgotten by the next morning, it excludes trivial bickerings, and it leaves out many bursts of temper, all of which could not possibly be recorded. On the other hand I feel confident that I have recorded every quarrel, both public and private, falling within the scope of my definition.

Although the quarrel which I described was between white people, the Eskimos on the whole were a more pugnacious group. Some seventeen out of the twenty-one adult Eskimos around Wiseman participated in fights while only twenty-nine of the sixty-one whites did so.

Perhaps one reason for this undue representation of Eskimos in the wrangles of the community was that, while the white fights seldom involved more than two people, the Eskimo troubles frequently involved almost every adult of that race in camp. Take the case of Annie Kayak, for instance. Annie had come over from the tundra of the Arctic coast with her husband Itashluk and two little children in the latter part of November. She spent a month getting used to the strange white community and learning the white dances from another Eskimo girl. On Christmas night she made her début on the Wiseman dance floor. She was a little bit clumsy at first, it is true, but she was a novelty and very beautiful, so all the men made a rush for her. She liked it so much that when her husband, who not only had a bad temper but was also impotent, insisted that they return to the Arctic immediately after New Year, she rose in wrath one night and hit him in the eye.

The next morning it chanced that I had an appointment to come down to the igloo and take pictures of their family. When I got inside I found Itashluk sitting on a bunk, scowling furiously through a blackened eye, and Annie sitting on

the floor, looking very defiant, and every adult Eskimo except four in the whole camp inside the igloo, looking very
worried and serious. Big Jim took me outside and explained
with a dubious smile: "Maybe better no picture to-day.
Everything all right, only Itashluk maybe no feel right."
Then he invited me back into the igloo.

I must have sat on the floor there for better than two
hours, listening to one speech after another in Eskimo,
almost all directed at Annie, urging her to go back to Itashluk. There were but two people to defend her. I could only
understand a little of all that was said, and there were very
few facial expressions or gestures to give a clew as to meaning, but at the end it was very clear to me as well as everybody else that Annie was not going back to Itashluk. Nevertheless two more mass meetings were held. In the first
urgings were replaced by threats, and Annie was told that
according to the white man's laws if you left your husband
you could be sent to jail. Just as Annie was wavering at this
appalling thought, one of her supporters pointed out that
Itashluk had never gotten a divorce from his first wife who
deserted him, and that if any one would go to jail by the
white man's laws it was Itashluk who had committed bigamy.
This meeting then broke up in confusion. The final one alter-
nated the tactics of cajoling, of veiled threats, and of furious
denunciations. But still Annie refused to return to her husband. Thereafter, except for her two friends and the four
neutral people, she was blacklisted, deprecated, and avoided
by every Eskimo in camp.

In spite of this harsh treatment she remained bravely ada-
mant, and there was nothing that could be done. After about
a month the other Eskimos, most of whom reveled in quarrels but hated them to persist, began to show Annie guarded
friendliness. They still refused to help her economically,

saying: "Well, she brought it on herself. She had a man to take care of her and she got away from him. Now let her take care of herself." This neglect of her needs on the part of the natives was made good by the whites and her two Eskimo allies. They raised a fund of fifty-seven dollars for her. They gave her their laundry to wash and paid double prices. They helped her saw wood. Two white men, having a facetious dispute as to which loved her most, even bought her three cords of wood as testimony of their affections. In particular, every one had a glorious time discussing the pros and cons of the case. Finally Itashluk went back to the Arctic, Annie's enemies had other quarrels to occupy their minds, and by spring she was so generally accepted as a part of the community that no one remembered any more that her entrance into its life had caused the most furious dissension of the winter.

Perhaps this story, as well as the other I told, gives some notion of the joyful diversion which these fights make for the rank and file of the community. They take the place of the movie, the vaudeville, and the prize fight. "Oh, it tickles me; I like to see this jangling," says one man, rubbing his hands and laughing. Another remarks: "This country suits me fine as long as Martin and Mamie and Biddy and Joe and Harry and Jim put on a show like they've been doing every little while. They're as good as any show you could see Outside, and you've got more background."

One peculiar feature of Arctic quarrels is their seasonal nature. The following figures indicate the occurrence of the forty-three fights by months, starting with the first month I was in camp:

September 2   November 4
October 2   December 6

January	5	May	3
February	6	June	3
March	5	July	2
April	3	August	2

Of course another year would not give exactly the same results, but I think the figures are sufficiently clear to indicate beyond peradventure the irritating influence of darkness. There seems, however, to be a lag in the peak and trough of the quarrel figures to the period of maximum and minimum sunlight.

Many of the Outside people to whom I have shown this table have tried to relate the results to other matters. They have suggested that the abnormal winter fights were due to too much idleness. Actually, as the reader is aware, there is fully as much work in winter as in summer. They have wondered if the December maximum of fights was not due to the great gathering of people for the Christmas hilarity, forgetting that the second greatest gathering came on the Fourth of July, month of fewest altercations. They have even blamed it on the difference in summer and winter mail service until informed that the latter was the more regular. Yet all the while the fact remains, obvious to almost every one who has lived through the dark months of the North,[1] obvious indeed to many people of temperate zones who become depressed by long periods of cloudy weather, that sunlight has a distinctly cheering effect on the spirit of the majority of people. The Koyukukers do not go around during the sunless days telling each other that the time for depression is at hand. They often have the gayest and most hilarious times imaginable. But subtly most of them sense the depressing effect of the short days, and sometimes under

[1] Stefansson dissents. See his *Friendly Arctic*, page 22.

this influence they behave more irritably than they would in the twenty-four-hour daylight of summer.

Closely related to the subject of quarrels is unpopularity. In order to determine what types of people were most unpopular in the Koyukuk, I recorded every enmity among the sixty-one whites who centered their lives around Wiseman. A dozen of these people had from eight to twenty-five enemies each, and they may fairly be considered as the most unpopular twenty per cent of the community. Were there any traits of character possessed by a large proportion of these people which were notably rarer among their less disliked neighbors?

I observed some eight different traits which seemed distinctly to fall in such a category. These were:

1. Being a snob;
2. Being a hypocrite;
3. Belonging to either of the two small cliques around Wiseman;
4. Stirring up trouble;
5. Bragging, vaunting one's own knowledge, or telling repeated stories in which one is the hero;
6. Being greedy;
7. Being dishonest;
8. Having bad outdoor manners, such as leaving cabins without wood, keeping dogs in the trail shelters, wasting game, and leaving traps unsprung.

There are also certain positive traits which are far more frequent among the dozen most popular men than they are among the rank and file of the community. These include the ability to make a joke, the ability to take one, cheerfulness and gayety, absolutely undeviating honesty, and above all a distinctive personality which makes one stand out as a unique individual. People with these characteristics seldom become disliked, rarely are involved in quarrels, and generally are regarded with the highest affection by their diverse fellowmen.

XXIV

INTER-RACIAL RELATIONS

AL WEST has told me that when he was living alone as
the only white man in Alatna, Little Mary would frequently
come around to invite him to her house for meals. "You no
cook for yourself, open cans all time, no good," she would
say. After a while, when he commenced to feel embarrassed
at the number of times she was inviting him without any
reciprocation on his part, she adopted a more tactful approach.
She would send one of her little sons just before lunch time
to ask Al to help her with some trivial matter, and then he
would have to stay for lunch. She would always have some
special reason. "You never eat whitefish eggs, you got to
try them," she might say, and of course Al could not refuse
such an invitation.

This story could just as well be reversed to illustrate the
innumerable acts of white kindness to Eskimos. Either way
it illustrates the fact that two such divergent races as the
whites and the Eskimos are actually living together in almost
perfect amity. They are continually exchanging visits in
each other's homes, mingling together in conversation, eating together at meals, sharing the same cabins on the trail.
At all social events they have standing of equal importance,
except that the Eskimo girls are in greater demand than the
white women at the dances because they are younger. There

230

are absolutely no legal inequalities set up, no restrictive regulations which do not apply to both races. From every standpoint the Eskimos and whites treat each other as equals.

This gives rise to the natural question whether the Eskimos and whites also think of each other as equals. I have attempted to obtain some measure of belief, not by questionnaire, not by the superficial method of direct oral inquiry, but by close observation and intimate personal acquaintance.

I have conceived of four different attitudes which the white people could entertain toward the Eskimos. Each of these viewpoints could be subdivided almost indefinitely, but I prefer to use rather broad categories. I have tried to augment my definitions with quotations expressing the viewpoints held in each of these groups.

I. In this class I include anybody who takes the attitude that the Eskimos are too low to associate with. It is the typical attitude of the Southerner toward the negro. I cannot give any quotations for this category because no white person in the entire Koyukuk held such views.

II. In this class I include those who believe the Eskimos are distinctly inferior to the whites in every way, who tend to treat them coldly, and who constantly make uncomplimentary remarks behind their backs. In spite of this attitude some of them have been exceptionally generous to the Eskimos when they have needed help. Here are a few of the expressions which typify the attitude of this class of people:

"Fancy treating the natives as equals! It's simply out of the question. They have nothing but children's minds. All I have to do is smile at them and be friendly and give them a little food now and then and they think I'm a goddess. Just like children. No, they're simply below the white man's level, that's all there's to it." (The Eskimos, who have secret nicknames in their own language for every white person, call this "goddess" by two titles. One means "she paints her lips red," with reference to her desperate efforts to maintain a youthful appearance. The other means "the camp robber.")

"I always considered an Eskimo a good shot, but of course he ain't good at nothing compared with a white man."

"When you try to compare the natives to the whites it's like comparing night to day. You just can't talk about the two together. Tell me, did a native ever invent a typewriter or make anything like a can of milk or a rifle cartridges? No, you're God damn right they didn't. There are thousands of things like that which whites have invented and not one did a native ever make. But they're so God damn conceited they think they're better than the whites. 'White man fool,' they always say. Why, they never have a thought which is more than skin deep."

III. In this class I include those who regard the Eskimos as inferior to the whites in intelligence and culture, though they treat them as equals. Their attitude may be summarized by the remark: "They're not quite our equals, but it isn't their fault." Here are a few sample viewpoints from this group of people.

"I get along with the natives fine, just as well as with the whites. But they're peculiar people in many ways. They seem to think it's wrong to save up any money. As long as they've got two bits they're never happy until they've spent it. It doesn't matter if their kids may be starving next month, they'll spend what they've got now on clothes, on useless contraptions, on drinking or gambling. Then when they've got it all spent they'll go back to work."

"She's a pretty good woman for a squaw."

"I figure the native is to white man almost just like a dog. You can train a native to be good or you can train a native to be bad. Bad native, it ain't his fault, it's because he's gotten mixed up with bad white men. A native could be the finest man in the world or the worst man in the world. It all depends on how he's brought up."

IV. In this class I include those who consider the Eskimos to be fully as admirable a people as the whites, though undeniably a very different people. This group may criticize various traits of the Eskimos, but they feel that other good points fully balance these defects. The following quotations are representative of the attitude of this class:

"The Lithuanians [from whom this man came] aren't my people any more. The natives here are my people. The land here really all belongs to them. They just let us live here through kindness. They have always been very kind to me. I want to do what I can for them. At first I wanted to destroy their superstitions, but then I thought of the superstitions of all the white men around me and I decided I'd better leave them alone. I think it's time we stopped patronizing the native. He's just as good as the white man and we ought to treat him so."

"They're fine people to get along with. Poor devils, they haven't got a thing in the world, but what they have got they'll share with you. I've lived with the natives here for thirty-four years and I've found them better people to live with than the whites. In all the years I've lived with them I've only found one who ever stole anything from me and that was only a ball of twine. No, I've bunked with them from Dawson to the Siberian coast for better than thirty years and I'd never ask to find a finer people."

"There's lots of things you can say against the Eskimos. They're forever squabbling and they're terribly superstitious and they don't think anything of a debt. But on the other side, look at all you can say. For all their little fights they don't ever carry resentments like the white people. They're not all the time scheming to get the better of you. They're the most honest people you can find if you treat them squarely. They know how to enjoy themselves to-day without worrying over what's going to happen to-morrow. And you know, I believe they have on the average greater mental capacity and more intelligence than the whites. Anyway, they're the most good-hearted people in the world, and that's a lot more important than whether they pay their bills at the store."

I think these quotations define the viewpoints qf the groups I have mentioned. It is now pertinent to present my census of how these different attitudes were distributed among the seventy-seven white people of the upper Koyukuk.

Attitude of Whites Toward Eskimos	Number Holding This View
I. Eskimos are too low to associate with........	o
II. Eskimos are distinctly inferior to the whites in every way	9
III. Eskimos are somewhat inferior to the whites but should be treated as equals	38
IV. Eskimos are fully as admirable a people as the whites	30

Included among the nine people who regarded the Eskimos as distinctly inferior were the whites with the first, second, fourth, and fifth most enemies among their own race. Not a single one of the nine people was ranked by his fellow whites among the top half in popularity. This hints at an interesting psychological relationship. A person is disliked by his own people, so in order to assuage the feeling of inferiority which this must at least subconsciously create, he bolsters his pride by stressing how much superior his entire race is to another race.

I thought it would be interesting to see whether on the
basis of the Stanford-Binet intelligence tests there was any
marked difference between the people entertaining the three
different attitudes. Although I only gave these tests to forty-
five of the seventy-seven whites, it accidentally happened
that almost exactly the same proportion of each attitude
group was covered by these tests. The following results
were found:

Attitude of Whites Toward Eskimos	*Average Intelligence Quotient*
II. Eskimos are distinctly inferior to the whites in every way	94
III. Eskimos are somewhat inferior to the whites but should be treated as equals	104
IV. Eskimos are fully as admirable a people as the whites	106

It will be seen that while there was no significant difference between the last two groups, the first one, if these tests
mean anything, had a distinctly lower average intelligence.

So far I have centered the discussion on what the white
people think of the Eskimos. It is worth paying some attention to the reverse relationship. I cannot go into as much detail regarding the Eskimos' attitude toward the whites, but
I can mention a few viewpoints.

If a white person treats the Eskimos as equals, is interested in and sympathetic to what interests them, is honest,
jolly, and fairly generous, is neither stupid nor conceited,
and does not try to get their women drunk in order to have
sexual intercourse with them, it is almost certain that he will
be regarded enthusiastically by the Eskimos. Just about one
quarter of all the whites qualify in this class, and the amount
of affection which the Eskimos heap upon them is enormous.

The majority of the white people fail to meet all these requirements. The Eskimos feel friendly toward most of these people, but they lack the great enthusiasm with which they regard the first group. It is also true that they are not averse to ridiculing many of these white people. I recollect an exceptionally gay evening in Ekok's cabin when one elderly man who was ardently courting a fifteen-year-old Eskimo girl, another fellow who was a terrible liar, a third who erroneously thought he was immensely popular with the Eskimos, and a fourth who was merely dull-minded, were successively derided.

As to positive dislikes, the Eskimos have surprisingly few. There is one white man who, when he used to be commissioner, heckled them pretty badly. Many of them hate him. But the whites who are most genuinely scorned are the ones who treat the Eskimos as inferiors. One of these people imagines that the natives are too childish to understand serious talk, so he only speaks nonsense to them. They laugh perfunctorily at his silliness, but behind his back they ridicule him and call him "the crazy old man." The woman, whom I have previously mentioned as being called "the camp robber," is a constant butt for their jokes. It is important to note, however, that all these instances of unpopularity are individual cases. Unlike most of the whites, the Eskimos almost never generalize about an entire race.

Of course one of the most interesting aspects of interracial relations is the sexual. I shall discuss this matter in considerable detail in the chapter on marriage. Here I merely want to mention that there is almost no prejudice in the Koyukuk against intermarriage and a sufficient amount of it actually occurring that a third of all the children in the Koyukuk have mixed blood.

WHERE RACE IS NOT CONSIDERED: Eskimos and whites mingling on terms of perfect equality after an all night dance at Hammond River.

In order not to confuse matters unnecessarily I have so far always mentioned as whites those people in the Koyukuk who were not natives. Actually among these seventy-seven people there is one mulatto negro who has been in the Arctic for a quarter of a century. It is interesting to note that his rating among both whites and Eskimos is not very high, though not quite low enough to place him in the most unpopular twenty per cent. He regards his relatively unfavorable status as a matter of race prejudice, but I believe he is mistaken. He exhibits several of the most unpopular traits which are enough to give any one in the region a low rating. Certainly he suffers from none of the prejudices which negroes generally encounter in the United States. He is welcomed in practically every one's home, has been a partner of many different white men, eats in the roadhouses, stops in the cabins along the trail, and participates in all the social functions just as freely as if he were a white man.

XXV

CHILDREN AND EDUCATION

THEY were having a big dance at the roadhouse, and the large room was crowded with both adults and children. Many of the latter were imitating their elders in gyrating about the floor. The fox trot record which had been playing was finished, and little Harry Jonas, aged six, left his five-year-old partner and came over to where I was sitting.

"I just danced with Mary," he said proudly.

"Good for you!" I said. "How does she dance?"

"Fine!" he replied. "My girl's a good dancer."

"How do you like to dance with Florence [aged four]?" I queried.

"Oh," he answered with much disdain, "I don't like to dance with little girls."

Which goes to indicate that these little urchins of the Arctic are not so much different from children everywhere, except perhaps for an abnormal sophistication. Thus, when this same Harry Jonas hears Jack Hood swear he says sympathetically: "I can swear too, God damn it. You feel better when you swear, don't you?" And Little Kapuk, aged three and one-half, said to me in surprise one evening: "What? You live all alone? You got no woman to undress you?"

This sophistication derives no doubt from constant, intimate association with the children's elders. Almost as soon as they

238

are born they are brought by their parents to the dances where they early commence to observe almost everything that is going on. As soon as they can walk they watch the men at work and hear their unrepressed language. Sexual matters are frankly explained to the children the moment they show any curiosity.

The upbringing of the Eskimo children is featured by a minimum of chastisement. The parents are genuinely anxious for their offspring to have a good time. They take no sadistic delight in disciplining them just because they think discipline is good for their health. "I had good time dancing and playing when I was a girl," said Bessie. "Now I only have one of my children left, I want her to have just as much good times as she can." The reciprocal reaction is given by another woman who says: "Mother let us do everything we pleased so her voice got just like music to us."

One mother says quite typically: "It's no good to tell children you punish them and then not do it. You say you punish them, you got to punish them. But I never have to punish Jennie. Charlie and I never spank her in our lives. If she do something wrong I just tell her she should not do it, nobody like her if she do. Jennie say: 'Nobody like me if I do that?' I say: 'No, nobody like you,' and Jennie say: 'Then I won't do it, Mom.'"

Nevertheless, the Eskimo parents do not fuss over or coddle their children. They do not try to protect them from contact with real life. Neither do they try to give them a false notion of their own importance. The children are allowed chiefly to grow up as they will, provided they do not make nuisances of themselves or shirk their share of the necessary family labor.

That they do have to help with the work is something which Eskimo children take for granted. Jennie started to guide her father's sled with the gee-pole when she was only six years old. This same girl, now fourteen, boasts that she can chop wood faster than any man in Wiseman. Oscar Jonas at the age of eight was a splendid axman and had already killed three caribou. Incidentally, he was in the fourth grade at school. It is so with practically all Eskimo children. Not only do they accomplish the school work of white children of the same age, but they also have the ability to perform most of the essential activities necessary for the maintenance of life.

Yet with all their work, Eskimo children have plenty of chance to play. They greatly enjoy games like "motion" and "pump-pump-pullaway," which they have been taught in school. They play tag with their parents from the time they are old enough to run, only they say "anguk" instead of "tag." They also play with their parents a game which they call baseball, but which really is about what we would call saluchi. Otherwise, most of their games are what they develop themselves. The Jonas boys of six and eight have as favorite summer pastimes: building great piles of rocks, wading in the water, making things out of mud, playing they are hunting, and pretending they are different animals by carefully imitating the habits which they have learned from much observation. Willie English, aged eight, enjoys most of all driving his diminutive sled in winter, wading in the water in summer, playing tag, running races, and riding on the caterpillar tractor.

This latter diversion was one of the most popular among all the children. When the cat was hauling freight last winter between Bettles and Wiseman, and the day for it to reach the latter place became due, the children would all be on the alert for the first sound. They would generally hear the tractor when it was a long distance from town, often when it was still down at Marion Creek, seven miles away. They would immediately set out across the river on the sled trail, a whole caravan of them, and maybe meet the cat down at Dry Gulch, three miles below the town. Here the driver would stop genially and let them climb on board, and then they would bump and bounce back to Wiseman in a high state of elation. When the tractor was not around it was considered great sport to ride behind Jack Hood's horses when he went out to haul wood.

But it is very dangerous to generalize about these Eskimo children, just as it is dangerous to generalize about any people. During one of the long evenings of last spring I was sitting with an Eskimo woman in her kitchen. While we were chatting together her three-year-old son came in, crying as if his heart would break, and repeating over and over again: "Poor puppy! Poor puppy! Puppy die! Puppy die!" At first we did not know what could be the matter, but in the intermissions between his sobs the trouble soon became apparent. During the winter this boy and his older brother had often played with the puppy of an elderly neighbor. When the dog died, it had been heaved over the bank into the river. The snow had soon covered it, and in the far below freezing weather it had been perfectly preserved. Now the snow had melted, but the flood water of spring had not yet come to wash the dog away, and thus it chanced that the boys, while wandering along the river bar, had suddenly stumbled over their former playmate. The natural conclusion after seeing the younger boy's anguish might have been that Eskimo children are very sensitive. But alas for such a generalized deduction, while we were still trying to calm the younger boy, his four-year-old brother marched into the house, swinging the dead puppy around and around by the tail, and throwing him down on the kitchen table, he exclaimed: "Here, Mommy, cook him!"

It is now time to return to the subject of child upbringing. I have so far only mentioned the enviable traits of the parents in relation to their children. To give a fair picture, at least two undesirable common habits of the elders should be mentioned. One is their fondness for teasing children. In regard to this practice I can add nothing to Jennie's reflection: "I don't think old people ought to tease children. It doesn't hurt them so bad then, but it hurts them long time afterwards."

The other bad habit is the fondness of many Eskimo adults for booze. "No good for kids," says one mother who abstains. "No good at all nothing kid see mamma papa act all the time like crazy. Maybe kid no forget. Maybe hurt kid pretty bad." Apparently she is right, for one girl who has seen her parents drunk tells me: "I hate to see my parents drunk. I don't mind seeing everybody else drunk, but I feel terrible if Mamma and Papa are drunk. It's awful on children when parents get drunk. I remember when Papa and Mamma get drunk the first time we're so scared Lucy and I run away to the hills and stay out all night. Think of Unakserak's poor children seeing their papa drunk all the time."

The most unfortunate trait which I observed in the majority of the Eskimo children was their habit of becoming hysterical when they were sick. Thus Oscar Jonas, who normally was the bravest, most grown-up boy of eight whom I have ever known, and whom I had never seen cry, no matter what the pain or disappointment, suddenly went all to pieces when he was suffering from tonsillitis and an earache. He whimpered constantly for days, made his mother sit up at nights, holding her hand on his head, and kept repeating, over and over, the ejaculation *ahnee* which is Eskimo for "ouch." Similarly, Oscar's sister of fifteen years acted like a little baby when she had tonsillitis, refused to gargle or eat even the least irritating things, and kept up a continuous inundation of tears. No doubt these children acquired the trait from their parents, who also tend to become hysterical when ill. Certainly it was much more usual among the full-blooded Eskimo children than those with white fathers who regarded sickness as something purely physical rather than as a creation of the devil.

Most of the white men, though they entered the wilderness in the days of "spare the rod and spoil the child," are very patient with these youngsters. When little Gitnoo threw a stone through the window of Jesse Allen's house, Jesse did not spank him or even scold him. Instead he sympathized with him, told him how much he used to enjoy throwing stones as a boy, and then asked him as a favor not to break any more windows. It worked perfectly.

In this discussion of Koyukuk children there remains the subject of formal education. For there is, as I have several times mentioned, a regular school at Wiseman. It is financed by the Territory of Alaska, managed by an elected school board of three Wiseman citizens, and taught by a white woman who must have at least the qualification of a high school diploma. Although some of the Koyukukers feel the children would be better off without this education, the great majority believe that as long as the Eskimos are living with the whites they are made happier by getting some sort of a white education.

The Eskimos, adults and children alike, are emphatically of that opinion. Parents with children of a school age almost all arrange to get back to Wiseman some time in the autumn so that their children may continue their education. As for the children, they are without exception enthusiastic about school. The very day they come to town they invariably report for classes, and every day thereafter, unless they are very ill, they eagerly congregate at the schoolhouse. Hooky is unknown at Wiseman. In the winter of 1929-30 the school made the remarkable record of not having a single absence for any child in town.

The school is run very much like any rural school. During my winter in Wiseman there was a primary, first, second, third, fourth, and fifth grade, each with two or three children. All sat together in one room. The teacher would assign each group its work, and then call each in turn to the front of the room for recitation. If any child wanted to ask a question in between he raised his hand, and the teacher came to help him. Some things the whole school did together, such as singing songs, reciting health rules, and playing in the school yard in a fifteen-minute morning and afternoon recess period. The school day was from nine to noon, and from one to three-thirty. The work included everything that would be embraced in the curriculum of similar grades on the Outside.

In at least one important respect, however, the school was radically different from any Outside school I have known. While many of the pupils started in the first grade at the normal age, there were several who had never had the opportunity of schooling until they were well along in years. Thus, a grandmother was in the Second grade, her son was in the Fourth grade, and her granddaughter in the First grade.

Several times during the course of the year the latter part of the afternoon was occupied by birthday parties for which the schoolteacher herself always provided the food. Twice a year, at Christmas and when school was out in the spring,

ESKIMO CHILDREN: Gitnoo, Manuluk, Kapuk, Johnie, Oscar. All are pure blooded
Eskimos except Johnie who has quarter white blood.

SCHOOL: Clara Carpenter, the teacher, is at the extreme right in the back row. In the center of the back row is Agorak, a grandmother. Her son, Willie, is directly in front of her, while her granddaughter, Mary, is in front of Willie.

the children put on splendid programs of acting and recitation at the Pioneer Hall, to which practically every person in the region came. The old white sourdoughs were almost as elated at the performance of these little Eskimo children as if they were their own, while the children's own parents sat in the front row, listening proudly to what many of them could not even understand.

The children were very enthusiastic about their teacher, Clara Carpenter. She had been in Wiseman for three years and in that time had established herself on terms of great intimacy in their lives. They came calling in her cabin at all hours, and it was considered a great privilege by the younger girls to be allowed to sleep with her. The older girls she taught much in the line of sewing, cooking, and general housekeeping. She played with all of the children, gave them cookies, joked with them, and distributed presents at Christmas. She did not have the slightest trace of snobbery nor was she in the least patronizing.

A few of her notions about teaching are interesting. She says: "I try to teach them to be independent and able to do things for themselves. If you just teach them facts that's not going to do them much good, but if you teach them how to use a dictionary that will help them all their lives.

"I like to teach them by games so that they don't know that they're learning facts but just having a good time. I teach them manners and health rules by giving them rhymes to learn.

"I don't believe in criticizing the children if they do poorly, but I praise them if they do well. When Willie and Oscar are up front together reading, and Willie is all jiggling around, I don't say: 'Stand up, Willie,' but, 'I like the way Oscar is standing.' Then Willie always stands perfectly straight.

"My most severe punishment is to have them stand on the floor or stay in their seat at recess. Whipping a child would be the last punishment I'd ever give him. Sometimes I talk to them, but never scold them. When they've done wrong they know they've done wrong, and it makes them feel badly without me saying anything.

"I find it on the whole easier to get along with these children than those Outside. They haven't got the background for doing things like throwing spitballs which the children Outside had. Then I could start right in with most of these children right at the beginning and teach them the way I liked. But of course it made it harder because they haven't had any discipline at all at home. They're much more eager to learn than children Outside because they haven't so many extraneous attractions. One reason I think they like to come to school so much is that their home environment is rather messy and they like the neatness of school.

"Some of them said I shouldn't allow the children to talk Eskimo in the school yard, but I never could see why. It's no use for them to forget their own language and culture just because they're learning a new one."

PART V

THE SEXUAL LIFE

XXVI

MARRIAGE

IN THE Koyukuk, where there are eighty men and only twenty-two women, it is obvious that marriage cannot play any very large part in the life of the community as a whole. Nevertheless, I will devote this chapter to discussing such marriage as does exist.

The marital history of the seventy white men in the region may be summarized in the following table:

Marital Condition		Number of Men
Married at some time		27
Living with wife	10	
Divorced	9	
Wife dead	6	
Separated from wife	2	
Never married		43

In the United States sixty per cent of the men, fifteen years of age and over, are married at present. In the Koyukuk only seventeen per cent are married. In the United States only thirty-four per cent of the men have never been married, in the Koyukuk sixty-one per cent have never been joined in wedlock.

Of the twenty-seven white men in the region who have

been wedded at some time, sixteen were married since coming to Alaska. Ten of these are still living with their wives.
Not a single one of the eleven men who were married when
they came to the North is married now, four having lost
their wives through death and seven through divorce. Most
of these divorced women never tried to follow their husbands
to Alaska, but the few who did found the life too severe and
too different from everything to which they were accustomed.
The following story typifies the experiences of these men.

Breakfast was over and we were waiting for the dishwater
to heat. We were seated in George's little cabin where he
had just finished reading me an original poem about a man
who had found Alaska but lost a wife in the process. He took
off his glasses, a look of mingled pride and inquiry on his
face.

"Gee, that's fine, George," I said, "that's simply swell. I
like especially those lines—over here—'The devil's deep voice
called me and damned if I could resist.' "

George's wrinkled face was all smiles.

"That's the part Mrs. Pingel didn't like at all, but it's the
truest lines in the whole poem. Of course you understand
that poem hasn't nothing to do with me really, and there's
a lot in there that isn't just so for any one. A person has to
change things a little to put them in poetry. But I'm a telling
you, Bob, Alaska's broken up more lives than any God damn
place in the world. There's Wod Perkins and James Long
and myself and God Almighty only knows how many thousands more in here lost their homes by coming to Alaska.
Of course I've had some awfully good times in here, but if
I never came in I'd probably have a small fortune, and I'd
have a wife yet and most likely children and something to
look forward to. My brother and his wife lived together forty

years, and he told me they never had let anything unpleasant pass between them in all that time, and I don't
know why it would have been any different with us."

George got off the bed where he was sitting and went over
to the wall. There was a badly faded picture hung there by
a pin. He removed the pin and handed me the yellowish
picture. It was of a woman sitting competently on horseback,
a broad hat on her head, a confident expression on her face.

"That's the woman that was my wife," George explained.
"She sent me that picture after I came to Dawson. She was
only sixteen when I married her, and I was thirty. I hear
some people say a man shouldn't marry a woman if she's more
than ten years younger than him, but God damn it, that's
all nonsense. Me and my wife, we were just as happy as
could be for seven years. We lived on a farm near Seattle.
My wife, she was a good one on the farm. Knew all about
everything. We had some neighbors, and they'd gone to
college, and one day when she first got there the woman
came to call on my wife. We had a young bull, and the
woman pointed to him and said:

" 'My, that's a fine cow you got; I bet you get lots of milk
from her.' "

"My wife told me about it that night, and she says: 'I've
never been to college, but at least I can tell a bull from a
cow.' "

"But I wasn't satisfied. We had to work too hard, I
thought. And then we had a baby girl, and I wanted her
nicely brought up. Well, it was late in 1897 that the reports
come in of the big strikes in the Yukon country, and I thought
all I had to do was to go to Dawson, and I could pick up a
fortune in a few weeks' time. I thought surely I'd be back
by fall, just loaded with gold. Then I was going in business

in Seattle, and it would be a much better life for my wife than on the farm.

"I left Seattle on February 14 and got to Dawson June 3. Well, I made good money right from the start. Not big money, but good money. I could have made big money too. There were two brothers, Benson was their name, and they wanted me to go into partnership with them, but I knew they were crooks, and I didn't want to mix up with them. So when Jim Benson, he was the older one, came up and says:

" 'George, you're the best mechanic in the whole Dawson country, and I want you to come in with us on 17 Below as a partner,' why then I says:

" 'You God damn dirty crook, I wouldn't work with you and your brother if you gave me the whole of the Klondike.'

"So I walked away, and that next summer they took $140,-000 from that ground. But I went ahead and did nicely, only you see how it was, I didn't want to go home until I'd made a real stake, $50,000, I set for myself. I would have made it too in a year or so. And then one day, about three years after I came to Dawson, I got a letter from a lawyer, and he said my wife was suing me for divorce on the grounds of desertion and that I should come back if I wanted to defend myself.

"Well, I got so God damn mad I tore the letter up, and I never answered the letter, and I didn't write to my wife again for better than fifteen years. But it really wasn't her fault, after all. I found that out years later. There was a bunch of bastards came back from Dawson to Seattle, and they went to my wife and filled her up with the God damnedest pack of lies you ever heard tell of. Told her I was living with another woman and that I was drunk all the time, and I don't know what all they didn't tell her. There wasn't a God damn word of truth in anything they said, but you know some people aren't ever happy unless they're stirring up trouble. But of course my wife had no way of knowing it wasn't so, and then there was the mail. Why, they'd think on the Outside you could write a letter and get an answer inside a week, and maybe it would be a year before I ever got her letter, and maybe I wouldn't get it at all. Why, when I was building my boat on Lake Bennett in the spring of '98 there'd be fellows would come around, and they'd tell you they was going out in a week, and if you had any letters to send Outside to have them ready in a week, and they'd take them out to the post-office at Skagway for a dollar a letter. Well, maybe they would, and maybe they'd just take them up the trail a couple of miles and bury them in the snow, and they might be $10,000 to the good. That was the way our mail worked in those days. So you can't tell, some of my letters might have gone that way, and she never heard of me, and with all those lies they gave her it wasn't her fault, and it wasn't my fault neither.

"Well, I commenced going with the sports then, not much, you understand, because I still expected to make a fortune and come back and shake it in her face. And then I'd take my little daughter back with me. She was seven years old then, and she used to write me letters all the time. She had a beautiful handwriting too, I'm a-telling you."

George got up and unpinned another faded picture from the log wall of his cabin.

"This was her. She was seven years old when this was taken, and a few weeks later she was drownded. Well, I never felt so terrible in all my whole life. Nothing seemed to amount to anything any more. I just went crazy. Yes, Bob, I'd be a rich man to-day if she hadn't died. But I'd been thinking ever since my wife left me that every cent I made would be for my girl's benefit, and when she died I just couldn't stand the thought of money no more. I just couldn't get rid of it fast enough. Why, I'm a-telling you, I gave away fifty dollar bills right out in the streets of Dawson.

"I'd always gambled a little, but now I spent all my time a-gambling, and I hoped I'd lose too. I went with the prostitutes every night. Only I never went crazy like some of the boys and paid them a thousand dollars just because they asked me. I've gone to bed with more God damn women than any man in all Alaska, I guess, but I never paid them more than their price. But they all liked me just as much as if I'd given them a fortune. I used to haul wood in Dawson right down the row, and there wasn't a one who wouldn't come out and smile at me. When I was out to Anchorage in 1923 I went into a restaurant with Sam Dubin and Murray. All of a sudden a woman came and threw herself around my neck and pulled me one side to the counter and kissed and kissed me. She said to Murray and Dubin:

" 'I never thought I'd see this man again. He's the best dancer ever come into this North country. We were pals together in Dawson twenty-five years ago.'

"And me not knowing her from a man only for the clothes she wore. But she told me her name was Sweet Marie, and I kind of remembered her name. When I got ready to pay she wouldn't take a cent of my money but she took Dubin's and Murray's.

" 'You don't spend a cent in here to-day, boy,' " she said.

"But there were hundreds of more like her. Some of the best-looking women I ever saw in my life were in those old dancehalls. When Dawson was at its height you could go into a dancehall and find a hundred beautiful young women whom you'd have to travel days and days and days to find their equal Outside. A woman who wasn't good looking, she just couldn't make a living, that's all. They were a pretty hard, cold-blooded lot, but they had some wonderful points at that. Take the Oregon Mare, for instance. Why when they had that flu epidemic in Fairbanks she worked night and day nursing people who wouldn't even look at her when they got better. Aunt Kate—she was a wonderful singer, you know—she used to offer her services free for the charitable entertainments in Dawson. She married Pantages, you know, and set him up in the show business, and then when he got independent he treated her like I wouldn't treat a bitch dog. She used to come to me—you know how a woman sort of seems to like to confide in some one when she's in trouble— and she told me all about this Pantages."

George stopped, and for perhaps a minute there wasn't a sound except his deep breathing and puffing on his pipe. Then he got up and knocked out the ashes.

"George," I queried, "have you ever met your wife again in all these years?"

George had started walking toward the stove, but he wheeled around.

"Well, I guess I have. I was riding in a street car in Seattle along First Avenue when I was out in 1917, and I saw a woman on the street wave at me. I started to get off, but she motioned me not to, so I stayed on. I thought probably she'd made a mistake, you know, and took me for somebody else.

"A few days later I was walking along Pike Street and looking into a store window when a lady comes from behind and grabs my arm. She says: 'Do you know me?'

"Well, I was just about to tell her if I wanted any prostitutes I knew where to go to find them and she needn't try to pick me up, when all at once I recognized it was my wife.

" 'Will you talk with me?' she says.

" 'Certainly,' I says.

"So I took her into a moving picture show where we could sit and talk together quietly, and she told me the whole story I was a-telling you about the lies that was told her and her never getting any letters from me. She was married again, but she hadn't no children. She wanted me to come and meet her husband, but I wouldn't do that. She said he was a fine man, but if she was on her deathbed I know she'd call for me. There's something comes between a man and woman when they've lived together, I don't care under what circumstances they separate, that never passes away."

The fundamental tenet of the Eskimos' sexual belief is that marriage should last only so long as there is mutual desire for it to persist. As soon as either partner wishes to suspend the relationship they simply separate. Since they have no such thing as an official marriage, it is unnecessary to bother about anything like a legal divorce. Of course, many Eskimo couples have been living together for years without any thought of separating. But if the desire does arise, each one can go his or her own way without further concern.

When there are children separations are less simple. Under such circumstances the other Eskimos frequently bring all sorts of suasion to bear on the one who is responsible for breaking the partnership. But if that person refuses to listen there is nothing which can be done to stop him or her from leaving. I have described this fact already in the story of Annie Kayak.

There is a sequel which is needed to complete that story. After a few months of living alone Annie discovered she could not support her two little children comfortably on the small amount of money she made taking in laundry, so she gave one of them away to Big Charlie and Bessie who, with only one grown daughter to support, had long desired a baby.

Although the whites have swung over strongly toward the Eskimo notion of marriage by mutual consent, although most of them are enthusiastic about the modern Russian and Swedish divorce laws, and although the majority thoroughly approve of the principle of companionate marriage, nevertheless many find it hard to tolerate this giving away of children. One of these men made this comment concerning Annie's donation: "It kind of gave me the creeps the other night when Bessie brought over that little baby. She was carrying it on her back, and Annie came up and kissed it, and then she went away and started laughing and joking. Not much feeling of motherhood there. I tell you, it made me feel funny, I just can't explain how."

If it has been hard for the whites to get used to some of the Eskimo marital customs, it has been equally difficult for the Eskimos to become accustomed to the white ways. In the very early days of contact between the two races some rather amusing difficulties occurred. Most of the Eskimos are very fond of ceremonies, so when they discovered the white ritual of marriage, with a large gathering to witness proceedings and an important man to say solemn words and a lot of writing put down in a big book, it seemed ever so much finer than the primitive Eskimo method of just living together. Consequently, when Binnayuk and Kitty decided to live with one another, they thought it would be splendid to get things done in the white way. A few years later when they wanted to split it did not seem so splendid. However, Binnayuk went up to the commissioner, Judge Howard, and told him he wanted a divorce. Judge Howard was noted for his cutting of red tape, so in good frontier spirit he simply tore the record of marriage from the official book and tossed it in the stove. But Binnayuk was not satisfied. "Me want divorce," he insisted. "You've got your divorce!" exclaimed Judge Howard. "What more do you want?" Binnayuk apologized, but he was very firm in explaining that what he wanted was the return of his $2.50 marriage fee.

Gradually, over the years, such misconceptions have vanished, and to-day most of the Eskimos understand the white man's marriage code as well as the white men themselves. They make numerous observant comments upon it, some of which seem worth repeating as being illustrative of general Eskimo viewpoints.

Forcing children to marry is very wrong. It was attempted last year at Wiseman, so one girl went out of her way to condemn it. "I can't see how any people can be crazy enough to force children to marry some one they don't love. If my parents ever tried to make me marry some one I didn't want I'd leave home right away. It's nobody's business except the two who are going to be married."

As a matter of fact, there is only one circumstance under which marriage is justified. "Anybody can get along if they love each other, but if they don't it's no good to get married at all."

The attempt, so prevalent among the white men, to marry an Eskimo girl thirty or forty years younger is roundly condemned. "Old man, young girl marry, no good. He wants sleep all time, she wants dance all time, they can't be happy that way. Young man, young girl marry, they have same laughs together, same jokes, same troubles, same happy, same everything, then they get along fine all the time."

In spite of the advent of the white culture with its custom of relatively late marriage, the Eskimos still consider that marriage is in order for girls any time after they have been sexually mature for at least one year. The Eskimo age of maturing seems to be about twelve or thirteen years. Consequently, though it sounded a trifle amusing to me, it was a matter of dead earnestness to an Eskimo girl of eighteen when she sighed: "I'm getting so old I don't think I'll ever get married."

There was one Eskimo man in camp who was a confirmed cynic regarding marriage. I should interject the fact that he was married once when he was sixteen and once when he was twenty, but he beat both wives so badly that they left him. Time has mellowed him into a kindly gentleman, but his early misdeeds still hang over him after twenty-five years, so that if you ask any of the Eskimo girls why they don't marry him the prompt reply will be: "Oh, he was married already, and he treated his wives terribly." Consequently, he seems doomed to a permanent bachelorhood which he rationalizes into a voluntary singleness by denunciations such as this:

"Too much trouble get married. You too much tied down, you no free, you always got kid coming, can't do nothing. Woman watch you all the time, you just like in jail. No good. Young man no good get married. All right when you get fifty maybe, but no good young man. Young kids get married together all same cat, scratching and fighting together all time. White people, native—all the same."

The attitude of the whites toward intermarriage is varied. A handful of the less tolerant people in the region hold views similar to the following: "I'd admire a man who rapes them, but I certainly look down on a man who marries one." There are quite a number who believe that from a genetic standpoint intermarriage is harmful alike to both races. "I won't ever marry a Siwash," says one of these. "I think they're just as fine people as we are, it isn't that, but I don't believe in mixing the breeds." A great many hold that the only serious obstacle to intermarriage is incompatibility of interests. Others claim it would be splendid to marry an Eskimo if one intended to spend the remainder of his life in the Koyukuk, but that it would be ruinous to do so if one ever expected to settle Outside. One of these admitted: "If I'd known when I came here how many years I'd spend in these black log cabins I'd have taken a squaw long ago."

There is one man who, although he is over fifty, is one of the most popular white men among the Eskimo girls. He could easily get a wife, but he refuses to marry one of them for still another reason. "I always feel," he says, "what have I got to give one of them fifteen-year-old chickens if I marry them. I'm their inferior in every way. I can't dance like they can, I don't understand their jokes, I'm not interested in hardly any of the things that interest them, I'm not attractive like they are. Christ, what they enjoy doing is getting out and sliding down one of these snowbanks. That's fine, and they ought to do it, instead of getting tied down to an old man."

The Eskimo attitude toward marriage with the whites is generally favorable, which is especially interesting in view of the fact that they frown very severely on intermarriage with the Indians. There are a few of the old people who prefer to see Eskimos marry Eskimos, but most of the elders are much influenced by the economic advantage of having their children marry the relatively wealthy whites. As for the children, they are tremendously eager to wed white men. It is a much easier life to have a permanent home all the year round than to have to spend half the year in a nomadic existence, hunting the caribou and moose and sheep.

Nevertheless, every white man does not suit these girls. As a matter of fact there only are nine or ten of the whites whom any of the six unmarried girls around Wiseman would even consider. The others were all too old, too stupid, too often drunk, too lazy, too selfish, or too dishonest to be approved. Most of the especially desired white men are relatively young fellows who expect some day to return to the United States, and consequently they do not want to become entangled in marriage with an Eskimo girl who would probably cause considerable discrimination in the outside world. Thus, a temporary impasse to marital developments has been reached, with Eskimo girls not willing to marry the white men who desire them, and white men not willing to marry the Eskimo girls who desire them.

When a white man actually is married to a native he seems to suffer practically no loss in social prestige. Even people who themselves would not think of marrying an Eskimo generally regard the matter as purely a personal one. Actually, the president of the Wiseman Igloo of the Pioneers of Alaska, most honorary elective post in the community, was married to an Eskimo girl.

There have been a total of fifteen intermarriages in the upper Koyukuk. Of these, four were terminated by divorce, three by death, while eight are still continuing. This seems to be nearly as high a percentage of lasting marriages as the records of whites married to whites, and an infinitely higher record than that of the white marriages made before the men left for Alaska.

Although there is a high proportion of sterility among Eskimo women, some of them are exceedingly fertile. Several methods to avoid the responsibility of children have been tried. One of these is abortion. However, on the frontier with its crude surgical equipment and training, this is a hazardous matter. One young Eskimo girl nearly lost her life in this manner about ten years ago, and she received permanent internal injuries. Her experience was taken so seriously that no abortions have since been attempted.

Before contact with the whites the Eskimos frequently practiced infanticide on superfluous babies. But the whites have never countenanced that practice. There have been rumors of the clandestine extermination of new born babies, but if true such cases are so rare as to be insignificant.

Theoretically, the easiest solution would be to prevent the problem of unwanted babies from arriving at all by having recourse to contraception. I believe that in the entire region there is only one white person, a very pious and sincere Catholic, who is opposed to birth control. Most of the whites are vociferously in favor of it and quite profanely denunciatory of all those who fight the dissemination of its knowledge. Nevertheless, the Eskimos almost uniformly regard it as nonsense. They have practically without exception been informed about it, but those who have attempted to practice it have had either poor instruction or inadequate equipment or both, and it has proved for them a consistent failure.

However, I am perhaps stressing too strongly the efforts to get away from children. There are many of the whites who are much more concerned by the fact that they have never had any. "My God," says one of these, "you know it ain't natural for a man to think of being snuffed out without having any children. It's just as if he'd never been on earth."

Another man conceives of children as the only binding factor in marriage. He says: "If a man marries an honest woman and they love each other and have children they should get on very well. Without the children they might get on together, but there is nothing to bind them."

A third is far more emphatic. "What's the use for man get married if he have no children? I never want to get married unless I get woman can bear me children. I might just as well keep dog as keep woman if she no will have children. Best one in the world, I wouldn't take her if I knew nature fixed it so she wouldn't have kids. If I no can have kid I don't want to get married at all. If you have kid there's part of you keeps living after you're dead so you not altogether gone. It's just like planting the seeds from the old plant and it lives again. I think I give anything in the world if I could have nice, clean, decent woman for wife, and she bear me a few kids."

XXVII

PROMISCUITY AND TABOOS

BOTH Eskimos and whites in the Koyukuk have long been accustomed to consider promiscuity as the normal sexual relationship.

The Eskimos have never believed that a person should be confined in sexual intercourse to one individual of the opposite sex. Occasional copulation with another man or woman meets no objection from one's partner unless it becomes a regular habit. One Eskimo woman phrased this concept quaintly to a Wiseman sourdough when she told him: "Any time, anybody, one time, that's all, any time." Often a couple will discuss together a prospective extra-marital coitus before it occurs. I know of one girl whose only condition was that her husband must not have intercourse with old women. This, she felt, would be a reflection on her own attractiveness. When the man expects to be away on a long hunting expedition he will sometimes encourage his wife to have intercourse in his absence so long as she tells him about it on his return. But if he first finds it out from some one else there will be plenty of trouble.

Clandestine intercourse and not adultery is the great sin among the Eskimos.

Of course in practice things do not always work out quite so smoothly. There are individual Eskimos, both men and women, who are intensely jealous of their mates. But they are exceptional cases.

The Klondike stampede of 1898 probably brought six or eight white men for every white woman who came to the North country. With such a sexual unbalance it was inevitable that long-established moral standards should be demolished. Several factors aided in the ease with which this overturn was accomplished. One was that the entirely new country eliminated many features of life which had borne well-established associations with chastity. A second was that in this frontier land there were practically no old acquaintances to gossip about one's derelictions and carry the news of misdeeds to pious relatives who would be shocked by a knowledge of them. A third involved the fact that very few wives came to the North country in the early stampedes, that if a man wanted any sexual intercourse at all he was virtually forced to patronize prostitutes, and that this constant association with promiscuous people tended to make one forget the old standards of purity. A fourth was that the people attracted to the North were in general adventurers who desired varied experiences. A fifth merely involves the truism that when no taboos are erected men everywhere seem to slip into habits of promiscuity. As a result of all these factors, as well as several lesser ones, an entirely different set of moral standards was evolved by these pioneers of the North, and promiscuity became the accepted pattern of sexual behavior.

Along with the acceptance of promiscuity came also the acceptance of prostitution. "It's necessary and they ought to admit it," is the viewpoint of at least nine Koyukukers out of ten, including even the ex-missionary. The remaining tenth, even though they may oppose it, do not look down on either the prostitutes or on those who have patronized them.

This acceptance of prostitution is a theoretical attitude to-
day, because there is not a single prostitute remaining in the
Koyukuk. In the boom days of 1914, 1915, and 1916, there
were from twelve to fourteen harlots practicing in the region
continually, but when gold production fell off rapidly in the
ensuing years the prostitutes departed in such haste that by
1920 not a single one remained.

I was interested in determining just how much of a change
in the sexual life of the Koyukukers this involved. In order
to obtain some quantitative measure I secured the coöperation of three of my most intimate friends at Wiseman. These
men, so far as I could ever observe, had absolutely no sexual
inhibitions. Two of them had been among the most regular
patrons of the prostitutes, while the third had probably indulged in more sexual intercourse with the natives than any
man in the region. These were obviously people who would
speak both frankly and knowingly about the sexual life of the
community. I asked each one independently to tell me just
what sexual activity he believed the present day white men
of Wiseman indulged in now and in the boom days of prostitution in 1916. Newcomers since that time were not considered. The answers of my informants coincided in all but
eight instances, indicating a high probability of accuracy. The
following table based on their views illustrates strikingly the
change in sexual activity which the disappearance of prostitutes and the passage of fifteen years have involved:

	No. of People Leading It	
Type of Sexual Life	*1916*	*1931*
Regular sexual intercourse	26	10
Occasional sexual intercourse	14	12
Celibacy	9	27
Total	49	49

Within the span of this fifteen-year period celibacy has increased threefold while regular sexual intercourse has decreased by almost as great an amount. This means a tremendous alteration in the fundamental tenor of men's lives. One naturally wonders how these people have been able to adapt themselves to such a sweeping transformation. I will let a few of these men answer the question themselves.

One man, who had formerly been one of the most constant whorehouse patrons, remarked simply: "It's wonderful what a man can stand if he sets his mind to it." Another said: "What's a fellow going to do if he can't get it? He's just got to control his mind, that's all."

"It's this way," explains a third miner. "When a fellow gets out on the Creeks, he's so busy and has so much to be thinking about all the time that he doesn't have much chance to worry about women, especially with the hard physical labor involved. It's only when a man's mind hasn't anything to occupy it and his body's got nothing to get it tired that he can't get along without women. Of course when you see them all the time and have a chance to flirt with them, that's different."

Another man, used to regular intercourse when he is around women, has told me: "If a man can go a month without it, he can go a year. It's the first month which really is the hardship. I was a whole year up John River without ever seeing a woman. But I was working hard and never seemed to think very much about them. Of course sometimes I felt pretty passionate, but it would pass off by hard work or in a dream."

In other words, when one does not see too much of women, has hard and interesting work to occupy him, and possesses a considerable amount of will power, he can change from promiscuity to celibacy without too much misery. But there has also been another important factor involved. "You must remember that between the time the last prostitute left here and now everybody has grown a dozen years older and that makes a devil of a lot of difference." In 1916 the average age of the men under consideration was about forty years, now it is approximately fifty-five. Consequently, even though several men vigorously deny that they have noticed any diminution in sexual desire, this unquestionably has been a very important factor in the group as a whole.

When the prostitutes disappeared so abruptly, a number of the miners replaced them with native women. However, this was not a solution of the difficulty for most of the men, both because there were not nearly enough native women to go around and because the Eskimo women cannot be bought into intercourse, but will only copulate for the joy of it. In addition, the Eskimo women were exceedingly wary about going to bed with men whom they suspected of venereal disease.

It is, of course, impossible to ascertain how much masturbation has softened the transition. Judging from the unreliable basis of conversation, the great majority of Koyukukers do not masturbate regularly because it seems like an inadequate method of gratification after having experienced real intercourse. There is no moral prejudice against it, and most people feel that if it does little good it also does no harm.

It is interesting to consider psychologically those ten Wisemanites who have made the most extreme change from regular sexual indulgence to complete celibacy. Seven of these men form as cheerful, uncomplaining, self-controlled, and happy a group as I have ever known, and all but one of them rank among the most popular twenty per cent in camp. The other three men who have made this abrupt transition show symptoms of irritability and nervousness, but certainly do not seem to be suffering from any serious psychopathic disorders.

Because people generally look upon sex as something with a unique moral significance, no account of this subject would be complete without some mention of sexual prohibitions. Among the Eskimos I could only observe two common taboos. One was simply that a girl must not indulge in sexual intercourse for a whole year after she matures.

The second taboo was most surprising to me in view of the usual promiscuity of the Eskimos. It involves the subject of what the Eskimos call *dadayluk*. The Eskimos will translate this word as "child without a father." If you proceed to refer to it as "illegitimate child" they will laugh at you, for to them one of the most ridiculous of the white men's notions is that a child who has absolutely nothing to do with the circumstances under which it was born should suffer for them. As for the father, they feel that he merits no real disgrace, although he may be slightly censured. They usually remark in resignation: "Men are men." It is the mother who, in addition to bearing the baby, has also to bear the brunt of the ignominy. The old people make life just as miserable as they possibly can for the girl. They scold her, they ridicule her, they try to make her feel as if she had done the most monstrous thing in the world. The chief force back of this custom is the jealousy of the older women who can no longer have their fling and so resent the younger generation of girls sowing their wild oats. A secondary motive for this prejudice is that the older men feel that they will have to help support one extra child in lieu of the father. If the derelict girl later marries, as she almost always does, her sins are largely forgotten, and she is accepted once more as a normal member of the community. Once married, she may also indulge without foreboding in the promiscuous intercourse which is normal to Eskimo women.

The old women apparently also feel that an ounce of prevention is worth a pound of cure. They are continually trying to keep the girls on the straight and narrow path. Even without overt sins, the girls are severely rebuked by a self-appointed board of withered censors for such perfectly innocent activities as going sled riding with the more dashing miners and choosing young men in the lady's choice dances. The most critical of these guardians of morality without exception led lives of unrestrained promiscuity until they became too aged to attract men. Here is an Eskimo jingle which the older women often sing to annoy the girls when they feel they are getting too wild:

> Why did I bear that baby?
> Why did I pack him on my back?
> Why did I pack him in my stomach?
> Why bear a son without a dad?
> He cries too much.
> He is no good.
> Don't cry!
> Don't cry!
> Don't cry!

This song is also used interchangeably as a lullaby.

The fear of having fatherless children is threefold to the girls themselves. They not only dread this unmerciful censure of their elders, but also shudder at the problem of raising fatherless children and realize that a *dadayluk* would practically nullify the hope of marrying a desired white man. Consequently, much as many of them long for sexual intercourse, they indulge, except in the case of one or two who are sterile, in very little copulation. Most of the sexual intercourse which the white men have with Eskimos must be adulterously with those already married.

Among the whites the closest approximation to a sexual taboo is against rape. However, this is inclined to be more theoretical than actual. Some of the men even go so far as to doubt whether there is such a thing as genuine rape among adults. "It takes a God damn husky man to hold a woman who don't want to; it's pretty near impossible in fact," says one man. There is only one actual instance of a man being punished for rape in the Koyukuk, and he merely had to pay some money to the family of the raped girl. Nevertheless, the fear of arrest as well as the severe criticism to which the perpetrator of rape would be subjected probably scares a number of men from attempting it.

Homosexuality is looked upon with considerable disgust in the Koyukuk, but it is not outlawed. Like almost all personal conduct, it is considered to be no one's affair except the individuals who indulge in it. As a matter of fact I have only been able to find a record of six homosexuals in the entire history of the Koyukuk. Three of these committed suicide.

There has never been any definite case of incest among the whites in the region. I have heard a couple of suspected cases discussed with so little feeling that I doubt if there would be any very strong taboo, although there would certainly be plenty of gossip. I know of two mother-son incest cases among the Eskimos, neither of which seemed to have roused any great disapproval. I am not aware of any instances of the reverse type of incest.

It remains in concluding this chapter to discuss the subject of conversational taboos. Among the whites about the only one of these is that a man will seldom tell a smutty story in front of a woman unless they are alone. Otherwise there is perfectly frank discussion on all sorts of sexual matters, and risqué remarks are indulged in by both sexes.

The Eskimos among themselves have absolutely no conversational reserve in sexual matters. Among the whites many of them are quite bashful because they have been taught by missionaries that white people think it is very wrong to discuss sexual matters. However, once you come on intimate terms with them all sexual reserve is dropped, and they speak without the slightest trace of repression.

XXVIII

CHICKENS

_____

IF YOU ask any Eskimo to translate their word *nivershak*, you will be told not *girl* nor *maiden* nor even *flapper*, but *chicken*. This word as used in the Koyukuk refers to any girl over fourteen years of age who is not married or has not gone through change of life. In other words it means any girl potentially eligible for marriage. Thus, when Annie gave Itashluk that black eye and left him, she thereby punched herself back into the front ranks of chickenhood.

During 1931 there were six Koyukuk chickens, all of them living around Wiseman. One of these was a white girl who, both because she did not dance and because she carried with her various of the inhibitions of the outside world, really was not representative. Nevertheless, her cheerful home which was always open to visitors was a favorite retreat for many of the old miners who were nearly starved for even the sight of a young white woman.

But when most people thought of chickens it was of the Eskimo girls, and they certainly formed a unique group. At one and the same time they were the bitterest of enemies, the most jealous of rivals, the most helpful of allies, and the dearest of friends. I recollect once hearing Annie make one of the meanest remarks imaginable about Ashagak. Yet a couple of nights later, when Ashagak was dancing with a man whom

Annie knew that she especially liked, Annie, following the usual coöperative practice of the Wiseman chickens, replayed the record so that her friend might get a double dance with her favorite partner. A few dances later Annie was waltzing with her reigning sweetheart, when Ashagak reciprocated. Similarly, I recall one week when Ashuwaruk and Jennie were hardly speaking together. It was a rupture over an Eskimo boy of their own age, so I assumed it would be long and bitter. But it was only a short time before I encountered the two recent rivals in the most affectionate embrace, giggling uproariously, and entirely oblivious of their recent dissension.

The mutual attachment of these girls is never better illustrated than when they gang together to tease some conceited white man. Often at a dance they will pick out some vain fellow for an uproarious disillusionment. As soon as there is a lady's choice, all the girls simulate a wild scramble to get the victim for a partner. This makes him proudly imagine that he is a great favorite among the chickens. Then, when he is thoroughly puffed up, they calmly prick his bubble and let him collapse, simply by rushing after some one else. By way of illustration, here is some news which one of these chickens wrote me all the way to Baltimore:

"If Hank comes down again we are all going to try to make him go crazy. We all thought he is easy to get crazy if us girls start on him. Us three girls is getting crazy too seems like. We was going after Emerson too and nearly made him go crazy this Xmas."

How is this possible with men whom I have painted as intelligent? As a matter of fact, the most intelligent are not usually the conceited ones, and consequently they are seldom the victims of such tactics. But anyway, practically every man in the community is so undernourished sexually that any young girl assumes an abnormal importance. Furthermore, most of these particular chickens are unusually winsome. They are not the stodgy, somber, fat-looking creatures which they seem popularly to be pictured. Their clean, olive skin, their heavy, black hair, their strong chins and high cheek bones, their happy smiles and jocular humor, and their bounding vitality give to them an exuberant attractiveness which is almost irresistible to many of the frontiersmen.

But, lest any one think that I have expressed the erotic appeal of the Eskimo chicken too strongly, I will let one seasoned Koyukuker, who has lived among them for thirty years, express his opinion. He says: "You know, if you lined up five native girls on one side and five white girls on the other, and asked me to pick between them, pair by pair, which one was most attractive, I believe in four cases out of five I'd pick the native girl. I don't know what it is, but there's something about them that's tremendously appealing. And they're such a healthy-looking lot. They have fine teeth, beautiful hair, no bad breath, none of these woman's ailments, not all shot to pieces once every month. When one of them laughs she doesn't give one of those looks she's practiced in the mirror. She throws her head back and *laughs*. There's something so genuine about them. They say what they really feel and they look what they really feel. They don't put on all this affected talk and they're not ashamed to show their emotions. If they were only interested in a few of the things which interest me most and weren't so terribly extravagant, I'd marry one every time."

To talk with these charming girls as a stranger you would think that they did not know what sex was. They are very reticent about the subject until one gets to know them thoroughly. Their language in public is always exceedingly discreet and proper, and one might easily suppose they were models of chaste mental virtue. It comes to many as quite a shock to learn that they not only are thoroughly familiar with everything there is to know about sexual matters, but that among themselves, even when they are still virgins, their language might well make a lumberjack or a longshoreman envious. I know one fourteen-year-old chicken who was caught by the teacher trying to teach a five-year-old girl how to spell a highly obscene word right on the school blackboard.

The sexual emphasis in the following letter from one of the Eskimo girls is typical of at least a dozen other chickens' letters which I have read. The writer was eighteen years old, but she had never seen a white man until seven years before, and she had received only three years of schooling.

Wiseman, Alaska,
Jan. 15, 1932.

DEAR FRIEND BOB OR OOMIK.[1]

Oh, you cut them off. I received your most welcome letters this fall and a picture of yourself you sent to me from Seward. It was wonderful picture of you. Last fall Ma and I started for town on 19th of Sept. and got here on 21st. I felt as if I had a big heavy stone in my heart when they say you had left yesterday.

Gee! But if you was here to hear what a talks they are talking about us girls for liking the mechanic came in here every plane. His name is Emerson. He is awful good natured and kind and he loves flirting more than anything else. Us girls just make believe that we just crazy for him and talk to him nice just acted awful nice around him and be dancing with him whenever he comes and walk around with him. And do every thing just to make these old mens say something about it. Gee! When they start talking how wild we was over him. And second time when he come again I gave

---

[1] Oomik Polluk was my Eskimo nickname, meaning "big whiskers."

up acting so nice to him. And he ask whats makes me so blue and I told him my sweet heart was dead not long ago. And he said did you have those too before? I said yes. He ask if he could do anything to cheer me up. I said if you could get him back to life again then you'd bring me back to the world. He was just about know I was just making believe. But he just keep on joshing. When he first came when Robbins and Martin introduce me to him he ask me to sit by him so I did and he start talking to me and ask question. And I talked to him was kind to him. After little while he start talking about sweethearts in town and ask if I've been married and I didn't know what to think of him.

Finally I say I am going home. I had a bottle of gas, and told him I was in hurry with it. And he ask if he could walk home with me. And I said he didn't have to. And he just coax me. So finally I say he may. I was rather afraid of him the way he was talking to me. Beside he was stranger. So we went out and walk down store. He didn't say anything hardly, that is I didn't say anything to him. We was just about to Big Jim house when he start to ask me— And I tell him us girls up here don't believe in drinking or flirting. He said lot more and I told him to start back. And he said don't get mad. I said I will if you don't go away right now. And he said all right and make me promise that I wouldn't be mad at him at the dance that night and ask me to be sure to be at the dance. I said yes. And he started back.

Gee! I was rather shame to see him that night but I was at the dance any way. All that evening I was wondering what he was thinking about me to act like he was going to kill me. Goodness I was a bashful but I hid it all away even though I was. Ever since that time he never try to do such thing to me again. But he is awfully kind to me and to everyone. All the other girls loves him dearly. And that makes me think he didn't show them his love yet. Made me laugh every time I think how funny it was to me that is.

Emerson is awfully nice boy too. Oh! you should of be here and see how the girls talks about him and love sick for him. They have right to I think. Because every one is welcome to him. I think I am telling you too much about this mechanic. Now I am going to start talking about one more new comer.

Julius Karlson came up on Dec. 15 and he had Hank Baumann with him. That evening when they came us girls didn't see him when he came we was in school yet. And that evening we all were so anxious to go up to the dance. Soon as we have our supper we started up for Roadhouse. Annie saw him before we did and she said Gee! he's awfully cute and pretty. Looks exactly like Emerson. Get all of us girls accided still more. Mrs. Green and I were the first one that reach Roadhouse. And when we went in Billy Burke introduce us to him. Gee! we was awful disgusted after we saw him. Although we had a dance that night and he got stuck on Lucy and I at the same time. And we both hate him. We had biggest laugh at him more than we ever did laugh in our whole lives. And we treated him just as cold as we can be.

Not long after wards Julius invited us for supper at his place so we went down with him. And when he opens the door a-most-surprising-side-we-ever-did-see-there was Hank Baumann and Sally Brown in bed. We did not give them a chance to get up or straighten their clothes. Goodness! Lucy and I were so shame we just turn right out and went home and ate our supper and Julius was mad. But we couldn't do anything. They've done it already. Ha! Ha! Mrs. Brown was scared. And we told her we wouldn't tell on her if she don't talks about us. I told you because you know you and I used to talk whole lot about same things. You know these people so I don't mind telling you any news. One wonderful flirtation had showed up here now are Kaypuk [2] and

[2] Aged about 57.

Nakuchluk [3] are almost fighting over Robbins.[4] Robbins likes Nakuchluk awfully well that is for friend and just to be kind to her not falling in love with her but Kaypuk thought Robbins was going over heels over Nakuchluk. So when Robbins left here Kaypuk said Robbins want her to be sure come to the dance next time when he comes. But Robbins didn't even know who Kaypuk was. And Xmas time plane came on 24th and Robbins and Emerson stayed here for Xmas Eve Xmas night. So us girls were awful anxious to watch see which one Robbins was going to dance with most. Nakuchluk has more show again. Gee! that made Kaypuk sore. Robbins didn't even know those two old ladies were almost fighting over him that night. Ha! ha! ho! ho! Nakuchluk didn't care much but Kaypuk thought so. Too much imagination in Kaypuk's head. Ha! ha! ho! ho! Kaypuk even order a suit case by Robbins just a excuse to talk to Robby. And she even payed $40 for bringing it in. Thats some lover isn't it? Now I am going to start on other story about love. Its more like in love this time.

Seven and ⅓ Fingered Wallace [5] is living with luckiest woman that ever lived in this town to find that Seven and ⅓ Fingered Wallace. That no other woman was good enough and pretty enough to win that Seven and ⅓ Fingered man's heart. They have been together for nearly one whole month now and they are together yet. Oh! Bob. It did surely look foolish to me. You know he have been fighting her and calling her all kinds of dirty names—and she go and make in love with him. Good God! she is some lady. They don't even dance very long now a days because they are awful anxious to get to bed early. Ho! ho! ha! ha! Theres nothing like being in bed to them. I wonder how long their honey moon is going to last. I suppose till their lives ended that is the way they are enjoying them selves any way.

[3] Aged about 61. [4] An aviator.
[5] The nickname is Kaaruk's, and is based on the loss of three fingers on his right hand.

Mr. and Mrs. Seven and ⅓ Fingered are in heaven every minute and enjoyed the nights the best. Oh! Bob. What's the use of being devil while you can find your heaven as Seven and ⅓ Fingered did. They think we're in hell since they got together. Every one have big laugh out of them at one time. Gee! Bob. What in the world makes me write so long a letter as this. And I have a whole lot more to tell you.

Now to tell you about the people we've lost. First we heard Ruth Edwards died and then Bob MacIntyre and we heard Ekok's new born baby died with measles. Every one in Tanana got measles. MacIntyre died Dec. 22. It kind a deaden our Xmas that poor old Bob died. But we forget when we start dancing with Emerson. Ernie Johnson made a coffin for him. And Pa and Big Jim dig his grave. We had funeral on Sunday, 27th of Dec.

Garry was stewed in Xmas and couldn't dance Xmas night. He was dancing in Xmas Eve. He walks around town with his underclothes. And it was about 40 or more below zero too. We have 48 and 50 below zero here to-day. And we have 5 to 6 feet of snow this winter. One of these Wiseman girls going to have *dadayluk*—some time toward spring. I wouldn't mention her name. Maybe later on I will. Any how I am telling you too much. It is very impolite to talk about peoples own goods. But I wish you wouldn't mind to get this terrible crazy letter. My brains have too much to think about these days can't help telling all this news. You would know it any way if you were here.

But please remember we missed you terribly bad. I am behaving very best as I can. I am not looking for no kind of man. Because if I ever start flirting why there is no one to stop me maybe. Mens wouldn't do me any good any way. Unless I get crazy and start flirting and just spoil my reputation. I am so glad that people talks I have thousands of different sweethearts and I haven't any. All I care is that my health is not destroyed by no kind of disease like some people has. If I had been crazy enough to welcome most every man maybe I would be dead by this time. Or have all kinds of *dadayluks* by this time or some things that is most terrible bad sickness any one ever did have.

Well Bob I am getting tired and sleepy. Besides I have to write lot more letter. Please be sure to answer soon. As I am always waiting to hear from you.

Respectfully yours,

KAARUK.

P.S. We are dancing those new records you sent to Martin. That (Beside the Dutch Canal) is favorite to every one. Will close this letter after the plane come. Because I wish to tell you who comes.

Jan. 18.—Air plane 2 o'clock. Emerson and Robby. Hurray we are to have big dance to-night!!!

PART VI

THE RECREATIONAL LIFE

XXIX

WHITE CONVERSATION

THERE is nothing unusual in the fact that conversation is the most popular pastime of the Koyukuk. It is so with almost every people. But it is just because of this universal importance of talking that it is a subject worthy of special attention in the study of any community. Indeed, I would suggest that there is nothing which characterizes men so distinctly as their normal conversation when they are neither inhibited by the presence of a stranger nor stimulated by some external factor to vaunt their erudition.

In this chapter I shall analyze the talks of the white people to find what subjects they cover and what fraction of their conversation each subject occupies. I obtained my figures by actually recording the subject matter of some 5,016 minutes of ordinary conversation as it occurred in the roadhouses, at the stores, in dozens of different cabins, and even in the mines where the men were working. In making this investigation it was necessary to take several precautions. First, I myself could not take any part in the conversation, otherwise the data I was trying to study would be altered. Second, I had to be especially careful not to arouse suspicion of what I was doing, because quite obviously if people felt they were being studied they would not talk naturally. A third necessary precaution was not to include any conversations until I had ceased to be a stranger and became an accepted member of the community. With the unusual hospitality of the Koyukuk, in addition to my two months' previous visit to the region, it did not take very long to reach this stage of familiarity.

The subject matter of conversations can be divided into two fundamental classes. People can either talk about matters which have a direct connection with their own lives, or they can talk about matters which are unassociated with anything which they have directly experienced. The former might be termed personal subjects, the latter impersonal or abstract subjects. According to these two primary groupings, the division of the 5,016 minutes of white conversation for which I recorded the subject matter, was found to be:

> Personal subjects 3,539 minutes—70.6%
> Impersonal subjects 1,477 minutes—29.4%

I think it will generally be admitted that it takes a higher level of intellect to discuss impersonal than personal matters. I myself have long felt that the ratio between these two divisions of conversation would give a better index of group intelligence than any of the standard mental tests yet devised. Unfortunately, I do not know of any adequate figures for conversations in the outside world with which to compare my Koyukuk results. However, I should estimate that very few groups with which I have associated have occupied as much as 30 per cent of their colloquy with matters not directly related to their own lives and experiences.

The subjects of a personal nature I have further divided into six secondary classifications, and most of these have been subdivided again. The following table indicates just how many minutes of the 3,539 were embraced in each of these classes:

Subject		Minutes
Social activities		1088
Recreation (dancing, drinking, cards, etc.) ...	255	
Sickness, accidents, and death	184	
Sex from a personal standpoint	152	
Personal reminiscences	152	
Quarrels in the Koyukuk	105	
Laws and crime in the Koyukuk	35	
General features of Koyukuk civilization	35	
How Koyukuk life compares with the Outside	34	
Morals and ethics applied to Koyukuk problems	34	
Alaskan politics	30	
Local history	26	
Child upbringing	24	
Domestic activities	22	
Personalities		914
Gossip and opinions about acquaintances	495	
Joshing	231	
The natives	148	
Human traits unique to the Koyukuk	21	
News about acquaintances away from the Koyukuk	19	
Economic activities		880
Work (mining, hunting, gardening, etc.) ...	440	
Travel and freighting	246	
Products used in the Koyukuk	71	
The store and the roadhouse	62	
Domestic animals	61	
Scientific observations		347
Events of passing moment (weather, trail conditions, arrivals, and departures, etc.)		300
Plans for more than three months ahead.......		10

Gossip, it will be observed, takes up more of the conversation than any other subject. If there is a scarcity of truthful gossip there are quite a number of rumormongers in the Koyukuk. Most of these are not malicious, but when people are "talked out" conversation may really be splendidly enlivened by saying something like: "They tell me the schoolmarm sent a telegram to Juneau, telling the Commissioner of Education there how Kelly got one of her pupils drunk. I guess they'll make things pretty hot for Green for not doing anything about it. Of course, I don't know, but that's what they tell me."

The rumor quickly spreads throughout the community. A man, returning to his home at Nolan Creek, may stop at every cabin he passes to chat and give his version of the tale. It is discussed as an accepted fact. Feeling against the generally well-liked school teacher runs quite high for several weeks until it is discovered that she never sent any telegram at all.

A favorite type of gossip, of course, is the sexual. The most trivial happenings are often pointed to as proof positive that some man has been having clandestine intercourse with some woman. Probably in nine cases out of ten the deductions are totally erroneous. The strange thing is that even if the rumors were true no one would particularly care. It is not considered any sin in the Koyukuk to have extra-marital relations. The reason for creating such gossip is not the sadistic one of getting some person into trouble, but the detective joy in exposing the recondite.

The *scientific observations* refer not to abstract principles but to direct, personal observations, such as Ernie Johnson and Charlie Irish recalling the geography of Sixty-mile Creek, Pete Davey and Martin Slisco arguing about the geological formation of the Hammond River benches, Vaughn Green and Poss Postlethwaite discussing the coldest weather in the Koyukuk, and Rosher Creecy explaining an ingenious experiment he performed on ants.

The fact that *plans for more than three months in advance* only occupied ten minutes out of more than five thousand minutes of conversation is typical of one of the most distinctive Koyukuk traits. People live and think emphatically in the present, enjoy life while it is passing without dreaming constantly about some future happiness, and do not spend their time in futile worry about what will probably never occur. It is interesting to speculate on how much this mental characteristic of the whites has been influenced by the universal Eskimo habit of leaving the distant future almost entirely out of their considerations.

The 1,477 minutes spent on matters not directly connected with the life and experience of the talkers may be broken up into the following classifications:

Subject	*Minutes*
Abstract scientific discussions	275
Economics and government	197
Religion and philosophy	191
Sex from a factual standpoint	121
Contemporary public life in America	116
Geography	66
History	65
The arts	63
Problems of morals, ethics, and tact	60
The liquor problem	43
Racial considerations	35
Foreign affairs	34
Curious factual information	34
Stories which are not reminiscences	31
Militarism	26
Civil liberties	26

Subject	*Minutes*
Transportation and communication in the outside world	25
Human traits	24
Laws and crime	20
Etymology	15
Exploration	6
Sporting events	4

The abstract scientific discussion shows a truly surprising knowledge of the more recent advances in many different fields. Among the topics which I have listed in my notes are:

the principles on which the auto-gyro works;

how does the sun maintain its heat?;

the indestructibility of matter;

the design of the hydrogen and helium atoms;

the optical principles of the new Mount Wilson telescope;

the physics of field glasses;

the influence of different wave lengths of light on plant growth;

the cultural similarity of the natives of Lake Titicaca to the ancient Egyptians;

the possibility of high civilizations before the earliest written record;

the fossil embryo just uncovered in North Dakota;

the influence of heredity and environment;

since mutations can be tremendously stimulated by X-rays, some scientist ought to be able to build up man from slime right in the laboratory if the theory of evolution is valid.

The economic beliefs of the seventy-seven white people of the upper Koyukuk may be divided into the following major categories:

Capitalists	37
Socialists	31
Malcontents	9

I have included communists among the socialists; fascists among the capitalists. Both socialists and capitalists vary all the way from rabidly enthusiastic, thoroughly convinced, active proselytists for their faith, to very slightly interested, unconvinced, passive followers. The minimum requirements necessary for a man to be considered a socialist are that he must believe in public ownership of natural resources, the major utilities, transportation, communication, and banking. The malcontents include those who feel that capitalism has broken down entirely, but that socialism is even worse as a remedy. Several of them are anarchists. I have already given in the *Conversational Introduction* chapter copious quotations from all these viewpoints, so that no further explanation is required.

Contemporary public life in America comes in for severe strictures. "Congress passed a law that no mosquitoes could enter McKinley National Park," sarcastically exclaimed one staunch individualist. Another, expressing the common contempt for American legislators, remarked: "If a man started in and picked seventeen or eighteen ten-year-old kids and put them in the Senate, and if he took about thirty-four teething babies and put them in the House, he'd get a lot better laws passed than they're passing to-day. If they just lay off an even hundred years and not make any more laws, and then spend the next one hundred repealing the ones they've got, we'd get down to the seven cardinal sins and not have to bother about anything else."

Among the foreign affairs discussed were matters as varied as the rise of Hitlerism in Germany, the Spanish Revolution, the influence of Chinese culture on Chinese economic conditions, the iniquity of United States' interference in Central American affairs, and the likelihood of a war between Italy and France.

The Koyukuk is strongly anti-militaristic. A few feel that "it's an impossibility to stop war," but the majority condemn unmercifully everything of a military nature. Here are a few representative remarks. "These generals and admirals and senators and people who shout that they're patriots, they don't ever sacrifice a thing and get all the glory, while the poor bastards who never wanted war get blown to hell."—"Always wars are fought for something which could be settled perfectly well peacefully. There never was a war that there was any justification for fighting, to my way of looking at it."—"When you see a camp like this get along with as little trouble as it's had and no gun packing you can tell that human nature if it's not excited isn't as pugnacious as they try to claim."

The variety of thought in the Koyukuk may be further illustrated by recording the news item from the Outside which was of greatest interest to each white person for the period of 1929 and 1930. In gathering this information I made my only use of the direct oral questionnaire. I admit freely the weakness of this method, yet the drawbacks were probably minimized by the fact that I did not question any of the people until I was on terms of genuine intimacy with each individual. The following list shows the varied subjects of greatest interest:

News	Number Most Interested in It
Hard times	11
Prohibition	5
Aviation developments	5
Other mechanical developments and inventions	4
Foreign politics and economic conditions	4
Radical activities and progress	3
The Russian experiment	3
Technological unemployment	2

News	Number Most Interested in It
The corruption in American public life to-day	2
Market reports and prices	2
Medical advances	2
Effort of Eastern civilizations to overthrow imperialism	2
War preparations in Europe	1
New evidence of Allies share in World War responsibility	1
Phil La Follette's fight for governor...........	1
Revolt of the soft coal miners against the Lewis machine	1
Stock market crash	1
Failure of the Bank of the United States	1
Economic conditions on Iowa farms	1
The new tariff and its effect on overproduction ...	1
The increasing concentration of huge fortunes	1
Radio driving the phonograph industry to the wall	1
Guns and ammunition	1
U. S. Government's activities in behalf of its native races	1
The new Swedish divorce law	1
The crime wave	1
Psychological developments in the treatment of crime	1
Marion Talley quitting the opera..............	1
The racing career of Gallant Fox	1
The Byrd Expedition	1
National Geographic articles describing strange lands	1
Coin Harvey's fireproof house to preserve the records of this civilization	1
Excavations in Ur	1

News	Number Most Interested in It
The curse of Rah and its devastating effect among the Tutankhamen excavators	1
The discovery of Vitamin G	1
The new Mount Wilson telescope	1

The varied interest in the affairs of the outside world which this list and the subjects of conversation have indicated would seem unbelievable among isolated pioneers if one did not consider the reading which they do. The seventy-seven white people in the region took seventy-six different magazines in 1930, the following being most popular:

Name of Magazine	No. of Copies	Name of Magazine	No. of Copies
Alaska Weekly	8	Ladies' Home Journal	2
Literary Digest	7	Good Housekeeping .	2
National Geographic .	7	Liberty	2
Saturday Evening Post	6	Current History	2
Country Gentleman ..	5	Nation	2
Pathfinder	4	Plain Talk	2
Atlantic Monthly	4	Progressive	2
Review of Reviews ..	4	Alaska Fisherman ...	2
Harper's	3	Reader's Digest	2
Scientific American ...	3	Time	2
Outlook	3	Cosmopolitan	2
Farthest North Collegian	3	Fairbanks Daily News-Miner	2

Among the fifty-two magazines of which only one copy came to the Koyukuk were: *Asia, Christian Science Monitor, Moody Monthly, Fortune, Century, Golden Book, World's Work, Liberal, Field and Stream, Nautilus* (the New Thought journal), *Child Life, Jack O'London's*

*Weekly, Kolnische Zeitung, Belgrade Politik, Volkzeitung,
N. Y. Sunday Times, Science News Letter, Airway Age,
Theosophical Magazine, Physical Culture,* and *Toberri* (a
Finnish communist magazine). The actual circulation of these journals in the Koyukuk
was much greater than the number of copies would indicate.
For instance, Jesse Allen was the only man on Nolan Creek
who subscribed to *Harper's,* but there were probably four or
five neighbors who borrowed it from him every month. I
know that Albert Ness' *Nation* had a regular waiting list of
three, while at least an equal number borrowed every issue of
Vaughn Green's *Saturday Evening Post.*

The people of the Koyukuk also took a great interest in
a surprising variety of books. The library of the Pioneers of
Alaska contained authors varying from Marie Corelli to
Plato, and subjects as far apart as Egyptian mythology and
principles of surveying. These books were frequently borrowed and read with avidity, as were also the volumes which
I had brought to the region. There were forty white people
close enough to Wiseman to make use of my library. The
following table shows the percentage of these forty possible
readers who borrowed each of the more popular books during the first nine months they were available:

Name of Book	Author	Per Cent of Possible Readers
The Strange Death of President Harding	Means	70
Humanity Uprooted	Hindus	40
Coming of Age in Samoa	Mead	15
Erewhon	Butler	15
The Friendly Arctic	Stefansson	15
The Ordeal of Civilization	Robinson	12½
The Universe Around Us	Jeans	12½

Name of Book	Author	Per Cent of Possible Readers
Middletown	Lynd	12½
Typhoon	Conrad	12½
The Sexual Life of the Savages	Malinowski	10
Kristin Lavransdatter	Undset	7½
Is Conscience a Crime?	Thomas	7½
The Magic Mountain	Mann	5
Elements of Scientific Psychology	Dunlap	5
Social Psychology	Dunlap	5
The Dance of Life	Ellis	5
The Rise of the American Civilization	Beard	5
The Life of John Marshall ...	Beveridge	5

It was obvious from the discussions which one heard that these books were not only borrowed but also read and understood. Ernie Johnson, who read all of *Anna Karenina* and *War and Peace* in two months while he was alone on the trap line, gave me a critique of these volumes which seemed to me considerably more intelligent than much that has been published on them.

XXX

ESKIMO CONVERSATION

THERE is one serious obstacle to any study of the Eskimo
conversation. That is the Eskimo language. I myself learned
between 700 and 800 words, yet I found that barely enough
to follow even the general trend of a conversation. As for
getting any of the finer shades of meaning, it was simply out
of the question.

The reason is obvious. Stefansson estimates that the average Eskimo has between 10,000 and 15,000 words in his
every day vocabulary. Compared with this massive total a
trivial 700 words forms scarcely a drop in the bucket. But
even a large vocabulary would not eliminate the difficulty
of the frightfully complex grammar. For example, I had
worked out for myself 182 different inflexions for each
Eskimo verb. When I got down to the Congressional Library, however, I found that thirty years ago Father Barnum, who lived among the Eskimos for nine years, worked
out a 400 page syntax for their language which showed
among other things some sixty-three different grammatical
forms for the present tense alone. As to how many forms
there may be altogether in the Eskimo language, Stefansson
says: "No man has ever worked out the number of possible
different ways in which a single Eskimo verb may be used,
but it is undoubtedly up in the tens of thousands." But verbs

are only one phase of the language. Even the relatively simple nouns have each, according to Father Barnum, 252 different inflexions.

Yet I know an Eskimo who had the temerity to tell me: "English langlidge more harder than Kobuk. Lots of things no name at all my langlidge, English give him all name. Lots of little bugs, no name Kobuk, lots of names each one English."

Although, with the language limitations I have mentioned, I was able to obtain no statistical record of conversation comparable to the one procured for the whites, nevertheless I did observe in a general way some of the most frequent subjects of Eskimo conversation. Two of these which attracted an unusually large amount of notice compared with the attention they were paid by the whites were the matters of game and geography. One frequently heard long discussions of such propositions as where the caribou were, how far you might have to go at a particular time to get a sheep, or the unusual tactics which Big Jim had employed on some moose hunt on the Iniakuk twenty years before. Geography often involved detailed descriptions of all the forks of some minor drainage by a man who had thoroughly explored it. Perhaps one other man in the room might have been up the same creek, in which case he would accompany the narrative with frequent nods of the head and sounds of approval, while those unfamiliar would occasionally stop the speaker to ask specific questions.

Just as among the whites, local gossip occupies a prominent place in the conversation of the Eskimos. But bitter criticism of those of their number who are in temporary ill-repute looms out of all proportion to the representation of this subject in any other conversations I have ever heard. At the time that Itashluk was deserted almost entire eve-

nings were spent in blackening the character of Annie Kayak.
Jokes and humorous stories form an unusually large part
of the conversation of the Wiseman Eskimos. Any normal
evening in an Eskimo gathering is interrupted many times
while every one bursts into unrestrained laughter. I have
already told Big Jim's pancake story as an example of what
tickles the Eskimos' sense of humor. Sometimes a whole
evening is nothing but merriment. After Kalhabuk and Kaypuk returned last spring from a four day fishing trip to
Marion Creek they kept the former's daughters roaring
with laughter from eleven o'clock at night until three in the
morning with facetious accounts of their adventures.

At other times, however, the Eskimos are in a very serious
vein, and discuss together the whys and wherefores of life,
nature, and the world in general. Since they are in such
varied states of belief and disbelief, there is plenty of chance
for stimulating disagreement.

Finally, the Eskimos of Wiseman delight in telling and
listening to their time-honored legends, even though they
have all been narrated and heard on innumerable previous
occasions.

Much of the Eskimo conversation is now conducted in
English. All but three of the fifty natives speak that language with varying degrees of proficiency. Even the older
ones, who were already mature when they first came to live
among the white people, have learned to speak a broken
English. Nevertheless, their command of the language has
never been adequate to avoid many rather amusing mis-
understandings. As an example, one of the prospectors tells
the following story. He had camped for the night on the
bank of the Koyukuk, and was just cooking his supper when
an Indian woman known as Hog River Annie walked up.

"Have some supper with me," said the man cordially.

"No," replied Annie.

"Well, have some of my tea anyway."

"Thank you," said Annie firmly. "I don't want your tea. I have two babies already."

Such ludicrous instances, due to lack of a common language, worked both ways. Some of the whites tried to speak Eskimo, and in addition to the normal difficulties of the language the Eskimos gayly made matters worse by telling the white people the wrong words, just to get a good laugh. Many years ago one of the white freighters was trying to climb the steep river bank at Alatna. He was having a difficult time until Old Lady Tobuk came down and gave him a hand. When he got on top he tried to say "thank you," but they had fooled him, and what he really remarked was: "I want to marry you." She got furious and replied: "You dirty old thing, I'll push you down the hill again."

When Nutirwik first came to live among the whites nearly thirty years ago he decided he wanted a white name. *Nutirwik* meaning Blizzard, the whites suggested the name Snowden to him, and Harry Snowden he became. While I was up in Wiseman, Harry used to dictate letters for me to write to his friends and relatives in other parts of the Arctic. Here is one:

DEAR OKPIK:

I going to send over to you one caribou skin, you want it. The mail come in that time, I'm hunting above, want to send him in by mail but I'm not there. I kill him no caribou skins this summer only four. I got one left right now, I going to send him over to you.

I like to hear you send me letter. Anything you need, I get it, you get it. You tell me about it letter my brother die. Glad you tell me, sorry he die. Who come over from Kobuk which you hear my brother die? You get him letter? Somebody come over?

I go hunting but no luck at all. Got him one moose, kill him, go out 21 days, awful time.

Man and wife name Johnnie, Oxadak boy, come over from Arctic, two children, one girl, one boy. Arctic side says they're lots of caribou, lots of sheep, lots of them.

Where you got along with you children? You got along all right?

From your friend,

HARRY SNOWDEN.

When I read this letter back to Harry he exclaimed in admiration: "Jesus Christ, you write him letter pretty good! You got the fine education!"

On the other hand, those Eskimos who came as children to live among the whites have picked up the English language with amazing alacrity. In November, 1930, four-year-old Johnnie arrived in Wiseman, having migrated with his parents from the Arctic Coast. Up to that time he had never heard a word of English. For about two months he seemed to be lost, and then all of a sudden one commenced to hear unexpected English phrases from his lips. In September, 1931, shortly before I left, Johnnie was visiting in my cabin early one morning. I had one volume of Beveridge's *Life of John Marshall* on my desk and the other in the bookcase. Johnnie took the book on the table and placed it beside the one in the case, remarking: "I'm going to put him where his partner is." Being quite busy that morning, I had shortly to say: "Good-by, Johnnie." Now I used to take my laundry down to Johnnie's mother, so Johnnie's rejoinder was: "Good-by. Come again when you have some more dirty clothes."

In one respect it is remarkable that these children ever

learn to speak correct English. For many of the Eskimos who already know the language delight as much in teaching the newcomers the wrong English words as they do in teaching the whites wrong Eskimo phrases. "When I first came over," said Kaaruk, "Harry Snowden tried to job me and get me to say all sorts of dirty things to the whites. I would have said some awful things if I had not too much sense."

In order to give a more consecutive notion of the type of dialogue in which these young people indulge I shall conclude this chapter with a verbatim reproduction of the conversation of three Eskimo girls as they sat outside Ekok's cabin on a sunny afternoon in June.

Dishoo—Isn't it funny Edythe has gotten so terribly lazy you say. She used to do lots of work when she was up here.

Ekok—Yes, she sit down and talk how she used to work up here.

Kaaruk—But she don't do anything any more at all hardly. I remember one time we go out berry picking together with the kids. I pick and pick and pretty soon I have my pail all full. Then I look to see how much she has done but she did not even pick one berry. She said she had awful time with the kids. When she's home she will tell me she is going to cook supper this time, and first thing I know she is lying down on the bed and she says she has awful headache. The only work she can do is run after that Theodore.

Dishoo—Theodore? Why I thought he was only a kid.

Ekok—He is. He is only seventeen and she is twenty-five and has four children. But that doesn't stop her. When that fellow comes she'd go crazy. She'd run after him and he'd run after her.

Kaaruk—And how she dressed up for him. It wasn't enough that she must wear a clean dress all the time when he was around. It would have to be a new dress. Then she would forget she had it on and lie down on the bed, and first thing it was all crumpled, and she would be too lazy to wash it so she would burn it up. Every time she got her dress dirty she burned it up and then she cry until Henry give her money to buy new one.

Ekok—Some days when that boy is away she does not get up at all. Two or three times last spring she sleep twenty-four hours. We tell her she's going to die she sleep so much, but she just start in to cry. She never smiles not even once at all when that kid is away.

Kaaruk—I talk and laugh and talk and laugh and try to cheer her up, but she's sad all the time until that kid comes around and then she's all smile and happy and silly as can be.

Ekok—Sometimes she had an awful temper. You couldn't hardly get near her.

Kaaruk—She'd get mad and throw things around, throw the kids here and there, and one time I think of that lady who live in the shoe, and I have to run out I laugh so hard.

Ekok—And then what was worst of all she never hardly used to wash her hair at all. If she wash her hair every week it's all right, but she goes months and months without washing it and it's awful.

Kaaruk—When the wind blows if I'm way over there I can smell her. I want to take a boat and go across the river.

Ekok—I wish there was some way she would know how terrible it is. You cannot tell her at all. She ought to be changed to a trout and then she would have to be washed all the time.

Dishoo—Didn't she know how much you were joking about her?

Ekok—No. She was too stupid to understand anything about it at all. Sometimes Cora used to put on the record which says "she combs her hair but once a year," and then lots of time Kaaruk and Cora and I would all be laughing, and she'd laugh without knowing what we was laughing at, and we'd be laughing at her, and she'd be laughing at herself.

Kaaruk—But worst of all is how lazy she is (*pausing and laughing*). And here I am, and all I want to do is dance, and now I talk about how that lady down there won't work.

Dishoo—Wouldn't it be nice if we could all be born again and be something that we wouldn't ever have to work.

Kaaruk—I'd like to be grass, it's so pretty and has nothing to worry about, but then horses would eat me up.

Dishoo—I'd like to be little bird, they're so happy.

Kaaruk—Yes, but big bird would eat you up.

Dishoo—No matter what you are, they're always big bird try to eat you up.

XXXI

DANCING

A HOLIDAY in the Koyukuk has two principal attributes. It involves a general assemblage of the people of the region and it involves a dance. On Thanksgiving, Christmas, and New Year's it involves in addition a certain amount of gorging. But as for any original significance which the holiday once possessed, that has largely disappeared.

The matter of assemblage has an importance in Wiseman out of all proportion to its moment in any of the more heavily populated regions. The diggings centering around this Koyukuk metropolis are so widely scattered, the extreme distance between Jack Rooney's hole at Big Lake and Dutch Henry's sniping on the South Fork being over seventy miles, that many men who have been in the country for over a quarter of a century have never even visited their friends' operations. Without some general congregation one would rapidly lose contact with most of one's fellowmen. But by these periodic gatherings of the citizens from all over the hills the gregarious instincts of the Koyukukers are assuaged, and this geographically scattered community becomes socially a most closely knit organization.

There were eleven major dances at the Pioneer Hall during the year I was in the Koyukuk. They occurred on each of the eight major holidays: Election Day, Thanksgiving,

Christmas Eve, New Year's Eve, Washington's Birthday, St. Patrick's Day, the School Picnic (when school is over for the year), and Fourth of July. In addition there were big dances Christmas night, just before the spring breakup, and on the occasion of one farewell party. The following figures are averages for all of the eleven big dances:

Time of beginning	8.20 P.M.
Time of ending	7.15 A.M.
Length of dance	10 hrs. 55 min.
Number of men dancing at height of celebration	20
Number of women dancing at height of celebration	11
Total number of dancers at height of celebration	31
Total number of dancers at 3 A.M.	26
Total number of dancers at end of dance ..	16

The longest dance, on Fourth of July, commenced at 6.40 in the afternoon and lasted until 11.00 the next morning.

While the big dances were the most spectacular, they were very much in the minority compared with the smaller affairs which were held at the roadhouse on 159 different nights during the course of the year. These varied in formality from the unpremeditated dancing which might ensue any evening a couple of Eskimo girls happened to drop in at the roadhouse, to several celebrations which brought out most of the people in town when the mail arrived, an airplane pilot spent the night at Wiseman, or some well-liked person arrived or was about to depart. Such dances generally broke up by twelve or one o'clock, often with much encouragement from the sleepy roadhouse man, but on New Year's Night it was three o'clock before the party disbanded. The music was supplied by the roadhouse phonograph and records, many of the latter also doing service at the dances in the Pioneer Hall.

Since there is so much similarity between the different holidays, I shall describe the first one in detail to serve as a sample for all. As much as a week before Election Day the first man drifted in to Wiseman, and from then on by ones and twos and threes they came, many of the nearer ones not until the day of voting. In town they grouped together and discussed many matters, but it was interesting to observe that the subject of most animated conversation was their work.

By Election Day most of the fellows had started their holes, and there was eager inquiry and recital in regard to what sort of digging was encountered, how deep it was going to be to bed rock, how the hole lay with reference to the position of the river channel in the geologic age when the gold was deposited, whether it would be necessary to use timbers. There was discussion of how the gold might have washed down, different geologic theories being expressed and sometimes sharply contested, and reasons were advanced why such a spot should be just as good as one 300 feet away where $80,000 had been taken out.

Voting took place at the Pioneer Hall. The polls opened at 8 o'clock in the morning and closed at 7 o'clock at night. There were three judges: Harry Foley, a Republican because his father had been a Democrat; George Eaton, a Democrat because he and Jim Ham Lewis had years ago been delegates to the same Democratic state convention in Washington; and Albert Ness, a Socialist because he never could see how a person could be anything else. The voters straggled in all day long, and there was much good-natured banter between themselves and the judges. The most important election was for territorial representative to Congress, but nobody took the voting seriously, and I think the general sentiment was well expressed by the following random remarks:

"Whatever way the vote goes, things will be just the same as ever on the Koyukuk when it's all over and the world will keep turning once in twenty-four hours."

"Whichever one's elected, we know both of them ought to be in jail."

After the polls closed and the votes were counted there was a meeting of that most democratic fraternal order, Igloo No. 8, Pioneers of Alaska. Strangely enough, it opened with a ritualistic prayer in spite of the fact that not more than one or two of the twenty men present believed at all in the efficacy of supplication. Thereafter, the secretary read the minutes of the last meeting, gave an elaborate financial report, and read two letters received recently from old timers who had left the region many years before. The members then discussed the matter of sending a complaint to the Post Office Department about the wretched summer mail service of the past year. The secretary was instructed to write the third assistant postmaster. After that some minor repairs in the Pioneer Hall were approved, and the session ended as it had begun with a formal prayer.

About half of the men left the hall when the meeting was over, while the remainder waited for the dance to commence. After a few minutes there was a stamping of feet on the steps leading up to the ante-room in the rear of the hall, and a moment later three Eskimo girls entered, followed by a cloud of snow. The girls wore fur parkies, and in strange contrast had their feet covered with zippered overshoes. They had kerchiefs covering the tops of their heads and tied under their chins. They took off these outer garments in a leisurely way, revealing beneath fresh cotton print dresses, cotton

THE NEW YEAR'S EVE DANCE: The man in the center is old George Eaton who at 70 is still generally regarded as the best dancer in the Koyukuk.

MIDNIGHT SUPPER: In spite of the flags, the Wiseman roadhouse is decked to celebrate the advent of 1931 and not the Fourth of July.

stockings, and most beautifully beaded moccasins. As soon as they entered the main room of the hall, which was about twenty-five by forty feet and perhaps fifteen feet high in the center, one of the men went over to a large orthophonic phonograph and turned on the record *Bye, Bye, Blackbird.* He then walked up to one of the girls and asked politely: "May I have this dance, Lucy?" The girl smiled and promptly rose, and they swung gayly into the rhythm of the fox-trot. Meanwhile, two other men had garnered the remaining girls, and the dance was on.

The hall filled rapidly with men, women, and children, who sat on the benches around three sides of the room, the women against the south wall, the men on the north and east, and the children anywhere when they sat down at all. The west side was occupied by the phonograph on a low platform, a large, iron heater into which frequent chunks of wood were fed, and the door into the ante-room. By eleven o'clock the crowd was at its height with nineteen men and eleven women dancing, as well as some eleven additional adults merely watching and chatting. Every one of the fifteen children in camp was at the hall, and most of them were racing around, playing tag, shouting, and constantly slipping under the dancers' feet. The babies under three had fallen asleep by this time, and were laid out on the benches in the ante-room where they would not get in their dancing mothers' way.

With twice as many men as women, the males had a relatively easy time, for they had a rest on the average of one dance in two. They spent this leisure sitting along the side of the hall, chatting with each other, and occasionally shouting some jocular remark to those on the floor. The women, however, had no rest at all. The men even followed them out to the ante-room to get them to dance. Often when an especially good tune was being played almost every masculine dancer would jump up. There would be a great dash for the youngest and prettiest girls, a lesser rush for the older women, and a good-natured trek back to the north wall for those who had lost out. On the whole the men were very fair about dividing the available women, and few there were who tried to get more than their share of dancing, a self-restraint which was not entirely altruistic since rest was a pleasant diversion in the long night. The way the women were able to do without any rest during the ten hours which this dance lasted was one of the greatest marvels of stamina I had ever witnessed. But I was inexperienced then and thought ten hours constituted a long dance.

There was something pleasantly exotic in watching the dancers glide along the smooth, spruce floor with their whole preoccupation in having an exuberant time. The unpretentious dresses of the women, and the prevalent flannel shirts and overalls of the men fitted ideally with the simple good humor which pervaded the entire hall. Three out of every four people were smiling broadly as they moved rhythmically past, and loud chuckles and giggles frequently rose above the music of the phonograph. They did not dance for social prestige, for show, for duty. They danced because it was the greatest joy in the world at that precise moment. "I could dance if I didn't have any leg at all," said little Ashuwaruk with a wrenched ankle. "I could dance if I was dying."

As one looked around the floor it was amazing at first to see the number of elderly dancers. Three of the Eskimo women were between fifty and sixty. The one white woman was well along in the forties. Among the men seven were over sixty, and three of these were in the seventies. One fellow in the latter class told me: "What little joy a man has in life, he'd be a fool to ever miss a dance. I'd like to

dance till about ten o'clock in the morning. That's the way
to get the most out of life."

The dances, in contrast to the Outside, were delightfully
varied. The standard fox-trots and waltzes, though most
numerous, were only a beginning. The old two-step, with
its almost unlimited opportunity for the display of energy,
was romped through in joyful abandon to the tune of many
a stirring march. There were Circle City two-steps, heel-and-
toe polkas, highland flings, several complex schottisches, and
one Virginia reel. Several times during the evening the hall
rang to the commands of the square dance. "Honor your
partners right and left and don't forget the opposite lady.
All join hands and circle to the right clear around the hall."
And dozens of other similar orders followed each other in
rapid succession.

Some time during the course of the evening the local
talent was called upon to perform. Bob MacIntyre sang the
songs he had been preparing for weeks. Floyd Hyde and
Frank Miller each followed with a vocal solo. Roy King
then obliged with a humorous dialogue; Jennie Suckik, after
much coy refusing, danced the Charleston; and Minnie Wilson responded with a vigorous piece on the piano. It was all
impromptu, except for Bob's painfully rehearsed arias.

Old Bob MacIntyre fancied that with a little training he
could have surpassed Caruso as a singer. In spite of this
optimism, one of his friends told me: "I'm awful fond of
music, but I'd sooner some one give me a good, swift kick
than to have to hear Old Bob sing." This attitude was shared
by almost every one in camp. Nevertheless, as another man
said: "We all know he's terrible, and it's an agony to have
to listen to him, but the poor old fellow gets more happiness
out of those solos of his than anything else in life, so I guess
it's worth ten minutes of our suffering a few times a year

to give the old boy his fun." Consequently, he was always called upon for a recital to which he joyfully responded with such songs as the *Gay Caballero. The Little Black Mustache,* and *Only a Pansy Blossom,* while all around the hall people were grimacing, unknown to him, and choking down laughter.

At about midnight Big Jim jumped up at the close of one of the fox-trots and said in a loud voice: "Now our turn." At this the whites all clapped, and everybody around me whispered what I already knew, that they were going to stage a Kobuk dance. Six of the older Eskimo women, who had been dancing the white dances continuously since ten, filed out to the dressing room. Jim sat down by his big bass drum which had been sent him from Outside, and Harry Snowden, Jonas, Riluk, and Oxadak sat on either side of him.

Then Jim started beating the drum, lightly at first, while he and the other four men sang together a song which in the beginning sounded like nothing but cacophony. Fairly soon, however, I began to notice a strange rhythm, and the sense of discord vanished. In perfect time to the rhythm Nakuchluk, Utoyak, Kaypuk, Agorak, Kalhabuk, and Selina entered the room, all dressed in their most magnificent parkies. They swayed back and forth to the music, arms waving gracefully in slow motion. They formed a semicircle on the floor around the men who were now singing louder than ever as Jim kept beating the drum harder and harder. Suddenly Harry got up and went through the wildest gyrations, jumped up and down, threw his arms from side to side, twisted his body, and emitted the most dismal yells, which constantly increased in fervor as did the entire dance. But everything here, too, was done in perfect time to Big Jim's beating and singing. Indeed, they all followed Jim as carefully as an orchestra would follow its conductor. After Harry was through Riluk jumped up and danced, and then Jonas, and then Harry returned again. In all the variety of contortions through which the three men went, they consistently kept their bodies in cubistic shapes, the arms and legs as they jumped around being held either straight or at right angles, but never in curves. The women, on the other hand, kept always in harmonious curves as they swayed back and forth, going through a violent muscle dance.

At about one o'clock the roadhouse man announced that the midnight luncheon was ready. Every one slipped on overshoes, several donned their parkies, and under the cold splendor of the aurora all trudged through the snow to partake of the meal at the roadhouse. This consisted of sandwiches, cake, and coffee, for which fifty cents a person was charged. At the table it was delightful to note the heterogeneous nature of the group. In the picture which I have reproduced of just such a feast the people seated haphazardly around the table include in order an old Eskimo woman who cannot speak a word of English, a Montenegrin, two Iowa Methodists, two Eskimos, a Swede, an Eskimo, an Irishman, an Eskimo, an Indian, a Canadian, a Dalmatian, a Pennsylvanian, a Michigan Irishman, a Herzogovinian, a Finn, a half-breed Eskimo-Indian girl, an Ohio boy, an Eskimo girl, and a Norwegian. Among those varied races there was not the slightest trace of discomfort, but only joyous jocularity and wholesome appetites.

After about three-quarters of an hour of feasting and rest the majority of the dancers returned to the hall. Most of the people who had merely been watching retired, and several of the younger children were put to bed. This left more room in the hall, and it seemed to stimulate the dancers to increased vigor. At three o'clock some twenty-two people still survived, including all of the women. Shortly after this hour the less energetic commenced to drop out, but the resulting survival of the fittest seemed to increase the speed of the dance to new heights. Men and women whirled through fox-trots and waltzes and two-steps with a celerity and *élan* wonderful to behold. By five the women commenced to taunt the men good-naturedly that they were playing out, and the men reciprocated the slander. About this time the two sides of the hall lost their sexual distinction, and men went to sit among the women between the dances as well as women among the men. By six o'clock almost every one began to appear sleepy, but no one wanted to give up. There was an adventuresome joy in lasting out to the end. At seven, just ten hours after it commenced, the dance was finally adjourned by general consent. Exactly half of the original thirty dancers were still on the floor, and this number included all three of the old men over seventy.

The breakfast at the roadhouse was an all-masculine affair at which the dance survivors were joined by half a dozen men who had been engaged in an all-night poker session. The biggest loser had only dropped twenty dollars. After breakfast several of the men lay down for a few hours' sleep. Those who were working on the nearby creeks returned in the afternoon; the more distant miners waited a day or two before departing. I think practically all agreed with one of their number who remarked: "Even if you do get all worn out, it's a diversion that sure breaks you out of your rut. After such a recreation you don't mind going back and working like hell till next month."

XXXII

THE ARTS

THE SUM total of the creative artistic efforts of the white people of the Koyukuk includes several sincere but undistinguished oil paintings of both landscapes and portraits; one paper-covered book of reminiscences, with numerous flowery passages, which is ridiculed by almost every person in the region; and a number of attempts at verse.

The best of the latter was one facetious poem written by an anonymous author many years ago. It formed a sort of epic of the Koyukuk, replete with the quaint local slang, and was boomed out by many an inebriate voice in the old saloons and whorehouses. Here is how it went:

Come all you jolly snipers[1] *and listen unto me,*
A story I will sing to you, with me you will agree,
About a jolly sniper who never did have luck,
Who fooled around for forty years in the good old Koyukuk.

An easy kind of a going man with a sort of a swindling smile,
Who worked a hunch on a North Fork gulch that went a
      penny a mile.
And every fall he had his gall his hard luck to lament,
How the heavy rains washed out his drains so he couldn't
   make a cent.

[1] A sniper is one who reworks old mining ground.

He has told me his hard luck stories of how he near starved and died,
On his empty guts he had frozen his nuts crossing a high divide;
How he and his dog got lost in a fog at the head of Buncombe Slough,
And how he went broke losing a poke paddling his own canoe.

He never would keep sober whenever he came to town
For he was a charter member of the good old Slap-her-down,
And the first rule of that order was to always drink your fill.
He was so conscientious that he never paid a bill.

He'd poled up every river and he'd panned on every bar,
He'd been in every mining camp from Nome to Chandalar,
You could tell by a glance at his caribou pants he'd been out in the hills for years,
And the dirt on his face was a howling disgrace, it had only been washed by tears.

One day he cursed the Koyukuk from the head clear to the mouth,
He cursed it East, he cursed it West, he cursed it North and South.
"I'm leaving for a country where the wealth is yet untold,
Where there are no laws and there's lots of squaws, I'll hunt for sunburned gold."

So the last time that I saw him was on the Arctic slope;
He was bound for the MacKenzie, primed with gall and hope;
A great big pack was on his back, consisting of bacon and beans,
While the legs of a goose and a big chunk of moose were slung to the seat of his jeans.

At last I heard he hit it rich at the head of the Swan-uk-tuk,
But he fell ill and pined away, he could not survive his luck.
He wrote his friends before he died: "I bid you all adieu.
Put a pick and a gold pan in my grave and a brand new
    Number 2." ²

He sent a spirit message back that he was doing well,
He'd started in a-sniping on the high old rims of Hell,
But there it's all dry washing, for it never rains or snows,
But there ain't no damn mosquitoes and a cold wind never
    blows.

The Devil was quite angry, thought it was a great disgrace
That a man should be contented while stopping at his place,
But when he found that forty years he'd roamed the Koyukuk
He said: "You had your Hell on earth," and wished him
    better luck.

In a semi-creative way, five or six men play somewhat crudely on the violin. They say it is a great help in maintaining spirits when one is living alone, and that it helps particularly to cheer one during the long nights. One woman plays the piano of which there are two in Wiseman, both relics of the old saloon days.

By far the greatest share of the white enjoyment of the arts is in a non-creative rôle. I have already discussed how eagerly the people of the Koyukuk read many of the great works of literature. Their enjoyment of pictorial art hardly keeps pace. Most of the cabins in the region have pictures on the wall, but I did not see a single picture which was better than a colored print, a newspaper or magazine clipping, or a photograph. The colored prints were mostly very commonplace, having generally been received as advertisements, cal-

² The Number 2 shovel was the one almost universally used by these miners.

endar illustrations, or religious society propaganda, although
a few were bought. Of course there are some famous repro-
ductions, such as the Mona Lisa. The most frequently encountered picture, found in about one out of every five cabins,
is of a wolf howling above a sleeping, snowbound settlement.
The most common types of pictures are: first, girls; and second, western mountain scenery.

It was in listening to phonographic music that the Koyukukers received their chief artistic diversion. About one out
of every three homes had a phonograph, and those who were
without such instrument frequently enjoyed the concerts
of their neighbors, or if stopping in town visited the roadhouse to play its semi-public machine. The records in the
region numbered well into the thousands, including many
which dated back to the days when only one side of a disc
was used. The favorite records reproduce sentimental songs,
humorous songs, and especially dance music.

There were also eight or ten out of the seventy-seven
white people in the region who were genuinely enthusiastic
about the classical music. One of them remarked, after hearing the *Gymnopedie:* "Oh, it's wonderful, but it doesn't
mean anything to use such a word. It reminds me of climbing a hill in Germany and getting a big panorama with
woods and run-down farms and all those old castles crum-
bling to ruins." A second said to me: "I don't see how anybody can like any music better than one of the symphonies.
You just can't help yourself, it carries you right away, while
I believe you have to cultivate a taste for sentimental songs
and jazz. But they never can begin to stir every emotion
like that music you just played [Schubert's *Unfinished Symphony*]." Old Carl Frank, after listening to the *Ride of the
Valkyries,* said simply: "Music like that I could listen to

forever. It puts something there in my mind above everything else in the world."

But these were minority viewpoints. About the same *Ride of the Valkyries*, Vaughn Green said: "I suppose some people call that music, but it's just a lot of noises to me. What is there about that you could call musical, tell me that? What's it called? Oh, I supposed it would have some high-sounding name like that."

Here are a few additional remarks gathered from people not over-appreciative of the classics:

Following Beethoven's *Eighth Symphony*—"I know it must be very fine if a person's trained to it, but it's above my head."

Following Schubert's *Unfinished Symphony*—"Play that *Springtime in the Rockies* now. That's the most beautiful music I've heard in a long time."

Following Liszt's *Hungarian Rhapsody*—"It reminds me of the picture shows at home."

The Eskimos were on the whole more appreciative of the classics than were the whites. Ravel's *Bolero*, which in many ways resembled their own music, aroused unbounded enthusiasm. I will never forget the first time I played this piece for Harry Snowden. He had previously sat through half a dozen popular songs with the most complete lack of expression on his face that I can imagine in a human being. His high cheekbones, his protruding lips, his half-closed eyes, his completely immobile countenance might have been a model for some painting of the god of boredom. Then timorously I tried the *Bolero*, and almost at the first notes Harry was completely transformed. He broke into a broad grin and said with great feeling: "That's good, Bob." A little later he muttered: "Gee, that's fine music." At the end he was in ecstasy and exclaimed:

"Gee, isn't there a lot of playing, isn't there a lot of music going on there! Play it again, Bob!"

One October night, a few weeks later, I was stopping at the abandoned village of Coldfoot. Just at dusk I walked out across the snow to the point where Slate Creek joins the Koyukuk. Upstream it was almost dark, and even with snow on them the mountains which hemmed the river as far as one could see looked black. But downstream to the southwest the twilight persisted for a long time. Twelvemile Mountain stood out black and clear against it, the deep valley of the Middle Fork to its left, the brightest of the orange sunset sky to its right. I kept looking around up- and down-stream, watching the darkness creep down from the north and the stars come out, watching the orange fade slowly in the south. All the while, as an accompaniment to what was passing before my eyes, the wind and the unfrozen waters of Slate Creek were putting on a symphony, sometimes rising to a great crescendo, sometimes dying down so that I could hear nothing but the unending, but constantly varying, rushing of the water. It reminded me of the drum undertone which runs through the entire *Bolero*, never the same at any two instants, but still exactly the same throughout the whole composition. All at once it occurred to me why the Eskimos were so enthusiastic about the *Bolero*. Because the *Bolero* is a perfect counterpart of the music they have heard from earliest childhood out in the wilderness of the North. The drums are the rivers rumbling unvaryingly, and the rest of the orchestra is the wind howling, the ice cracking, snow-slides coming down the mountains, rocks tumbling over one another, the wild animals howling. It represents to the natives all the chaotic music of nature in its wildest moments.

Like the white men, the Eskimos delight too in much non-classical music. However, the sentimental songs have relatively little appeal to them. It is in the rhythm of the dance music that they find their greatest joy. I have never seen an Eskimo who did not have an exceptionally well-developed sense of rhythm, and this they satisfy not only in their own dancing and singing, but also in all the music to which they can possibly listen. It is interesting to note that an even higher percentage of Eskimos than whites have phonographs.

Like the white men also, the Eskimos go in for pictorial ornamentation on their walls, whether in cabin or igloo. The esthetic urge which governs their selection is sometimes a trifle difficult to comprehend. One old Eskimo who had got religion from the missionaries had tacked on the wall of his cabin pictures of one tiger, two bears, Abraham, and Jesus. Here is the strange collection on the inside of an igloo:

Dr. Peters, health commissioner of Cincinnati;

Two colored furniture advertisements of luxurious city rooms;

Three pictures of orchestras; and

A humpty-dumpty cartoon;

all clipped from magazines.

It is, however, in creative art that the Eskimos are really distinguished from the whites. First of all, they put a great deal of esthetic endeavor into their clothing. Their parkies have different colors of skin pieced together in simple but alluring patterns. Some of their beadwork on moccasins and gloves is beautiful. Conventionalized flowers and leaves are always used for their designs which are less complex than those of the Indians farther south, but to my mind especially attractive for this very element of simplicity.

All of the younger Eskimo children, as I have mentioned in the chapter on intelligence, have better than normal ability at drawing with paper and pencil. One fourteen-year-old girl, Jennie Suckik, manifests a genuine talent which shows both imagination and a splendid sense of humor. Three of her sketches are reproduced in this book.

The greatest creative artistic efforts of the Eskimos are devoted to their songs. These include love songs, dance songs, narrative songs, moral songs, and nonsense songs. Of the latter there are many. Big Jim once explained them to me by this simile: "Just like telegraph, sometimes he sings, means nothing." Here is an example of the words of one, commonly recited while juggling small stones:

> *"There's a big seagull*
> *And I was afraid the mother*
> *Might swallow me or chew me*
> *And my tears are running."*

The origin of such a song may have been ritualistic when these people's ancestors lived on the coast, but to-day it has no more meaning than "Ring-around-a-Rosie" to the white people.

The Eskimos around Wiseman had about half a dozen dance songs of which the following was the music of the one they used most commonly:

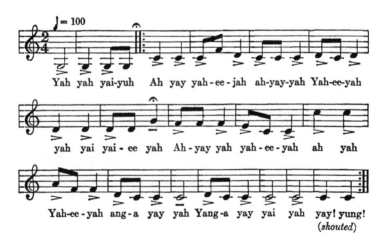

The sounds shown with the notes are meaningless, being equivalent to our tra-la-la-la which we often hum to familiar tunes. After one round with these yays and yahs and the like, words are substituted here and there as they fit with the rhythm, until after several more stanzas a whole song is completed. The following is an English translation of one which Bíg Jim made up for the Christmas celebration, being a sort of an Eskimo Christmas carol:

> *I am lonesome,*
> *I want to feel better.*
> *I want to warm myself,*
> *So I go to Wiseman.*
> *I go.*
> *All of us go.*
> *All of us sing.*
> *My arms aren't washed.*
> *Take my arm in the dance.*
> *Shake my hand in the dance.*
> *Christmas comes pretty soon.*
> *Roadhouse man,*
> *Busy all the time.*
> *Every one drinks coffee.*

These songs were hummed by both men and women at their work. The girls, however, were not content to hum merely the songs which some one else wrote. There is hardly an Eskimo woman in the entire region who has not composed her own songs as well. These always take the form of love songs, which however are not sung to the men for whom they are composed but to other women who can sympathize with the singer. And sympathy the singer surely needs, for every love song I have heard has celebrated some unrequited passion.

I should mention here that the translations of all the songs I shall quote were made by two Eskimo girls, though none of the compositions were their own. You can rarely get a love song from the woman who makes it up. You have to approach some friend who has listened to it repeatedly.

Here is a song written by a married girl who was momentarily and desperately in love with a boy several years younger than herself. The boy liked her, but was not sufficiently enamored to try to get her to leave her husband.

> *You're a crazy kid,*
> *And I'll never forget what you said.*
> *I'll love you always*
> *And want to see you always,*
> *You kid.*

As sung in Eskimo, the song has these words and this tune:

There is one lyric to commemorate a wholesale jilting bee. It seems that five Kobuk boys had gone over to the Koyukuk and remained, leaving behind them five heartbroken maidens

Drawings by Jennie Suckik.

JENNIE SUCKIK: The artist of the preceeding pictures is a splendid axeman and can outchop most of the men in the Koyukuk.

with nothing but memories and voices which they put to this use:

> Well, such crazy boys as you are,
> Leave us here and make us lonely,
> Go to Koyukuk, so far off.
> But if you ever come back here
> You'll be tied up here forever.
> Such crazy, crazy kids.
> Why did you say such foolish words?
> Oh, but we want to see you boys.

Some fifteen years ago one of the Coldfoot Eskimo women, then about forty-five years old and living with her third husband, fell violently in love with a good-for-nothing white man named Harry Horton. All that interested this fellow was the amount of sexual intercourse he could get from the Eskimo, who, since she copulated exclusively for love, was much cheaper than a prostitute. In order to be assured of her affections as long as he wanted intercourse this Harry Horton kept telling her he would marry her when his summer's work of freighting on the river was finished. She believed him implicitly, and composed the following song to relieve her loneliness:

Darling darling Harry Horton,
Why do you always leave me alone in this big house?
I always miss you at night time.
You know that I miss you more than any other men, darling
*   darling.*
Why don't you stay here with me and quit working on the
*   scow, darling darling?*
We have enough money to live on, darling darling Harry
*   Horton.*
Quit your work and come to me and we'll have fun.
I am lonesome without you and wishing you were here with
*   me, darling darling Harry Horton.*

Why did you start working on that old scow, darling darling
  Harry Horton?
When you're not around it seems there is nobody around
  here, darling darling Harry Horton.
I wish we have little baby boy, look exactly like you, darling
  darling Harry.
I would be so happy when I started to pack around our own
  baby boy, darling darling Harry Horton.
Come on, come on, darling darling Harry Horton,
Come on here to Coldfoot and live with me, darling darling
  Harry Horton.
I can't sleep when you're not around, darling darling,
Because you've promised me that you're going to marry me,
  darling darling Harry Horton.

But Darling Darling Harry Horton, when his summer's
work was finished, departed for the Yukon without ever
even saying good-by to his expectant bride. When she realized what had happened she composed this final plaintive
lament:

Darling darling Harry Horton,
Why did I say yes to you, darling?
When you wanted to —— me I said:
"Yes, darling, darling, darling."

Come on! Come on!
I wish we were —— now, darling Harry.
Oh, my, oh, my, I want you, darling.
We used to —— together every night when you were around
  here,
Darling, darling, darling.

Why don't you live with me?
Come on! Come on!
There's lots of room for you in my house.
You could have anything you want if you only live with me,
Darling, darling, darling.

PART VII

KOYUKUK PHILOSOPHY

✹ XXXIII ✹

THE HISTORY OF THE WORLD

WE WERE sitting together on the bank of the Alatna on a
hot afternoon in July.

"Human life is different than any animal that ever lived,"
Old Tobuk was telling me through the interpretation of his
son, Jimmie. "We shall see another life after we leave this
one, though I don't know where. A leaf falls to the ground
but another leaf grows, and he never dies forever. He never
forgets his life; he lives the same way next year. Lots of
people think that man dies, but he does not die, he lives again,
goes same way like the leaf.

"One time I dreamed a man come and lay down right
alongside me. I wanted to see him, I wanted to hear him,
but I could hardly hear him, hardly turn my head to see
him. He was only about two feet high. Maybe that's what
we are really like when we die.

"The nature that we see is all simple, if we have no one
to try to mix us up. But lots of people think they know just
how everything works, and they try to make us believe that
no one else is right. All of those different missionaries—
Episcopal, Quakers, Catholic, Methodist, Baptist—all tell
different stories. There can't none of them be right except
one. Perhaps not that many. I wonder which? They do good
things for people when they're sick, but they teach people

things that make them crazy. Their life is working against each other. Maybe there's one good judgment that we should follow, but how do we know which?

"Everybody's all the same as one. We are nature and we should live according to nature. Nature never hurts us if we live its way. What suffering comes to us we make ourselves. Nobody else will make it for us. We suffer for our own mistakes. That's the way the world was made. If the sun falls down some day as the missionaries say and the natives believe, we won't suffer unless we make it fall itself.

"When we're young we hear an old man say something and we don't give a damn. I never paid no attention to what no man said. I always lived my own life myself. My mouth has always been open and I say just what I feel. I am not a medicine man and I'm not supposed to be, but my grandfather and great-grandfather were great medicine men. They know many things we don't see. But I don't adopt anything from their life. All I know is through my brain. I see lots of things now that I'm old man that I didn't expect to see, and young men don't believe me. But young men should be that way: only believe what they sees through their brain.

"Now that I'm old man this is what I think. Maybe you think I'm wrong, but maybe when you are old man you'll think I'm right. The life that we live is all the same as play. All the same as if we go out and run race. If we win it's all right and if we don't win it's all right too.

"I believe in nature. I believe in all I see nature do. I see a tree grow with sunlight and water and dirt, and I believe that. I see my grandchild grow too, and I believe that. But I don't believe stories old Eskimos tell, and I don't believe Bible stories that tell the lessons either.

"I know my own life. I know you. I know white people. I know natives. I see and I can tell you about them, but I don't believe any of the stories old men tell about what I don't see."

This philosophy of Old Tobuk shows clearly the three major influences which to-day affect at least to some extent the belief of every Eskimo in the region. These motivations are the original legends of the Eskimos, the recently acquired teachings of the missionaries, and that independent thought which affects the faith of all human beings.

The Eskimos differ greatly in their attitude toward their traditional legends. Certain stories have unquestionably influenced every Eskimo, but their feelings are as varied toward these tales as are the feelings of ordinary American citizens toward the Bible. There are a few of the Koyukuk Eskimos who are fundamentalists and actually believe that the myths are literally true. A number believe that parts are true and parts are merely allegorical. Probably the majority do not take them to be the literal truth at all, but have a sentimental fondness for them as a part of the tradition of their people. Finally, there are several ardent atheists who regard all the legends as pure nonsense, and repeat them, if at all, with an accompaniment of satirical comments.

In the following pages I shall present some of these tales in the exact English words which these Koyukuk Eskimos themselves used in telling me their stories.

"Nobody," said Old Tobuk, "knows how the world started. After the start Eskimo people have it same way whites— man made first. The first man live all alone. One man alone cannot increase so they got to have pair. That's why nature made woman. But woman is not enough unless she can bear child. They tried all over where nature could find that child could come from. They try forehead—no good. They try breasts—no good. They try under arm—no good. They try between legs—O.K. Nature finally invented right place and then man do the rest.

"Nobody will ever know what nature was like then. It was not written and no story was ever handed down. Nobody know who made man and woman and who made little worm. Nature started in the beginning, but nobody know who started nature. Nature must be greater than we if we cannot figure how nature started.

"Man start first, then woman. The male was the nature in the beginning. Nature and the man all the same. But woman was the hardest to make."

Now I will let Tobuk's daughter, Ekok, continue the narrative:

"It used to be dark all the time. In those days there was a village almost at the mouth of the Kobuk River. A crow was one of the people living there, and all sorts of animals and humans were all mixed together. But in the dark they thought it was all people. The crow heard some of the people crying for light, because they used to have a hard time getting their fish and making their nets and finding their wood in the dark.

"Once the crow was flying up the river, just to see what's up there, and he heard the people getting their wood saying they were tired smelling the wood or feeling it with their mouth to see if it was dry. So he kept flying up the river until almost at the head he saw an igloo, bright as can be, so he went and see what was in there. He could look through the window on the top and see a very bright ball of light inside. He could hardly look at it, it was so bright. From that light it was bright all the way around the trees, and, oh, how nice it was, and he wish he had some of it. So he start thinking of ways he could get hold of this ball of light.

"In the igloo there was an old woman and an old man named Digillibeark and a daughter living. When this girl is getting wood and packing water they open the door enough so she can see where she is working. The girl came out to pack water once again, so the crow turned to a little feather of eiderdown, and he wished that the wind would blow him toward her while she was filling her buckets. As that little thing was coming toward her she felt like drinking water, so she dip a cup of water, and she took it, and start to drink, and as she did so this thing fell in her cup of water. But she wanted the water so badly she didn't bother to take it out, but drank it right down. From then the girl started to have a baby.

"Her parents didn't know what was the matter with her and kept asking her, but she said she wasn't sick, only not feeling good. At those times they were not supposed to drink in the dark, but they were supposed to carry it into the light of the igloo and drink it, so the parents think maybe that is how she got sick. But really the crow had thought of every possible way of coming close to this ball of light, and the only one which seemed possible was to come as a baby and be loved by the grandfolks.

"Soon a baby boy was born, just as the crow wanted, and the grandfolks was surprised. The girl told them she drank water from the river once, and swallowed something down with it, and since then she started having baby. The grandfolks loved the baby very much. As he was growing older and was big enough to sit and crawl they loved him more and did everything he wanted. When he was big enough to crawl around he started crying for this ball to play with it every once in a while. The grandfather used to take it to him and let him play with it, but he always held it and watch every movement the baby make to keep him from breaking it.

"This baby used to wish for the grandfolks to turn their heads away from him so he could break the ball. So one time he wished his mother would fall down when she was going out to work so the old folks would get excited and turn their eyes away. Just as he wished, once when she was going out to work she fell down in the door and hollered, and the grandparents were terribly frightened. They turn their heads away, and old Digillibeark who was holding the ball took his hands off just for a second. In the meantime, as soon as they got their eyes away, the baby got hold of the ball. At the same time he turned back to a crow and flew up through the window on the top of the igloo and he bust the ball. Right away, as soon as he bust it, it went out everywhere and became daylight all over the world.

"The grandfolks started looking for the baby, but they couldn't find him anywhere. As they were looking they heard that crow talking. He called out, *shooshukbunga ublooshukpunga,*[1] *Digillibeark kawk kawk kawk,* three times, making fun of him, and when they look where this come from there was the crow on top of the tree. He heard his grandparents scold the girl for falling down and blaming her for their misfortune. He heard the old man saying that the girl fell down and he lost the ball of light and now it's all over and he don't know what to do. The crow hollered back at them again before he flew that he didn't come for nothing but to get the light for the world, and that there shall be some dark nights at times as well as light. And from then on there were nights and days.

[1] "I didn't come for anything except the light."

"Even after they got the light the weather was still very cold in them days. There was not enough daylight after they got used to it, and no light at all at nights. The trappers when they went out on the short fall days had a hard time traveling when they came home late in the evenings. Lots of them would get caught in the storms at night and lose their lives.

"Not very long after the crow bust the ball of light there was a family in a big town by the coast, a man and his wife and a son and a daughter. The boy was just a little older than the girl. As the boy and girl grew up this girl became very pretty and lots of men wanted to marry her. But she had no use for any of the men because she had everything she needed at home. She would only marry a man who could outrun her and beat her at playing tricks, and none of the men in that town could, so she had no use for any of them. Some men from a long ways off across the ocean heard of this girl and came to marry her, but she had no use for every man she saw. All this time there were some men her parents had picked out for her to marry, but she wouldn't marry any of them. But they cared so much for their daughter that even when she turned down the men they picked for her they wouldn't get angry.

"The Eskimos always think it's very bad if girl and man lie together for first year after girl becomes woman. They say if boy comes to girl for first year after she becomes woman the boy will die or have bad luck all the rest of his life. They used to make their girls sleep all alone by themselves during this year in a little igloo back in the woods where the men couldn't see them to want to sleep with them.

"One night while this girl was sleeping in this place, something woke her up and there was a man lying alongside of her. She didn't think nothing of it and let this man sleep with her all night. Before she woke up in the morning that man left her. That happened again with her for several nights, and every night he slept with her he would keep feeling her breasts all night long. She used to wonder who this man was because she loved him very much, but she couldn't find out because he always came to her in the night. One evening when this man comes again she began to think if she could mark him some way when she was with him at night so she could tell him when she saw him in the daytime, and maybe she would marry him. In those days the girls used to have dark blue marks put under their eyes for a whole year after they became women so the men could keep away. So she marked him on his face with this marker she had used on herself which was hard to get off. Next morning when it's daylight she was anxious to find out which man it was, and she cooked the best breakfast she could for him, and went over to the hall where every one ate together, and when she came through the door she start to look all around, and as she looked around she saw her own brother.

"She was surprised, but she took it cool all right, and brought this breakfast to him. She went home downhearted and broke into crying. At noon, when she got ready to take dinner to him, she cut off her two breasts and put them in the wooden platter with his dinner and hand the dish to him and told him: 'Here's what you've been after for several nights now.' Right after she handed him this dish she burst out crying and started for home. When she got home she grabbed her knife, and she went right back outdoors, and started running for the hills, and she thought she wouldn't stop until she died. The blood was pouring down from her breasts and that's what makes the cranberries.

"In the meantime her brother ran right out behind her and started tracking her as fast as he can. He kept tracking her, and the people from town all started behind them, tracking the two. They ran and they ran and they ran and finally they came to where the girl wasn't touching the ground much any more she was going so fast, just the tips of her toes, and her brother the same. Pretty soon they lost the tracks, they couldn't track them any more. When they couldn't follow any more they hollered to them: 'Well, be a help to the world!' Then they told the first one to be the light for the day and the second one to be the light for the night.

"And that's how they became the sun and the moon, and the moon kept on chasing the sun around and around and they're still chasing each other yet. And she kept on bleeding and her blood drops now made the stars. And the girl grew so pretty and bright you couldn't see her any more with your eyes."

For the conclusion of this history I will return to the words of Old Tobuk.

"The story is told before the flood this world was full of animals we know nothing about. These animals were some of them as big as mountains. They ate all the other animals until there was nothing else living and they had to be vegetarians. But these stories are just imagination. The story of how the light came to the world and how the sun and moon started is all imagination too. It's the way people are made. They like to have a story for everything, and if they didn't know anything to tell about it they just imagined it. They find these big bones in the ground, much bigger than any bones we have to-day, so they imagine those monsters I tell you about.

"Before these big monsters all died out there lived a man named Kayaktawingyaktawk. The Indians have story about

him too, but they call him Kitchitallikanni. This Kayaktawingyaktawk showed all the people, Indians and Eskimos, how
to make boats, snowshoes, everything they need. Nobody
knew how he died or what happened to him. He was the
greatest man who ever lived. He could hypnotize any man
who ever lived. He could be both Kobuk and Indian. Even
he can talk to ptarmigan, otter, wolverine, and become one.
He could become anything, but he acts like a human. The
world was ignorant and they don't know nothing. They kill
each other and they try to kill him but they have no chance
to get him. He can run everywhere and meet everybody.
All over Alaska everybody know him. Maybe Outside people
know him too.

"After that they have civilized people. They have their
own house and their own sled and everything people can
make. But then there comes the big flood and destroys everything. Just a few saved their lives by crawling on rafts and
boats and climbing on high mountains on the very top. Before
that the country was full of people and animals and they
were wiped out. All the big animals were drownded because
they couldn't climb on mountains.

"The Yukon Indians built a great big raft as big as an
island. They suffered lots on the raft and pretty nearly
starved before land showed up. The Eskimos didn't suffer so
much because they had good boats. They saw the flood coming so they built their boats to meet it. It didn't take long to
come, but with lots of people working they built their boats
quick.

"It was a long time they didn't see any land at all. Then
finally just one niggerhead start to come up. When the
niggerhead was just coming out of water old Toolawak [the
crow] hit it with a spear. The niggerhead bobbed back and
forth and made it so rough that some of the boats tip over

and lots of people drownded. But pretty soon all the land come up and Toolawak bring it back. Every one tried before but it didn't do any good, and then Toolawak tried and brought back the land, but maybe it was coming up, anyway. Still, Toolawak always did his best.

"This was only time that the world was flooded. That must be the same time as Noah story, but of course the story of the ark is crazy because everybody and all the animals couldn't have gotten on one boat.

"My father once found the ribs of an old boat covered with red stone paint, way up on top of the mountain. It was made of very strong wood. It must have been one of the boats they used in the flood. There was no signs of water action on it which shows it must have been left there when the flood was over. The only way to find out whether something has come before or after the flood is to see if there are signs of water action on it. The wood and bones they found on Nolan Creek, way down below the surface of the ground, were water marked and must have come before the flood.

"After the big flood the people started to increase again and got so thick they start to fight and kill each other off. They never fought before that, but now they got so thick they all learned to fight. They stopped fighting six generations ago, and they never have picked fights since then. When the Kobukers sign peace they keep their word, but other natives don't keep their word. They do lots of dirty tricks to us, but even so we don't fight.

"Now we have white government, but before government rule the Eskimos they feel things like honesty and truth and act accordingly. Now we just live according to our government, and don't feel these things so strongly."

XXXIV

MEDICINE MEN AND THE SUPERNATURAL

THE KOBUK Eskimos had no gods, but thousands of devils or spirits or *Dooneraks,* as they called them. These *Dooneraks* might be beneficent, but generally they seemed to delight in making trouble. Their jealousies and their desire to prove their strength caused no end of bother to mankind and especially to the medicine men who controlled them. For it was only a special class of people, the *anagoks* as the Eskimos call them in their own language, or the medicine men as the white people usually refer to them, who could deal directly with the *Dooneraks.* Through these spirits the medicine men were able to heal injuries, cure disease, right wrongs, get revenge, and perform many miracles to indicate their power.

I could readily write a lengthy treatise on this interrelation of medicine men and *Dooneraks,* for I have heard about it from many sources. However, I think it would be much more impressive to give Ekok's succinct account in the exact English which she used in telling the story.

"If you follow what the medicine man tells you and believe in him you will get well. The medicine man may tell you not to eat something or not to do something: he may tell you not to eat berries or certain wild meat, not to eat off birch bark dishes or wooden dishes, not to wear certain clothes from certain animals, just for a while until you get well. Always he will say not to let anybody in the house, only the person who takes care of the food and feeds you. When a man's sick he can't let any one come in the house for four days, with a woman it's five days. These four or five days are the main things that decide if you're going to get well.

"The minute you send for the medicine men they can tell you whether you will get well, and if they can't do anything for you they won't even try. I guess that's why so many people die, they lose hopes when the medicine man gives them up. In the old days I never heard of any one getting well when the medicine man wouldn't help. Of course some medicine men are stronger than others, and they may pull you through when the weaker ones fail. If a medicine man once starts to help you and you follow everything they say I never yet hear of them losing any one. But if you cross their orders you may die in a flash.

"You've got to pay the medicine man what he wants: skins, food, or anything else he asks for. If a man is broke he must borrow from his friends to pay. Money's no good, it must be skins, food, bow and arrow, spears, something like that.

"Ever since the white people came and a new generation grew up that doesn't believe in these things the medicine men have all gotten weak. Even if the old person does believe, if the children don't why the medicine man can't help the older person very much. My father prophesied a year ahead that Clara would die. He said: "If she believed me and followed my orders I could cure her, but she won't. She will go to a doctor and he can't help her, and then she will die." Every one laughed at him, and I felt ashamed of him, he acted so foolish, but she died inside of four months although she was perfectly healthy and laughing then.

"A medicine man does his work by getting *Doonerak* to help him. There are thousands of *Dooneraks* in the world. Each medicine man, if he's strong, might have twenty or thirty. My great-grandfather had the most *Dooneraks* of any man who ever lived. No *Doonerak* can serve more than one medicine man at one time, but one person can transfer his *Dooneraks* to another. When a strong medicine man dies he becomes a *Doonerak*. My great-great-grandfather became a *Doonerak* when he died and brought all his *Dooneraks* with him and helped his son, who became the most powerful medicine man ever known.

"The *Dooneraks* live somewhere else until the medicine man want them and call for them. Some live up in the air, some under the ground, some in the water. They used to be able to hear the *Dooneraks* of this great-great-grandfather of mine talking around the igloo. They would hear them talking right back of his bed when they were sitting around the igloo after supper. Every one in the house can hear *Doonerak* talking, but only the medicine man can talk to them and get them to help.

"The medicine man with the most number of *Dooneraks* can overcome any other medicine man, but if two have just the same number the one with the most powerful ones can win. But sometimes the one with the most powerful *Dooneraks* is caught by surprise and then he is overthrown.

"My great-great-grandfather died because some other medicine man overcame his *Dooneraks* when he wasn't watching. Before he died he told them to lay him out in a special way and wrap him in a covering of skins and put him on a sled. He was going this side of where the spirits go, and then he was coming back in four days. They were to build a snow house for him when he awoke and he would live there four more days without any one touching him. Then he would be perfectly all right.

"He told two persons to feel him every morning at daybreak to see if he's frozen. It was very cold weather, maybe fifty or sixty degrees below zero. He told them if he's frozen to the guts they should bury him. These two go over there every morning to see how he's getting along. The first morning just his hands and legs was frozen, the second day a little more, the third day just the stomach wasn't frozen. The fourth morning, before they came close he asked: "Is it daylight yet?" They both were astounded, but answered: "The day is breaking." He answered back: "Do not touch the cover on me. Just pull the sled by that thong and take me home." Then he told them to make a snow house away from where there were any people's tracks in the snow. They made the snow house and put him in there without touching him at all. He told them to leave him alone for four days more, not even bring him food to eat, because his *Dooneraks* were feeding him. He told them he would be among them in four days. On the fourth day he was up working with them again just like before.

"When my great-great-grandfather finally died for good he told them to dress him all in furs sewed a special way with sinews, and they must hang a brown bear skin, a black bear skin, a wolf, a wolverine, two reindeer, and fifteen marten skins inside of a great big house made of poles all leaning together. They must not put any clothes under these poles, and they must build a cache inside for the body. Every spring they go by and build a big fire right near the cache and throw in food and pieces of skins. They pay him that for him to talk and give advice what they should do. After the fire dies down he would start to talk from his coffin. The medicine men would ask all the questions they wanted to know, and he would answer just as plain as you and I talking together now. He kept that up until the missionaries came to Kotzebue, and the people start to pray instead of come to him. Then he and the skins, as soon as they stop coming, start to rot, though he and the skins had been as fresh as when he died, not even faded, and the man looked as if he had died just last night. He stayed that way for two generations, all during the life of my great-grandfather and my grandfather. In all that time there wasn't a word he ever said which didn't come true. Other medicine men tried their best to get around it but they couldn't. He proved to them all that he was the strongest of any of them, which the people hadn't wanted to believe when he was living."

There are hundreds of legends indicating the power of the medicine man. Here is a typical epic in which an heroic medicine man saved the Kobuk nation from extinction:

"Once, long time ago on Kobuk, bunch of Koyukuk people came over mountains to murder Kobukers. Made him camp at head of Kobuk River. Kobuk medicine man meet them; tell them go back home. No go back home, they say. Chase him away and try to kill him; he run away up very steep mountainside, climb cliffs so steep they no follow him, even sheep no follow him. Koyukuk people go back to igloo then, go to sleep. Bimeby in night medicine man get strong *Doonerak* to help him make medicine. Bimeby people in igloo wake up, cough up lot of blood from stomach, pretty soon all of them dead, Kobuk people all saved."

But by far the most interesting phase of these medicine men stories is the fact that the majority of them were actually witnessed by the people who recount them. They are not miracles taken on faith, but miracles which the narrators swear they have seen with their own eyes. A few of these stories are worth repeating.

One Eskimo at Alatna still remembers when he was a very little boy how his grandfather had a marten skin in the igloo. As long as the skin remained, no matter how much the family ate, the amount of food always stayed the same in the house. Then some other medicine man's *Doonerak* stole the skin and the family nearly starved.

There is a very old man at Alatna who swears that he actually saw the following incident occur. An Eskimo had just chased a caribou into Kalooluktuk Lake at the head of the Kobuk River. He took after the animal in a canoe which he had beached on the shore. All at once a tremendous fish came out of the lake and ate the caribou, and then he ate the canoe and man together. Even to-day many of the Eskimos absolutely refuse to go on that lake.

Akaylyak is very certain that he witnessed this sensational revivification when he was a little boy. He was lying in an upper bunk in the igloo and saw every motion that was made. A very powerful medicine man wanted to give a demonstration of his strength. So he took a long, moose-hide thong and looped it around his neck. Then he got two big Eskimos to pull on one end of the thong and two on the other. As the loop tightened more and more around his neck his face became all puffed up and its color turned to a horrible purple. Little Akaylyak, lying in his bunk, could hardly bear to watch, yet there was something about the whole process which fascinated him, and he could not turn his head away. Suddenly the swelling and the purple all disappeared, and a moment later the head dropped off and rolled across the floor of the igloo. Then, according to previous instructions, "they grabbed the man and laid him out on a caribou skin and set the head back on and wrap it with seal gut and put him out in the cache in front of the igloo. Pretty soon some one was talking in the cache, and it was same fellow who lost his head. Then he came in as if nothing had happened and started to beat his drum and make more medicine."

"It seems impossible, but look at some of the things you people believe Harry Houdini really did," Ekok added significantly.

The most vivid of all the tales of the supernatural was the one which Nakuchluk told me over a period of two long evenings while she and I and Kupuk sat together on the floor of her cabin. It is about the disappearance of her first husband, Peluk. I got the story about one-quarter from her Eskimo, about one-half from her English, and about one-quarter from Kupuk's graphic translations.

The whole trouble commenced one spring, some thirty-three years ago, when an unknown Eskimo, encamped on the tundra along the Arctic Coast, heaved a stone at his dogs who were barking. Now it chanced that the trajectory of this missile, instead of carrying it to the ribs of one of the canines, collided with the skull of a passing Eskimo named Mukollik. Mukollik dropped unconscious to the ground, and his loving wife, Missonik, rushed post-haste to Peluk, who was a great medicine man.

As soon as Peluk saw Mukollik he realized his case was very grave. But extraordinary conditions may sometimes be cured by extraordinary measures, so he prescribed this unusual treatment: that he, Peluk, should have sexual intercourse with Mukollik's wife. Nevertheless, Mukollik died.

Now *Doonerak* was exceedingly wroth for he did not approve of adultery with the prospective widow as a treatment for a fractured skull. So he gave Peluk to understand that he had better beware. Then Peluk explained to Nakuchluk that *Doonerak* would surely get him if she ever allowed Peluk out of her sight, that to circumvent *Doonerak* she must always follow Peluk wherever he went. Peluk also told Nakuchluk that if *Doonerak* ever did capture him he would try his best to get back, but that she must never allow any men to live with her or he could not return.

In the autumn of that year Peluk and Nakuchluk decided to try their luck on the Koyukuk. They crossed the Arctic Divide at the head of John River, and food having run short, spent some time there snaring rabbits and ptarmigan. One day they spied some caribou on the hillside a short distance above them. This was rare luck, and Peluk hastened to get his gun. He left Nakuchluk to attend to the snares, but cautioned her to keep an eye on him constantly.

She watched him mount the hill, but as he approached the caribou they started to walk away and soon disappeared behind a little hummock. He followed them, and she continued working on her snares, expecting him to reappear at any moment. But he did not. The short December day drew to a close and still no Peluk. She spent a sleepless night in their skin shelter, and at first daylight started out to hunt for him. But the wind had blown during the night, and Peluk's tracks were all covered over, so she saw not the faintest trace of him. The next day she set out again, and the next day, and the next. But all in vain. Peluk had vanished as completely as the flowers of summer.

A few days later a couple of hunters from the Arctic passed by her camp. They joined her in the hunt, and slept that night in her shelter. Next morning when they went outside they saw Peluk's fresh snowshoe tracks coming almost to the shelter, and then abruptly ending. There were no back tracks. *Doonerak* had snatched him again when he was almost to safety.

The hunters wanted her to come with them, but she refused to go. Maybe she could still find Peluk. Maybe he would try to come back again. She would stay there without a gun, living on what ptarmigan and rabbits she could snare, and hunt for Peluk every day.

"Me look round, me look round lot, me look round every day, me no find him. Me no find him at all nothing. Every morning, me wake up, me go outside, put him ear on snow, listen, maybe me hear him come. He no come. Me hear nothing, me hear nothing, only wind, only wolf howl, only ice break him. Me snare few ptarmigan, no more rabbit. Dog die, no nuff ptarmigan [for] me [and] dog. Me get pretty poor, pretty near me die too. Bimeby sun come up, pretty soon lots people come along. Me pretty glad, me so glad me forget Peluk."

Of course they came into her shelter, men and women alike, and she told them the story of her misfortunes. While they were talking they heard a sound outside like the wind, and saw a man's shadow on the snow.

" 'Ha! Peluk come home!' everybody say. Me run out, look, nobody, just black shadow. Bimeby me look again, no shadow at all, nothing. Me never see Peluk again, me never see him no more."

For a person who has not been brought up with the requisite background to be able to accept medicine man marvels in pure faith, there are several logical explanations of these stories. The most obvious, of course, is the explanation which Ekok's comment suggests, namely, that all medicine man performances are simply magicians' stunts such as one might see performed in any vaudeville on Broadway.

But this explanation does not quite account for everything. It does not stress the very important fact that from earliest childhood the Eskimo minds have been prepared to expect the supernatural, that a special, psychological receptivity has been set up for the acceptance of medicine man phenomena. If there are not occasional miracles brought out by the medicine men, then the ordinary Eskimos will provide them. A few years ago, when there were forest fires at Big Lake, several of the Eskimos imagined they saw men dancing around the flames all night. This was so real to them that when a white man, camped near by, insisted he had been right at the fire and saw no people, they interpreted this as meaning that nature had given some things for the Eskimos to see which were beyond the ken of the whites.

It is also necessary to point out that competent medicine men are exceptionally keen observers of nature. They literally know which way the wind lies, and they fit their efforts accordingly. For example, in 1922 it rained all summer and the natives begged Big William to stop the rainfall. He agreed, but warned them that if he did it would snow all the rest of the summer. The natives thought it was worth taking this chance, and told him to go ahead and stop the rain. So he went ahead and stopped it, and sure enough, just as he said, it snowed almost constantly until autumn. Of course the principle of his success was the same principle which gives every locality its old timer with an uncanny knack of predicting what the weather will do. The same familiarity with nature which makes it possible for these men to prophesy correctly with unusual frequency also plays a great part in the Eskimo medicine men's weather control.

Medicine man success in dealing with sickness depends on both close observation and the psychological condition of the person on whom the medicine man practices. The close observation makes it possible for the medicine man to tell when a case is hopeless and thus refuse to treat it. The domain of psychology is obvious from the admission of the

Eskimos themselves that if a person does not believe in the medicine man's potency he cannot be cured. It is a sort of Christian Science, a faith healing. It may also be a faith hurting, for some of the injuries the medicine men bring about are as surely due to faith in the minds of the injured that the medicine man has power over them.

Before concluding this chapter on medicine men and the supernatural, I want to mention briefly the Eskimos' beliefs about death and its aftermaths. Here again, instead of trying to mesh together in my own words the host of different accounts which I have heard, I shall employ instead this abstract which Big Charlie once gave me of Eskimo beliefs concerning the hereafter:

"Eskimos all believe when you die you spirit goes away where the sun rise in the morning. Person drown, he go to dry land where no water to drink and suffers forever and ever. If he hang himself, always hang forever and ever, wind swing him body every direction. Man gets killed, goes to moon. Man murders somebody, sinks right through ground. Other bad people too, medicine man watch, spirit go right in ground. Other not so bad people, spirit hang around grave for year maybe before go away. If man kill himself spirit hang between sunrise and earth forever. If spirit looks back when it leaves means relative die. If it looks to left woman going to die, to right man going to die. Spirit of man stay in body four day after die, spirit of woman five days."

This idea that spirits normally go upward and eastward when a person dies has an interesting corollary. The Eskimos believed that some day the spirits of the dead people would go all the way around the world and come back at last from the west. When the first whites came in boats from that direction the Eskimos became very excited. "They didn't

know what to make of them, they were so white," Ekok
has told me. "At first they thought when they were a long
way off that they were the returning spirits, but then when
they see them closer it didn't take very long to find out that
was wrong."

XXXV

CHRISTIANITY AMONG THE ESKIMOS

WHEN Big Jim was still a young man in his native Selawik country he fell under the influence of the missionaries. Their teachings became the dominant force in his life. All the complexities of nature, all the problems of how the infinitely varied world he knew came to be, all the fear-provoking superstitions, were simply resolved in a perfect faith that a beneficent God, not so different in character from Jim himself, only infinitely greater, had created the universe for the happiness of mankind. In a severe life in which young friends were continually being carried violently to death, in which beloved parents died and apparently rotted away, it was very consoling to learn that after death everybody would be reunited in an existence infinitely happier than that on earth. "Me know nothing about all this, me no know how earth come, till me learn God business. Now me learn God business, everything fine."

This "God business" has come to the upper Koyukuk from three sources. The most important one is the Episcopal mission at Allakaket, which was established in 1907 by Archdeacon Stuck and ever since has striven to convert the natives to Christianity. It has also given them medical aid and schooling, regardless of the state of their faith. It has encouraged dancing and entertainments, and has even taken the lead in the erection of a hall where the natives can meet on festive occasions. It has tried to make Christianity seem like a pleasant religion, more friendly than the old medicine man beliefs, and (with the aid of a trained nurse) more successful.

A number of the Eskimos have received their first contact with Christianity from the missions along Kotzebue Sound and the Arctic Coast. These have generally preached a much grimmer faith than is taught at Allakaket. Dancing, cards, and many other of the chief joys of Eskimo life are forbidden. Medicine men are entirely outlawed. I have been told of one very sad concomitant of this latter action. The Koyukuk Indians, taught by the more tolerant Episcopal missionaries, were never forced to give up their medicine men. One spring these decided to make all the caribou, which normally congregated in the Eskimo territory at the head of the Alatna River, leave that region and migrate to the Koyukuk. The Eskimos, having given up their faith, were powerless to influence any *Dooneraks* to stop this migration. As a result they got no meat at all during their hunting expedition of that year, and several of them died of starvation, all because they had given up the means of circumventing the *Dooneraks* of their rivals.

The third source of Koyukuk Christianity has been Mrs. Pingel, the ex-missionary who lives on Nolan Creek. Every Sunday when the Eskimos are around Wiseman, winter and summer, fair weather or storm, she trudges the six miles to town in the devoted belief that she has lessons to teach which will bring them a life of eternal bliss. Partly because they enjoy the stories and especially the singing, and partly because of Big Jim's influence, most of the Eskimos are regular attendants at the services. As a result they know Bible stories backward and forward, and can pick up Biblical references in a general conversation much more quickly than most white men of the region. As to just how much of the fundamentals of Christianity they have actually acquired, even Mrs. Pingel has enough sense of humor to be skeptical.

As a matter of fact, it is an exceedingly difficult question to answer just how seriously the Eskimos as a whole take Christianity. I imagine the missionaries at Alatna would say that at least three out of four Eskimos were sincerely converted to the faith. At the other extreme, one prospector who has lived more intimately with the Eskimos than any white man in the community tells me that he does not believe a single native in the region really believes in Christianity, not even Big Jim and Nakuchluk who pray before every meal. This man explains the seeming religious fervor of the Eskimos by the fact that they genuinely like the missionaries, that they enjoy ceremonies and consequently delight in the religious services, and that they truly desire the medical help and the schooling which the mission gives them. Being very tactful people, the Eskimos strive to avoid hurting the feelings of those who have befriended them, and consequently they feign a belief in Christianity which does not really exist.

I think this is a reasonable statement of the attitude of the majority of the Eskimos toward Christianity. They like it for the celebrations, the medical aid, the schooling, and the friends. But few of them really believe its teachings. I would not put the number quite as low as the prospector does, but I think that twenty per cent is a generous allowance for the proportion of adult Eskimos of the Koyukuk who honestly embrace Christianity.

Nevertheless, both believers and non-believers conduct a prayer meeting every Wednesday evening when Big Jim is in Wiseman. They read a prayer book which some missionary once translated into the Eskimo language, and often Big

Jim will also preach a sermon. It sometimes happens, however, that after the prayers and sermon are over these children of the Lord will indulge in great conflict. The one prayer meeting which I attended was followed by a most bitter verbal battle concerning whether the gossip of the Jonases was responsible for Itashluk becoming estranged from his wife. I observed that several of the Eskimos who appeared quite sleepy all during the prayers were roused to instant liveliness as soon as the wrangling commenced. It was not until two hours later, after Jim had made an impassioned plea that Jesus did not like them to fight, that the warlike aftermath of the prayer meeting ended.

However one may doubt the Christianity of such belligerent worshipers, of Jim's sincerity I think there can be no question. Nevertheless, it is obvious that the festive phase of Christianity is of great importance to him. "I like God business right away pretty bad," he says. "Lots of fun Christmas time." He objects strenuously to the missionaries from his native Selawik country who have tried to teach the Eskimos a puritanical religion. "Over where I come from too much God business. No dance, no sing, no smoke, no drink him black tea, no fun at all. My brother come from Selawik, tell me: 'That's bad you dance, you sing. You no go to heaven.' I tell him: 'You help him poor man, help him cheechawker,[1] you be kind to every one, you go to heaven, no matter you smoke, dance.' "

In the outside world people discuss the conflict between science and religion. In the Koyukuk Big Jim discusses the conflict between medicine man belief and Christianity. "No like him *Doonerak*, God," he says. "Jesus no like him *Doonerak*. Medicine man all right before God. Get him God, no

[1] The Alaskan vernacular for "tenderfoot." This word is usually spelled cheechawko.

want him medicine man any more. Something wrong, God he help you."

There are many of the Eskimos, however, who frankly ridicule such notions. One of them told me amid great laughing: "You can tell people Outside that white people had to get some one to save their lives [Christ], but natives know enough to save their own lives."

Sometimes these diverse viewpoints meet in heated argument. One Sunday morning Annie Kayak tried to convert the atheistic Mamie Green. Annie wanted Mamie to confess all of her sins, just as Annie had done to the minister at Point Barrow. Mamie replied that she hadn't ever committed any sins, and even if she had she didn't see why she should confess them to Annie. To this Annie answered that if Mamie didn't she would go to hell which was all made of hot rocks.

When a bad person died, Annie continued, he went to this hell. Jesus came down from heaven to investigate whether the newly arrived sinner had confessed his sins. If he had, Jesus called on the angels who were all white and had wings, and they came down and carried the person to heaven. Annie told Mamie if she confessed her sins the angels would carry her to heaven.

Mamie wanted to know how Annie got this information. Had she ever seen the angels or Jesus or hell? Annie said she knew it because the Bible said so and because the people at Point Barrow had told her. Mamie answered that the Bible was just a silly, outworn book and the people at Point Barrow old fools. She said she'd never seen Jesus or hell or known anybody who had seen them, and the only white things with wings that she knew about that could come down and take her away were the airplanes, and they would charge her $150 fare.

There are undoubtedly more Mamies than Annies in the

OLD TOBUK: "White people had to get someone to save their lives, but natives know enough to save their own lives.

BIG JIM: "I like God business right away pretty bad."

upper Koyukuk. Many of them not only do not accept Christianity, but they also reject most if not all of the medicine man beliefs of their fathers. One might well suppose that they would be in a very upset condition. Actually, however, they seem to suffer from remarkably few neuroses, and those which do disturb them seem directly traceable to sexual maladjustments rather than to spiritual worries. After all, they still retain that most fundamental of Eskimo philosophical traits, the belief that life should be taken as it comes along without any worries for the unpredictable future or any remorse for the unalterable past, but with every effort to get the maximum joy possible out of the passing moment.

XXXVI

THE RELIGION OF THE WHITES

THE RELIGION of the white people of the Koyukuk varies from the strictest fundamentalism to the most blasphemous atheism. The preponderance of opinion, however, is away from either of these extremes, in a zone of tolerant agnosticism. Only eleven of the seventy-seven white people hold any belief whatsoever in a formal religion. Out of this number, six are Catholics, four are Protestants, and one is a member of the Apostolic Faith. The remaining sixty-six whites completely disregard church affairs, supplication, worship of God, and all the other matters customarily associated with religion. Even among the eleven believers, only one Catholic, one Lutheran, one Methodist, and the member of the Apostolic Faith take their religion seriously enough to read the Bible and recite prayers regularly.

The remaining seven have no living religion at all, but merely surviving habits from the training of early childhood.

I shall present a number of remarks which illustrate far more vividly than statistics the attitude of the Koyukukers toward formal religion. These remarks are arranged in series from the most thoroughly believing to the most thoroughly disbelieving, except that I have omitted the most blasphemously anti-religious extreme.

"I never worry about anything. Everything is made simple for me just by trusting in God."

"The great theologians lay out the rules and regulations for all of us to follow, but if you got a great theologian today he'd be kicked out of his church like Norman Thomas was. Norman Thomas is greater than any man in the Presbyterian Church, but he was too good for them."

"I consider myself a Catholic, but the only reason I would observe Friday as a meatless day if I went Outside would be because I like to eat fish and it's easier to get on Friday than any other day."

"We don't know anything about God, but there can't possibly be one with a personal ego. If you want to call the laws of nature God, then I would believe in one."

"The sun's my God. You can talk about all your artificial and man-made Gods, but I'll take that old fellow every time."

"Faith doesn't amount to anything. You must find everything for yourself."

"The life a person leads, that's what counts. This getting down on your knees and wearing out your pants legs doesn't amount to very much."

"There never was a good priest or a good preacher."

"I tell you what I figure on religion since I grow big enough to think. I figure the religion's just the same as the politicians, to keep the people poor and down and slaves. Nature gives everything for everybody, and every hardship the people have they make for themselves, and it's the politicians and preachers make it most of all. It's laughable when you think. It's just like you have a dog team, and they fine all the time, and never get tangled up or fight, and then you get one old bitch in, and she fights all the time, and then your whole team gets fighting, and you don't have no peace and comfort any more at all. Well, that's just the way I figure the politicians and preachers are, like that old bitch."

"All the kids learned in the old country was this devlish religion, all about Christ and that stuff. It makes me sick just to think of it. All the heaven and hell there is comes right here on earth. When the old man got the universe going he said: 'Here it is. Now it's for you to do with it what you want.'"

"The only really heartless man I've ever seen in this North country was a Presbyterian minister and the head of the Good Samaritan Hospital in Dawson. He turned down a woman, wouldn't even let her enter the God damn place, all because she was having an illegitimate child. But if you'd gone up the Creek you wouldn't find a miner, no matter how poor or how drunk he was, who wouldn't move out of his cabin to give her a place. He's the man who stopped all the horses moving in the town on Sunday. Later on he quits the church and goes down to Coal Creek where they're putting in a million dollar electric plant. He puts a lot of money in the plant and he's in a hurry to get it done. The men working there, they wasn't in no hurry though, and they wouldn't work more than six days a week, six days was enough for them. But this preacher, he tells them if they don't work on Sunday also he's going to fire them. Oh, I tell you, this religion is the biggest fake out."

There are several of the irreligious majority who hold special philosophical views. Quite a number believe in some sort of reincarnation. One man belongs to the New Thought school which he describes as "the power of mind over matter: psychology, in fact." A certain woman believes very seriously in thought transference. The most sensational secret of life was abstracted for me by the hermit who held it in these three words: *Everything moves Southwest.*

A number of the old sourdoughs have attained a highly objective philosophy. Harry Foley expresses the thoughts of this group when he says: "It's nice to sit on the sidelines and look at life as it goes by and wonder what it's all about. If you're right in the turmoil you don't have a chance to think and see how ridiculous it is. It's all in being on the sidelines."

The beliefs of the white people in the Koyukuk regarding what happens after death have been fairly well set forth in chapter V. Considering the white men's ideas about immortality from a numerical standpoint, it appears that there is an almost equal division. Out of seventy people whose views I was able to determine during the course of many different conversations which we had alone together, thirty-three believed in some sort of an hereafter and thirty-seven felt that death meant oblivion.

In spite of the prevalence of this latter viewpoint and the advanced age of the community as a whole, there seems to be little morbid fear of approaching death. It is simply disregarded. One man on his seventieth birthday told me: "If science got so they could make a man over again I think I'd be a pretty good subject to work on." Another old fellow who was seventy-three and suffering from palsy said: "Age never bothered me. It doesn't to-day. I'd just like to get out with the children and play marbles." A wrinkled veteran of seventy-two years admitted only this sign of the advancing years: "I feel just as well as I ever did, but my mind isn't so willing for me to buckle into hard work as it used to be." Quite a number who worry not at all about death, feel that the worst imaginable possibility is that some day they may be helpless. "So far as dying is concerned," says one active fellow of sixty-three, "that doesn't worry me in the least, but the only thing on earth that I'm afraid of is a long, lingering illness before death. I'd rather do almost anything than have to depend on some one for a living." Another remarks: "That's the only dread I have in this world, the dread of some day not being able to work."

It is not in coldly reasoned theory, however, but in the actual shadow of death, that men's real beliefs are most clearly divulged. I had a splendid opportunity to observe a man under such conditions. While engaged in road construction work last June, old George Eaton was run over by a heavy wagon. He was in genuine agony, and no one knew for sure but that he was fatally hurt. I took him immediately to my cabin where he stayed for a whole week until he was definitely out of danger. During the entire time he was lying painfully in bed he did not emit even a passing reference to God, the hereafter, his soul, or any religious matter. He talked plentifully about how much his side hurt him. He told me very clear-headedly that if he died there was plenty of money to bury him, and that his will was in a friend's safe. He grumbled: "When a man gets so he can't help himself he ain't much use in this world." He soliloquized philosophically that "it makes no difference how well a man is one hour, he ain't got no insurance on life." But he never once mentioned anything of a spiritual nature, and he never once showed the slightest fear of death. "We'll soon die and be forgotten," he said defiantly, "but I don't care. I've had my fair share of good times and more too."

Fame does not matter. Piety does not matter. Immorality does not matter. The thing that counts when you are brought face to face with death is whether you have had your "fair share of good times." This Epicurean doctrine, influenced no doubt by the typical Eskimo philosophy of getting the maximum pleasure out of life as it passes along, is tempered always by a strong social corollary that one must not attain his fair share of good times at the expense of somebody else.

But good times, unselfishly attained, are the fundamental considerations of existence. "When you come right down to it, about the only things that are worth while in life are to be happy and to make other people happier for having associated with you."

That statement, made by an old sourdough, can well stand as the major tenet of the religion of the Koyukuk.

XXXVII

WHITE HAPPINESS

IF HAPPINESS, then, is the principal goal in the philosophy of the Koyukukers, it is important to consider how well they seem to have attained their objective. Therefore, I have recorded for practically every white person in the region some remark made during the casual conversation of many months, which I feel reflects truthfully the reaction of that person toward his frontier life. In analyzing these statements it appears that fifty-four people are in general favorably inclined to their life in the Far North, twelve people are discontented, and nine take a neutral stand.

It would be much too tedious to repeat all of these quotations, so I have abridged them for convenience to a third of their number. I have, however, carefully preserved the original ratio, and consequently I believe that the general impression which these statements give remains sincerely representative of the composite happiness of the Koyukuk.

To have something to do that you're interested in, that's the main thing in life. Up here in the Koyukuk there's almost nothing you ever do that doesn't interest you. I wouldn't give that up for all the comforts and conveniences of the Outside.

Life is such a series of circumstances that looking into what might have happened if I'd gone East instead of North is a sheer impossibility. But I wouldn't call any life really successful where you haven't got a wife and children.

I used to like to go Outside to visit my mother when she was living. But since she died back in 1903 I've had absolutely no desire to go back again. There's nothing out there for me. I've been away too long. This is my home.

Sometimes when I remember I've thrown thirty-three years of my life away in here I feel so sore I want to kick myself all over the place. But the thing is the time passes so God damn fast you never realize how long it's been. When I went Outside for the first time I'd been in here twenty-one years and it didn't seem like more than five or six. You've always something planned ahead. In summer you have a whole winter of work planned, and in winter a whole summer. And first thing you know twenty years are gone. I've made several good stakes and almost made a fortune several times, but now I'm not much richer than when I came in. But I wouldn't have done any better Outside, and I'd have worked for wages all my life, and never been my own boss a minute. And then I love the wild mountains and the unexplored country and the fighting through hardships. There's no people in the world have overcome as many hardships as the Alaska pioneers. Why, the dangers and discomforts which these Arctic and Antarctic explorers have stood is just a joke in comparison with what thousands of Alaska men and women have gone through. If Stefansson could get to the North Pole and discover gold there'd be 500 Alaska whores there inside three months. There's no hardship in the world which any man can stand that a real old time Alaskan couldn't bear, and I'm glad that I was one of them.

Of course, everybody in here has some idiosyncrasies. They wouldn't be in here if they were normal. Outside at least a person has a chance to see something and hear something and learn something, even if they're not making any money. But God damn it, when a man gets in here he just can't get out.

I like this country well enough. But I don't peddle to myself that I'd live here if I had plenty of money. Why in hell should a man? There's so much more to live for out there. If I could live out there I'd be perfectly willing to give up Alaska, even though I'd always like to come back for a visit. But I've always said that if I had to rustle a living I'd a lot rather do it up here than Outside.

It's six and one-half years to-day since I first arrived in Wiseman. Gee, I've had a lot of fun since I've been here. I haven't missed the time at all. It's seemed like about six and one-half months. There's so much to do, and I don't know, there's something about it when you meet another fellow he's always good natured and jokes and kids you. Only excepting a few sons-of-bitches like Carter, every one's just as fine as they can be. And I don't suppose there's any place where you could get better hunting.

I've had plenty of opportunities to go Outside but I never wanted to go. Every one is elbowing one another and putting on fancy airs, and a poor man can't hardly make enough to eat. Here you always have plenty to live on at worst, lots of caribou and small game to eat, and you can grow all the potatoes and garden truck you want. There's no rent to pay, an easy chance to get at least a share in a good claim, and nobody in God's world to boss your life except yourself.

Outside it's a rush and a push and a jam all the time, and if you drop something somebody else is going to pick it up. Here you've got time to read and to think and to enjoy yourself. And anyway, I like these hills, and I've lived around here thirty-three years, and no place else could ever seem like home.

When a person gets as old as I am he doesn't look forward to very much any more, so hard work and reversals don't bother him. If he had any great joys or fortunes he'd just be oppressed by their transiency and the knowledge that at any moment they might be gone. That's why this life seems as good as any to me, living each day for itself, without any hope for the future.

If I had $100,000 to-day I wouldn't quit this life in the hills. I would get a little better equipment and I'd go Outside to get married, but I would come right back in here again. I know what that life Outside is like, and it don't appeal to me. I've lived this free life in here so long I couldn't live Outside for good, and I know I'd never get over being homesick for the beauty of this country.

I'm perfectly happy. That's all I care for. That's all life is.

Outside you've got your nose to the grindstone all the time, and the boss is looking down your neck. No, mining's the worst sort of gamble, it's a labor gamble, but you've always got expectations and that means a lot. If I had it all to do over again I wouldn't go through with what I have the last thirty years, but still I wouldn't ever live where I'd have to work all my life for some one else.

It's a hard life up here, so many hardships, and you have to deprive yourself of so much. You've got to miss all the fine music, and then you don't have any women hardly. There's no chance for most men to live with a woman. Anything that's unnatural is bad for a man. And then there's no chance to keep up with the times either. But life in here's a thousand times better than the life of the working man Outside. You have so much freedom, and you work for yourself. By gosh, I hate to work for anybody else worse than almost anything there is.

Summer time the mosquitoes are suicide, and winter time you're always running risk of losing your hands or feet. If I ever made a stake I'd get out of here quick as I could.

I've had a lovely time in here. Everything is so free. A man gets up and he feels as if he owned everything. Outside somebody else owns everything.

I like this damn country. Why, God Almighty, man, you were a hell of a lucky bastard if you got $2.50 or $3.00 a day, working Outside. In here you may make 100 times that in one minute, and even when you're making nothing, it's fascinating.

No country on the earth, in the globe, under the sky is better for poor man to live at in my way of look at it if ain't for mosquitoes in summer, than Alaska. The bastards, little fellows, mosquitoes, that's the only drawback I can see in all Alaska. Only I rather fight with mosquitoes than be trembling all the time for fear I lose my freedom. Freedom is the main thing of everything. There's no freest country in the world outside Alaska. The man who's got no freedom on earth, what's he got, poor bugger? Misery worse than hell because he's got such a short time on earth. If you take from man liberty he might just as well be dead right on the second. In here you're really free. There's nobody to hold you up or tell you what you can't do. I left 1903 from old country, and I figure in all that time I only work thirty-six months for other man, and all the rest of time fight my own way and work for myself. I wouldn't have any more money all this time if I work for other man, and I've been free man besides.

Outside all you learn is what you do: raise chickens, build fence, plow. In here you got to learn something about everything. Outside if you're broke you starve. In here, no matter how broke, I know lots of places I can always make grubstake. Outside you always work for other man. Here in North Country I'm my own boss. Even if I only make three or four dollars a day, I'm my boss.

I came here for adventure like I read about in books, and I found it.

If I had lots of money I'd prefer Oregon, but when I'm broke, as I usually am, it's much better up here. I'm too proud to be any one's cook in Oregon; in here where every one else works I don't mind.

Memory's a thing if a person doesn't use it, it goes back on him awful fast. A person's got to cultivate his mind if he wants it to remain keen. There's not much chance for a person to cultivate it out hunting. And there's lots of other things a man misses, being shut off out of the world up here. Why, I could have more good times in one year out in Wisconsin than in a lifetime up in the Arctic.

You've got to write back that there's no poverty, no bread-lines, and no hard times, and even the hard, savage, gut-eating Eskimos are better off than seventy per cent of the population Outside. All a person has to do in here if he gets hungry is take a rifle, and a box of .30-.30 shells which only cost $2.25, and a few pounds of beans, and a little salt, and maybe some flour and sugar and coffee, and an old can which he can pick up anywheres, and he's all set to live in luxury.

I'd like to take a trip around the States some day if I ever got enough money, but I don't think, even when I get old, that I'd ever want to live Outside. I can't see why I should anyway. I don't believe any work Outside a fellow'd be likely to get in would be as interesting as this in here, and I know he'd have nowhere like the independence and the good times.

Yes, even the hard times are good times. I remember once, about a couple of years ago, when we danced all night here, I think it must have been the St. Patrick's Day dance, how I had to rustle right back to Hammond to keep the fires going. So as soon as the dance was over, just about day-light, I picked up my snowshoes and hit her off to Ham-mond. It was blowing and snowing like hell, and the wind had drifted in the whole trail, so I sank, even with big snow-shoes on, up to my knees at every step. But you know, I got a great kick out of all that.

I remember one night in June there were a bunch of us went down to the mouth of the Kiwalik River and we lay on a sand spit to sleep, looking north across the bay. The sun sank low in the west and came down toward the top of an island in the bay, but even at midnight it never touched the island, it looked to be about fifteen feet above it. Well, you know there was something so beautiful about it all that

I just couldn't go asleep, so I lay awake, watching the sun commence to rise again. I thought to myself, my God, I'm glad I came to this country.

(This concluding item is not a quotation, but an excerpt from a letter which Mrs. Pingel wrote me about a year after she had left Wiseman to settle with her husband on an Iowa farm which he owned.)

We are living among nice people who spend all their days here and have attained to a certain perfection in furnishing and upkeep of the modern home, while I roamed the hills in search of wild flowers and berries. While I walked to town to hoe my potatoes or get the mail, they dusted, polished, garnished. While I sat down by Big Jim or Nakuchluk or Jonas or Kalhabuk or Kaypuk or Dishoo or Mamie or Lucy, they sat around a polished front room table, playing cards. While the hills and the mountains, the valleys and the creeks talked to me, they only beheld their neighbor's house.

And now comes the measuring rod of what they call civilization. All the things they do must be done—the quilt blocks sewed, the house ready for invited guests who will invite them again; while for years we had the latchstring out to any old boy who was hungry. What a good time old Bob and I had when he came from town after some dance, telling his side of the laurels he had won—the eyes sparkled when he said, "They asked me to sing."

People here are so impatient with our love for Alaska as a land of scenic beauty when they hear you have to walk to see it. And mining is madness as long as you haven't made a lot of money, the pleasure of hunting treasures in the bosom of the earth is folly unless you know where to dig and where to pick up gold. The wild flowers by the roadside as we walk to town are not interesting to them if thereby you must walk.

Oh, these people here have everything a person could wish for—modern homes, electricity, radio, all the good things like eggs, milk, butter, fruit, berries, gardens. I wonder what they would wish more in heaven. Still they are only half-awake—dull, routine slaves, tied down to follow each other.

When I picture the life in the North and here I say— my stomach is better off here but my mentality lives its best up there. The big open spaces are alluring, the lovely air, the near-by rainbow, the friendliness of the people. How interested we are up there in everyday occurrences and each other; helpful, ready to do all we can.

IKE SPINKS: "Well, you know there was something so beautiful about it all that I just couldn't go asleep, so I lay awake, watching the sun commence to rise again, and I thought to myself, My God. I'm glad I came to this country."

PETE HASLEM: "Outside you've got your nose to the grindstone all the time, and the boss is looking down your neck. No, mining's the worst sort of gamble, it's a labor gamble, but you've always got expectations and that means a lot."

CONCLUSION

CONCLUSION

IN CONCLUSION, I want to discuss my own opinion about the happiness of the people of the Koyukuk. Before considering this subject it is necessary to define what I mean by happiness, for the uses of that term are so varied that unless a precise meaning is chosen any discussion will inevitably end in misunderstanding. By happiness I mean how much more worth while than oblivion all of life seems to the person who is leading it. In other words, oblivion, extinction, or death (if one does not believe in a hereafter) is taken as the base from which the value of life is measured. This value is not considered for merely a moment or even a few years, but for the total effect of all of life. It embraces everything which tends to make living more worth while than extinction.

Such a definition precludes the possibility of any precise measure of happiness. One can only express a subjective opinion. Consequently, in evaluating the happiness of the citizens of the Koyukuk, the only measure which I can use is my personal reaction to their composite happiness. This reaction is that I believe the average value of life rises higher above the dead level of oblivion to the people of the Koyukuk than it does to any of the other groups of American people whom I have known.

If the foregoing seems vague and unsubstantial, I can be

more concise in explaining the reasons why I think the Koyukukers are so happy. Their life is featured by certain peculiar attributes which most of the people in the outside world either lack entirely or possess only to a limited extent. I shall summarize what seem to me to be the most important of these special values.

The people of the Koyukuk themselves, as the preceding chapter has indicated, stress their independence as the most precious component in their lives. "I'm my own boss," one hears repeated over and over, and this means that each man has the privilege of working out his own destiny. No person needs to depend on anybody but himself for his means of livelihood. As a result, instead of being hopelessly bound by the interplay of economic forces over which they have no control, the inhabitants of the Koyukuk have their economic destiny within their own direction. This gives them a buoyant self-reliance, an emancipation from other men's restraint, which immensely enriches the entire pattern of their lives.

There are two important corollaries to this matter of economic independence. The first is that a person can always make a living. There is no horror of unemployment in the Koyukuk, no constant fear that one's chance of livelihood may at any moment be removed. Even if a person has had a disastrous year in his mine and does not possess a dollar of his own, he can always get his subsistence through hunting, fishing, berrying, and gardening until fortune deals more kindly with his quest for gold.

Also closely associated with economic independence is the fact that the work is tremendously interesting. It requires skilled manipulation, continual planning, and genuine mental exertion. It has almost no dull and purely routinized jobs, and generally is featured by the lure of the unknown.

Furthermore, much of the work is not done merely for money, with which one may proceed to buy the necessities of life, but it is directly concerned with securing those tangible, exciting, and intimate necessities. There is not only economic independence in the Koyukuk, but also the most complete liberty one can imagine. A person is free to say anything, read anything, write anything he desires. He is even free to do anything except commit murder, robbery, and perhaps rape. Any other controls there may be over his actions have strictly voluntary sanctions, and consequently he may act in any way which satisfies his own conscience. For most people with minds sufficiently vigorous to do their own thinking this freedom of thought and action seems to be a genuine incentive to happiness.

Because there are so few people in the Koyukuk, the individual takes on a peculiar importance. Every person can really feel that he is a vital element in the world in which he lives, not merely one infinitesimal soul among millions of his fellowmen. Thus the Koyukuker, in order to satisfy his ego, is not constantly under the neurotic strain of trying to be important: of striving to rank as the leading merchant, the wealthiest citizen, the president of something or other, the greatest poet, the most persevering flagpole sitter. Every individual in the Koyukuk is important just because he is alive, and thus there is eliminated from his life all the nerve-racking striving which accompanies any effort to be distinguishable among the overwhelming numbers of the outside world.

Perhaps this fact that the citizen of the Koyukuk fills an assured niche in his world makes it unnecessary for him to bolster his ego with a race hatred which seems to be almost as conducive to misery for the person who does the hating as the one who is hated. Consequently, with sweeping prejudices non-existent, a great deal of what frequently upsets men in normal parts of the world is automatically eliminated.

The average person, living in a mechanized civilization, has small opportunity for genuine adventure. But there is not a person past infancy in the entire Koyukuk who cannot look back on repeated adventures which would put to shame the imaginative tales consumed by millions of thrill-starved citizens of the United States. There is an exultation in snowshoeing at mid-winter to the Arctic Divide, in meeting the hazards involved in the passage of some swollen wilderness river, in subsisting a hundred miles from the closest human being, which adds tone, vitality, and color to the entire functioning of life.

It is not only in adventure that variety is added to the civilization on the Koyukuk. The peculiarity of Arctic climate which causes such a tremendous contrast between winter and summer gives a cheerful dissimilarity not only to the entire appearance of the country, but also to every action. Thus each person has at least two different settings for whatever he is doing, two different types of labor, and two different methods of getting about, and this greatly reduces any likelihood of monotony.

It is impossible ever to evaluate just how much beauty adds to what is worth while in existence. I would hazard as my opinion that beautiful surroundings have a fundamental bearing on most people's enjoyment. Consequently, I believe that the happiness of the Koyukuker is greatly enhanced and his entire life is made richer by the overpowering loveliness of the Arctic wilderness.

Most important of all, happiness in the Koyukuk is stimulated by the prevalent philosophy of enjoying life as it passes along. The absence of constant worry about the future and remorse about the past destroys much that tends to make men miserable. The fact that happiness is frankly recognized as a legitimate objective removes at once much futile pursuit of false ideals, and makes it possible for men to live openly as well as subconsciously for what they primarily desire.

Of course there are also factors which tend to make the Outside a happier place than the Koyukuk. The variety of goods which one may purchase, the every day conveniences unknown in the northern region, the diversified possibilities of entertainment, and the wider opportunities for personal acquaintanceship are clearly advantages for the outside world. Especially, the family life for which most of mankind seems to yearn has very little possibility of fruition among the white men of the Koyukuk.

Nevertheless, the inhabitants of the Koyukuk would rather eat beans with liberty, burn candles with independence, and mush dogs with adventure than to have the luxury and the restrictions of the outside world. A person misses many things by living in the isolation of the Koyukuk, but he gains a life filled with an amount of freedom, tolerance, beauty, and contentment such as few human beings are ever fortunate enough to achieve.

APPENDIX

IT IS necessary to qualify the results which I obtained with the Stanford-Binet test by mentioning that I had little practice in giving it before going to the Arctic. Because of my lack of experience I probably followed Terman's standard rules for giving the test somewhat more strictly and marked more severely than would an examiner with greater experience. When I returned to Baltimore all the tests I gave were checkmarked by Bertha Brewer of the Psychology Department of Johns Hopkins University.

The Eskimo children were handicapped by the striking difference between their background and that of the white children for whom the test was devised. Of the eighteen Eskimos, seven came from homes in which the Eskimo language was spoken exclusively, and four more from a home in which it was used at least half the time. The Eskimo boy of 5½ who got the lowest mark of any of the younger children had never heard the English language spoken until six months before I gave him the test. A little girl who got a low normal grade could only speak the most broken English. In view of these language difficulties I uniformly omitted the vocabulary test.

Certain substitutions were necessary because some of the questions were meaningless to children with the Eskimo background. Thus in test III-2 a safety pin was substituted for a penny which none of the children had ever seen. In test V-4 the children were asked to define an ax instead of a fork with which several of them were not familiar. In test VI-4 they were asked what they would do if they missed the scow instead of the car, which of course had no significance in the Arctic. Test VI-5, involving the naming of a nickel, penny, quarter, and dime was omitted because a quarter is the lowest coin in circulation in the Koyukuk. The alternate test for this age was given instead. Test VIII-4 involved so many things the children had neither seen nor heard about that it was omitted and Alternate 2 given.

Among the adult whites there were just two changes. Test XIV-3 was omitted because it seemed to me that a wrong answer to this test might indicate considerably more intelligence than a right one. The fourteen-year alternate was substituted. The sixteen-year alternate was used instead of XVI-4 because of the difficulty of transporting the necessary equipment on long mushing or snowshoe trips.

The Stanford-Binet was given to forty-five of the seventy-seven whites in the region. These were not especially selected, but included every one who would voluntarily take the test, except that four rather senile men, eight people with unusual language difficulties, two people suffering from psychopathic ailments, and one very deaf man were arbitrarily omitted.

In taking the test practically all of the whites were under the disadvantages inevitable with any men who have led lives primarily involving physical effort. On the other hand, whites and Eskimos alike were helped by the fact that there was perfect *rapport* between them and their examiner, and consequently bashfulness or nervousness had no influence on the results.

R. M.

GENERAL INDEX

Religion (Cont.)
  Tobuk's views concerning, 329-331
  of Eskimos in general, 331-357
  of whites, 358-363
Rent, 184
Review of Reviews, 294
Revolution, recommended by Koyukukers, 59-60
Ride of the Valkyries, 318-319
Ring-around-a-Rosie, 322
Rink, H., 372
Rise of the American Civilization, 296
River travel, 127-129
Roadhouse, function of, 17
  description of Wiseman roadhouse, 57-58
  number of, 39, 83, 110-111, 151, 181, 287, 306-307, 314, 323
Roads, for dogs, 103, 180-181, 362
  for autos, 136
Robbery, 189-191, 233, 377
Robbins, Robby, 134, 277, 279, 281
Rockefeller, John D., 59-60
Roofing, 152
Rooney's Lake (Big Lake), 214, 305, 349
Royalties, 104
Rural origin of Koyukukers, 51
Russian divorce laws, 257
Russian experiment, opinion of Koyukukers concerning, 61-62

Salmon, 172-173
Saloons, 39, 315, 317
Salvation, ridiculed by Eskimos, 356
Sanitation, 155, 210
Saturday Evening Post, 294-295
Savings, drawn on to meet regional deficit, 182
Scarlet fever, 209
Scenery of Koyukuk region, 5, 15, 367, 370-372
Schimberg-Lowe scaled information test, 54, 79
School, 240, 243, 246, 306, 352, 354
Schoolhouse, 151
Schoolteacher, 103, 180, 190, 191, 244, 246, 288
Science, 65, 287-290, 361
Science News Letter, 295
Scientific American, 294

Scientific observations, 287-289
Scurvy, 31, 201, 209
Seal oil, 138
Seasons, definition, 21-22
  description of, 22-28
  effect on transportation, 118-119
  influence on quarrels, 226-228
  make life varied, 378
Seattle, 18, 118, 251, 252, 255
Seattle Fur Exchange, 108, 170
Selawik River, 73, 252, 355
Self-sufficiency of Koyukukers, 114-115
Seward, 117, 276
Sewing, taught to Eskimo girls informally by schoolteacher, 245
Sex (see also chickens, marriage, promiscuity, prostitutes), in dreams, 67
  unsatisfactory life, 85
  intercourse, 235, 266-267, 277-279
  frankness concerning, 239, 272
  unbalance, 249, 265
  age at which Eskimo girls mature, 258-259
  taboos, 265, 269-272, 336
  preoccupation of Eskimo girls with, 276-281
  as subject of conversation, 287, 289
  pictures of girls found in cabin walls, 318
  in songs, 324-326
  origin of, according to Eskimos, 331-332
Sexual Life of Savages, 6, 296
Sheep, 167, 298, 301, 344
  hunting season, 192
Shelter cabins, 152, 217, 228, 230, 237
Shooting, accidental, 219
Siberia, 72, 233
Siberian Eskimos, 72
Sickness, of Big Charlie, 88-89
  government relief for, 181-182
  how treated, 204-213
  of Jack White, 210-213, 222
  communal responsibility, 199-200, 211
  deaths due to, among Eskimos, 221
  Eskimos become hysterical when afflicted, 242-243
  as subject of conversation, 287

INDEX OF KOYUKUK PEOPLE

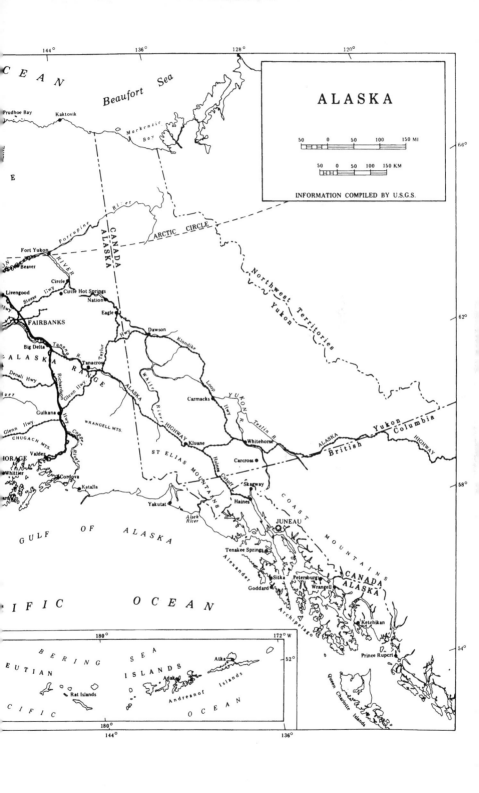

ALASKA

50   0   50   100   150 MI

50   0   50   100   150 KM

INFORMATION COMPILED BY U.S.G.S.

144°   136°   128°   120°

Beaufort Sea

OCEAN

Prudhoe Bay   Kaktovik

Mackenzie Bay

66°

E

Porcupine   River

ALASKA   CANADA

ARCTIC CIRCLE

Northwest Territories

Fort Yukon   Yukon

Beaver

Circle   Yukon

Livengood   Steese Hwy   Circle Hot Springs

Nation

Eagle

62°

FAIRBANKS   Dawson

Big Delta   Tanana R.   Klondike

ALASKA   Tanacross   Taylor Hwy

Denali Hwy   RANGE   Loop Hwy

White River   Carmacks   YUKON Hwy

Gulkana   Richardson Hwy   ALASKA HIGHWAY   Teslin R.

Glenn Hwy   WRANGELL MTS.   British Columbia

CHUGACH MTS.   Copper River   Kluane   Whitehorse   ALASKA

ANCHORAGE   Valdez   ST ELIAS MOUNTAINS   Carcross

Whittier   Cordova   Haines Cutoff   Skagway

Katalla   Haines   58°

Yakutat   Alsek River   COAST

GULF   OF   ALASKA   JUNEAU

MOUNTAINS   CANADA
ALASKA

Tenakee Springs

Alexander   Sitka   Petersburg

Goddard   Wrangell   Archipelago

PACIFIC   OCEAN   Ketchikan

54°
Prince Rupert

180°   172° W

BERING   SEA

EUTIAN   ISLANDS   Atka   52°

Adak   Andreanof Islands

Rat Islands   OCEAN

PACIFIC   Queen Charlotte Islands

180°

144°   136°